A PRACTICAL GUIDE TO

PERMITTED CHANGES OF USE

UNDER THE
GENERAL PERMITTED DEVELOPMENT ORDER

064236

ROYAL AGRICULTURAL COLLEGE

MARTIN H GOODALL *LARTPI*
Solicitor

BATH PUBLISHING

A PRACTICAL GUIDE TO

PERMITTED CHANGES OF USE

TO PHILOMENA

without whose love, support and encouragement
this book could not have been completed.

Published October 2015

ISBN 978-0-9567774-7-8

Text © Martin Goodall

Typography © Bath Publishing

Bath Publishing Limited

27 Charmouth Road

Bath

BA1 3LJ

Tel: 01225 577810

email: info@bathpublishing.co.uk

www.bathpublishing.com

Bath Publishing is a company registered in England: 5209173

Registered Office: As above

CONTENTS

CHAPTER 1

GENERAL INTRODUCTION

CHAPTER 2

CHANGES OF USE TO / FROM SHOPS OR 'RETAIL' SERVICES

CHAPTER 3

CHANGES OF USE TO AND FROM CATERING USES

CHAPTER 4

CHANGES OF USE TO AND FROM OTHER COMMERCIAL AND INSTITUTIONAL USES

CHAPTER 5

CHANGES OF USE TO AND FROM RESIDENTIAL USE

CHAPTER 6

RESIDENTIAL CONVERSION OF AMUSEMENT ARCADE OR CENTRE OR CASINO

CHAPTER 7

RESIDENTIAL CONVERSION OF COMMERCIAL OFFICES

CHAPTER 8

RESIDENTIAL CONVERSION OF 'STORAGE OR DISTRIBUTION CENTRE'

CHAPTER 9

RESIDENTIAL CONVERSION OF AN AGRICULTURAL BUILDING

CHAPTER 10

CHANGE OF USE TO USE AS A STATE-FUNDED SCHOOL OR REGISTERED NURSERY

CHAPTER 11

CHANGES OF USE TO AND FROM USE FOR ASSEMBLY AND LEISURE

CHAPTER 12

FLEXIBLE USES

CHAPTER 13

PRIOR APPROVAL APPLICATIONS

CHAPTER 14

PROCESSING AND DETERMINING THE PRIOR APPROVAL APPLICATION

CHAPTER 15

THE 56-DAY RULE

CHAPTER 16

TEMPORARY USE OF OPEN LAND

CHAPTER 20

OTHER CAMPING AND RECREATIONAL USES

APPENDIX A

LOSS OR REMOVAL OF PERMITTED DEVELOPMENT RIGHTS

APPENDIX B

THE PLANNING UNIT AND THE CONCEPT OF 'CURTILAGE'

APPENDIX C

THE USE CLASSES ORDER

TABLE OF CASES

TABLE OF STATUTES

TABLE OF STATUTORY INSTRUMENTS

TABLE OF CONVENTIONS

TABLE OF CURRENT MINISTERIAL POLICY GUIDANCE

TABLE OF FORMER CIRCULARS AND PPGs

AUTHOR'S NOTE

Until less than 30 months ago (prior to 30 May 2013), the changes of use permitted by Part 3 of the Second Schedule to the General Permitted Development Order could be summarised quite adequately on the two sides of a sheet of A4 paper. The government then chose this part of the GPDO as the vehicle for a significant liberalisation of the planning regime, so as to allow much greater freedom to convert existing buildings to other uses without the need to apply for planning permission. Further significant changes followed in April 2014 and in April 2015, when the previous amendments to the 1995 Order were also consolidated in a new GPDO.

Further amendments to the GPDO were announced in October 2015 and are expected to be made within the next six months. Those relating to Class O are expected to come into effect on 31 May 2016. However, at the time of going to press, the Department for Communities and Local Government were unable to say whether the other proposed changes would come into force on the same date, but this would seem likely. Such details of the proposed amendments as are currently known are explained in *paragraph 7.7* of *Chapter 7*. However, it has been decided not to delay the publication of this book to await these amendments. When the amending order is made, a supplementary commentary on these provisions will be published in the author's Planning Law Blog (http://planninglawblog.blogspot.com).

Most of the newly introduced permitted development rights are subject to a requirement to make a prior approval application to the local planning authority in respect of certain aspects of these developments. It is the substantial increase in the size of this part of the GPDO, and the complexity of its provisions, including the prior approval procedure, that has led to this book being written, so as to provide a single comprehensive and, above all, practical guide to these provisions and to the procedures that need to be followed in order to enable such developments to be carried out.

In order to provide background, the book starts with a general introduction to development orders, and to the General Permitted Development Order in particular, before dealing in the following chapters with the various changes of use permitted by Part 3, including the submission, processing, consideration and determination of prior approval applications. Further chapters then explain the temporary uses permitted by Part 4 and the provisions as to caravan sites and camping in Part 5.

This is not intended as an orthodox legal textbook, but rather as a work of reference which property professionals of all disciplines (and others) can consult in order to understand the rules and procedures that apply to particular changes of use. This has very much influenced the structure and organisation of the book, and in order to ensure that readers can easily find all the essential information relating to a particular type of development, material has where necessary been repeated, so as to minimise the need to leaf back and forth through the pages (or, in the case of the electronic version, to click on other links repeatedly) in order to gather the required information.

However, in order to ensure that all the relevant considerations that need to be taken into account are drawn to readers' attention, there are numerous cross-references alerting readers to the additional factors that need to be borne in mind, or where explanations of particular points are to be found elsewhere in the text which have not been repeated.

Nevertheless, it may be helpful to readers to read the General Introduction (*Chapter 1*) and, if they will be dealing with those Classes of permitted development that are dependent on a prior approval application, they are recommended also to read *Chapters 13* to *15*, in order to familiarise themselves with the relevant procedural rules.

Readers will be able to obtain a clear understanding of the scope and structure of the book by reference to the detailed Table of Contents. For the further assistance of readers in finding particular provisions in the GPDO, three Tables listing the various changes of use permitted by Parts 3, 4 and 5 of the Second Schedule to the Order are included at the end of *Chapter 1*. An index has also been provided for those readers who would prefer to find specific material by that means.

A Table of Statutes and Statutory Instruments is provided. Readers wishing to refer to the legislation itself should ensure that they have before them the fully amended text of the relevant statute or statutory instrument. The primary legislation has been repeatedly amended since 1990, and the subordinate legislation has been similarly amended in the same period. At the time of writing, only the General Permitted Development Order and the Development Management Procedure Order have been fully consolidated, both of them in April 2015. Important amendments have been made to other subordinate legislation, most recently in April 2015, but without consolidating that other subordinate legislation.

References in the text to "the Act" or to "the 1990 Act" are to the Town and Country Planning Act 1990 (as amended), except where the context requires otherwise. Similarly, the quotation of a section number without reference to any Act may be taken as a reference to a section in the 1990 Act, unless the context clearly indicates a reference to other legislation. References to "the 2004 Act" are to the Planning and Compulsory Purchase Act 2004, and the single reference to "the 1971 Act" is to the Town and Country Planning Act 1971.

References in the text to the "Listed Buildings Act" relate to the Planning (Listed Buildings and Conservation Areas) Act 1990 (as amended).

Chapter 19 refers to the Caravan Sites and Control of Development Act

1960. Further references in that chapter are then made to it as "the 1960 Act". References in that chapter to "Schedule 1" relate to the First Schedule to the 1960 Act.

Except where otherwise stated, references to "the General Permitted Development Order" or to "the GPDO" (or, in one or two cases, simply to "the Order") are to the Town and Country Planning (General Permitted Development) (England) Order 2015 (S.I. 2015 No. 596), which replaced the 1995 Order and its various amending orders with effect from 15 April 2015. Reference is also made, where relevant, to the version of the GPDO which it replaced. This has been referred to in the text as "the 1995 Order".

The other statutory instrument mentioned in the text is the Town and Country Planning (Use Classes) Order 1987 (as amended), which is referred to either as "the Use Classes Order" or simply as "the UCO".

A reference to "Article [X]", without more, is a reference to the relevant article in the GPDO. References to particular articles in the UCO make it clear that it is the UCO that is being referred to, other than where the context makes this obvious. Unless otherwise stated, references to "Part [X]" are references to the relevant part of the Second Schedule to the GPDO, where the various categories of development permitted by Article 3 of the Order are set out in detail - Part 3 in *Chapters 2* to *15*, Part 4 in *Chapters 16* to *18* and Part 5 in *Chapters 19* and *20*.

The Schedule to the UCO sets out various "classes" of use, and the several parts of the Second Schedule to the GPDO contain various "classes" of permitted development. In order to avoid confusion, references to classes of development in each part of the Second Schedule to the GPDO are simply referred to in the text as "Class A" [etc.], and classes in the Schedule to the UCO are mostly referred to as "Use Class A1" [etc.], unless it is clear from the context that it is the UCO that is being referred to.

A further distinction that may assist any readers who may be unfamiliar with this subordinate legislation is that classes of development in each part of the Second Schedule to the GPDO are identified by a single capital letter -"Class A", "Class B", [etc.] or, where a class is sub-divided, by a capital letter followed by lower case letters in brackets and, where further subdivided, by lower case Roman numerals, e.g. "Class M(a)(iii)", whereas use classes in the Schedule to the UCO are identified by a single capital letter followed by an Arabic numeral; thus "Class A1", "Class B8", etc.

Relevant judicial authorities are cited in case readers may wish to be informed of the derivation of various propositions stated in the text. A Table of Cases is also provided as an alternative means of finding relevant references to those judgments in the text. The names of cases have been shortened by omitting second defendants or interested parties in most cases, and by using well-known abbreviations such as "LBC" for London Borough Council" and

"BC", "CC" or "DC" for various other local authorities. Similarly the relevant Minister or Secretary of State under his or her various different identities has been referred to thus:

"MHLG" - Minister of Housing and Local Government

"SSE" - Secretary of State for the Environment

"SSETR" - Secretary of State for the Environment, Transport and the Regions

"FSS" - First Secretary of State (the name in which the Deputy Prime Minister was sued)

"SSCLG" - Secretary of State for Communities and Local Government

"SSS" - Secretary of State for Scotland

"SSW" - Secretary of State for Wales

A few planning appeal decisions have also been quoted as examples of the practical application of the statutory rules, but case references have been deliberately omitted, because these decisions depend on their own facts and cannot be treated as precedents. Decisions in planning appeals are of no binding legal effect, and should not therefore be cited as authority for any principles that they may illustrate.

The text necessarily assumes some basic knowledge of planning law and practice on the part of readers, but where points derived from other parts of the planning legislation may need some explanation, an appropriate passage has been included in the text in order to give context to the issue under discussion. For the further assistance of readers, the ways in which permitted use rights may be lost or excluded are set out in Appendix A, the important concepts of the 'planning unit' and 'curtilage' are explained in Appendix B, and the use classes defined by the Use Classes Order are briefly summarised in Appendix C.

It is practically unavoidable in a book of this sort that various other abbreviations and acronyms are used in the text as convenient shorthand for frequently used terms. The most commonly used abbreviation is "LPA" (local planning authority). Others include:

"ACV" - Asset of Community Value (designated under the Localism Act 2011)

"AONB" - Area of Outstanding Natural Beauty

"DCLG" - The Department for Communities and Local Government

"DEFRA" - The Department for the Environment, Food and Rural Affairs

"DMPO" - The Town and Country Planning (Development Management Procedure) (England) Order 2015

"LDC" - Lawful Development Certificate (under section 191 or 192 of the

1990 Act)

"MAFF" - The Ministry of Agriculture, Fisheries and Food (now replaced by DEFRA)

"NPPF" - The National Planning Policy Framework (published in March 2012)

"SSSI" - Site of Special Scientific Interest

The Latin phrase "*sui generis*" means "of its own kind" - a use that does not fall within any of the Use Classes defined in the Schedule to the Use Classes Order.

The meaning of the terms "planning unit" and "curtilage" is discussed in *Appendix B*.

The GPDO in its current form applies to **England only**. Following the devolution of planning powers to the Welsh Assembly Government, Welsh planning legislation has been steadily diverging from the English legislation, so that it was becoming increasingly difficult to explain the variations in the Welsh legislation at the same time as describing the English legislation. The GPDO 2015 represents the final break between the English and Welsh legislative provisions on this topic, and so the Welsh legislation on permitted changes of use (which is now substantially different from the English provisions on this subject) is not covered in this book. Scotland and Northern Ireland have had their own separate planning systems for many years.

The law (so far as it lies within the author's knowledge) is stated as at 1 October 2015.

Finally, I must express my thanks to my colleagues in Keystone Law's planning law team, and to many professional associates and correspondents who by their comments, suggestions and queries, and also by their responses to the questions I have posed to them in the course of writing this book, have contributed in many ways to the compilation of the text, as well as expressing my appreciation for the enthusiasm and efficiency that David Chaplin and Helen Lacey of Bath Publishing have brought to the production and publication of this book. I am also grateful to the directors of Keystone Law who, by readily agreeing to afford me a lengthy sabbatical in order to enable me to write this book, materially contributed to its speedier completion, and most of all to my wife whose unfailing support and encouragement has sustained me throughout the course of this writing project.

MARTIN H GOODALL

Bristol

October 2015

CHAPTER 1

GENERAL INTRODUCTION

1.1 Development orders – an overview

The requirement in section 57 of the 1990 Act to obtain planning permission to carry out development (coupled with the comprehensive definition of development contained in section 55) would lead to a vast number of planning applications for minor developments, which would entirely clog up the planning system if such developments had to be dealt with through the normal development management process. Development orders obviate this problem by granting 'deemed' planning permission for specified types of development, subject to the qualifying criteria being met, and subject to various limitations and conditions.

By section 59(3) of the 1990 Act, the Secretary of State is given power to make development orders in the form either of general development orders, which are applicable (except so far as the order otherwise provides) to all land, and special development orders which are applicable only to such land or descriptions of land as may be specified in the order. Section 60 allows the inclusion in a development order of certain specific provisions, but this section is purely an enabling power, and it is the actual provisions of the development order that govern the relevant permitted development itself.

The principal development order made under these powers is the Town and Country Planning (General Permitted Development) (England) Order 2015 (S.I. 2015 No. 596) (usually referred to either as "the General Permitted Development Order" or simply as "the GPDO"), which replaced the much-amended 1995 Order with effect from 15 April 2015.

The GPDO 2015 applies to all land in England (but not in Wales). However, Article 1(2) provides that where the land is the subject of a Special Development Order, whether made before or after 15 April 2015, the GPDO applies to that land only to such extent and subject to such modifications as may be specified in the SDO. Special development orders are necessarily local or specialist in nature. There are at present just over a dozen of these still in existence, and they allow additional permitted development over and above that allowed by the GPDO and can also be used to vary or restrict the effect of the GPDO for specified areas or descriptions of land. They have been made in respect of the development of certain nuclear facilities and certain new town developments, and also in respect of development by one or two urban development corporations.

In addition, section 61A of the 1990 Act gives local planning authorities power to make Local Development Orders which may allow certain permitted development over and above that allowed by the GPDO. Such an order

1

can relate to all the land in the area of the relevant authority or any part of that land, or to a particular site specified in that order.

Section 61E of the 1990 Act (inserted by Schedule 9 to the Localism Act 2011) similarly gives local planning authorities power to make Neighbourhood Development Orders (in accordance with the procedure set out in Schedule 4B of the 1990 Act). A neighbourhood development order grants planning permission in relation to a particular neighbourhood area specified in the order, for development (or for development of any class) specified in the order. The Order can apply to a specific site or sites, or to a wider geographical area and may permit (among other things) material changes of use of land and buildings.

In Greater London, Schedule 4 of the Infrastructure Act 2015 (which came into effect on 12 February 2015) has inserted sections 61DA to 61DE in the 1990 Act, giving the Mayor of London power to make Mayoral Development Orders that grant planning permission for development specified in the order on one or more sites identified in the order. However, the Secretary of State may by development order specify an area or class of development in respect of which a mayoral development order must not be made.

The current work is confined to changes of use and other considerations relating to the use of land and buildings, and so a large part of the statutory regime for permitted development under these orders lies beyond the scope of this book. Similarly, special development orders, local development orders, neighbourhood development orders and mayoral development orders are too local or specialised in their effect to permit of their coverage here.

So far as the specific permitted changes of use are concerned, Article 3(1) of the GPDO grants planning permission for the classes of development described as permitted development in Schedule 2 to the Order. This is, however, subject to the provisions of the Order (and, where relevant, to Regulations 73 to 76 of the Conservation of Habitats and Species Regulations 2010 (S.I. 2010 No. 490) in respect of general development orders), as well as any relevant exception, limitation or condition specified in Schedule 2.

It is unlikely, in most cases, that a change of use permitted by Schedule 2 of the GPDO would raise issues with regard to the habitats regulations, but it is a condition of any planning permission granted by a general development order that in those cases where a development is likely to have a significant effect on a European site (such as a Ramsar Site or a Special Area of Conservation) or a European offshore marine site, either alone or in combination with other plans or projects, the development must not be begun until the developer has received written notification of the approval of the local planning authority under Regulation 75. This application must give details of the development which is intended to be carried out, and must be accompanied by a copy of any relevant notification of the opinion of an appropriate nature conservation body under Regulation 74, together with a fee of £30.

This condition relating to the habitats regulations is entirely separate from and additional to the provisions relating to development that may require an environmental impact assessment (as to which, see *paragraph A.11* in *Appendix A*).

Finally, by Article 1(3), nothing in the GPDO applies to any permission that is deemed to be granted under section 222 of the 1990 Act for the use of any external part of a building for the display of advertisements which is not normally used for that purpose, if the advertisements are displayed in compliance with the Control of Advertisements Regulations. The GPDO does not affect the display of advertisements in any way, which is entirely governed by sections 55(5) and 222 of the Act and by the provisions of the Control of Advertisements Regulations.

1.2 Loss or removal of permitted development rights

Permitted development rights that would otherwise be exercisable under the GPDO may be excluded in several ways. It is important to check these factors before embarking on development in reliance on the permitted development rights granted by Article 3 and Schedule 2 to the GPDO, and before making any prior approval application in respect of such development. The various ways in which permitted development rights can be lost or excluded are discussed in *Appendix A*.

Paragraph A.1 in *Appendix A* also points out that in order for a change of use to be made as permitted development under Part 3, 4 or 5 of the Second Schedule, the relevant building or land must be in use for the specified qualifying purpose at the relevant time and, as explained in *paragraph A.4*, this pre-existing use must also be a lawful use. *Appendix A* also stresses that the pre-existing use must fall wholly and exclusively within the Use Class (or the appropriate part of that Use Class) which is specified in the relevant Class of development under Part 3, 4 or 5.

All the factors discussed in *Appendix A* need to be considered in order to ensure that the proposed development does qualify as permitted development under the terms of the GPDO.

1.3 Changes of use under Part 3

Prior to 2013, the changes of use that were allowed under Part 3 of the Second Schedule to the General Permitted Development Order were somewhat limited in scope. However, as a result of amendment orders made in 2013 and 2014, and now consolidated and further extended in the 2015 Order, the range of changes of use that can be made as permitted development has been considerably widened.

It should be noted, however, that many of these more recently introduced permitted development rights are subject to prior approval by the local planning authority in respect of certain aspects of the proposed change of use and the operational development (if any) associated with it, and so the new provisions have in effect introduced a new type of planning consent, which is intended to represent a lighter form of development management, but which still allows local planning authorities to determine, within certain parameters, whether the proposed change of use should be allowed to take place.

Chapters 2 to *12* examine those provisions in Part 3 of the Second Schedule to the GPDO which permit a permanent change of use of various buildings used within specified classes of the Use Classes Order, and changes of use that may be made to agricultural buildings, and to certain other buildings whose use is *sui generis* (of its own kind), and which are not therefore within the scope of the Use Classes Order. The use classes defined by the UCO are briefly summarised in *Appendix C* at the end of this book.

The individual Classes of development permitted by Part 3 of the Second Schedule to the GPDO are summarised in *Table 1* at the end of this Chapter, in the order in which they appear in the GPDO. The detailed provisions in respect of each of these Classes of development are explained in *Chapters 2* to *12*. Several of the new permitted development rights reflect the changes made to the Use Classes Order in April 2015, by which Betting Offices and Pay Day Loan Shops have been removed from Use Class A2, so that each of these uses is now *sui generis*. Others represent a further significant expansion of the permitted development that is now enabled by the GPDO, in addition to the changes previously made in 2013 and 2014.

In the first column of *Table 1*, an asterisk in front of the Class designation indicates that a prior approval application is required (as explained in the relevant chapter). The second column shows the corresponding Class of development that was permitted by the 1995 Order, from which it will be seen that Part 3 has grown considerably. The Classes shown in brackets in that column - (A), (C) and (CA) - indicate that those Classes of permitted development in the 1995 Order were not coextensive with the corresponding provisions in the 2015 Order.

The paragraph numbers in the last column on the right in *Table 1* refer to the paragraphs in the text of *Chapters 2* to *12* that explain the relevant provisions in detail.

1.3.1   *The physical extent of changes of use permitted by Part 3*

The extent of the property to which the planning permission granted by Part 3 applies varies according to the description of the development which is set out in each of the Classes of development specified in the text of this statutory instrument. In the absence of any more precise definition, development which is permitted in respect simply of "a building" or in respect of "land" can be taken to apply to the whole of the relevant planning unit (in accordance with the criteria discussed in *paragraph B.1.2* in *Appendix B*). In the case of "a building" the planning unit may include any land occupied together with the building as part of one and the same planning unit, and in the case of "land" it would clearly apply to the whole of the land comprising that planning unit (including any buildings erected on it). The same would apply to the term "a building or other land".

In relation to the change of use of a "building", it should be borne in mind that the definition of "building" in Article 2(1) of the GPDO includes any part of a building. Thus there is no reason in principle why a change of use permitted by Part 3 should not be made in respect of part only of an existing building (thus creating a new planning unit), leaving the remaining part of the building unconverted. In practice, however, this may raise an issue relating to noise impact in certain cases (see *paragraph 14.4.7* in *Chapter 14*) or other impacts (see the example given at the end of *paragraph 14.4.11*).

Furthermore, where the permitted development defined by a particular Class in Part 3 refers to "a change of use to a use within Class [XX]" of the Use Classes Order, this is not confined to the creation of only one new planning unit. In the residential conversion of office buildings under Class O it is quite usual for a single development to create a number (in some cases quite a large number) of new dwellings within the building. There is, however, a limit to the number of dwellings that can be created under Class Q (residential conversion of an agricultural building) - see *paragraph 9.5* in *Chapter 9*.

In some cases, the permitted development relates to "a building and any land within its curtilage". The permitted development specified by those Classes will not necessarily cover the whole of the pre-existing planning unit (as explained in *paragraph B.2.1* in *Appendix B*). In these cases, the area of land which may be included in the permitted change of use is clearly restricted to that part of the property which falls within the area that can properly be defined as the "curtilage" of the building and, in those cases where "curtilage" is not defined, the generally accepted definition of the word discussed in *paragraph B.2.1* should be applied. However, "curtilage" is given a specific (and extremely restrictive) meaning for the purposes of Classes P, Q, R and S, which allows only a very small area of land adjacent to the agricultural [or storage] building to be included in the permitted change of use in these cases.

There are also passing references to "the site" at various places in the text. Paragraphs P.3 and X in Part 3 define "site" as "the building and any land within its curtilage". "The site", wherever it occurs, is therefore to be construed in the same way as that term, as explained above.

One point which may arise in a number of cases is that if the permitted development in question does not subsume the whole of the pre-existing planning unit, then a new, smaller, planning unit will be created by the permitted change of use, leaving the remainder of the pre-existing planning unit as a separate planning unit, the lawful use of which will be unaffected by the change of use of the part of the planning unit which has been separated from it by the permitted change of use.

1.3.2   Commencement and completion of the permitted development

Several of the Classes of permitted development in Part 3 are subject to a condition imposing a time limit on either the commencement of development or its completion. In the case of those Classes that permit operational development in addition to a change of use, there may be no difficulty in determining when a material operation is carried out so as to constitute the commencement of that development (by analogy with the well-known judicial authorities dealing with the interpretation of section 56 of the 1990 Act). Similarly, there will be no difficulty in determining whether or not the operational development has been substantially completed (by reference to the House of Lords decision in *Sage v SSETR and Maidstone BC* [2003] UKHL 22).

Except where operational development is a necessary component of the permitted development which is to be carried out, 'commencement' (or 'beginning the development') and 'completion' will, in the case of a permitted change of use, be effectively one and the same event, because a change of use is a single event; it is not a gradual process or a continuing state of affairs (see *Cynon Valley BC v SSW* (1987) 53 P. & C. R. 68). The question then arises as to precisely when that change of use actually takes place, particularly where that change of use is to use as a single private dwelling.

It is clear that, in the case of a residential conversion, it is a prerequisite to such a change of use that the building must, as a question of fact, be constructed or adapted for use as a dwellinghouse as normally understood, that is to say, as a building that provides for the main activities of, and ordinarily affords the facilities required for, day-to-day private domestic existence (*Gravesham B.C. v SSE* (1984) P. & C. R. 142), but it was accepted in that case that *Scurlock v SSW* (1976) P. & C. R. 202 was authority for the proposition that regard must also be had to the actual use to which the building has been put.

However, the judgment in *Impey v Secretary of State for the Environment* (1984) 47 P. & C. R. 157 suggested that a change of use to residential use can take place before the premises are used in the ordinary and accepted sense of the word (for example, where operations have been undertaken to convert premises for residential use and they are then put on the market as being available for letting). Whilst nobody is using those premises in the ordinary connotation of the term, because they are empty, there has plainly, on those facts, been a change of use (although, as always, this will be a matter of fact and degree in each case).

The correctness of the judgment in *Impey* was doubted in *Backer v SSE* (1984) 47 P. & C. R. 149, where the deputy judge expressed the view that, were it not for *Impey*, he would have had no hesitation in accepting an argument that physical works of conversion cannot by themselves give rise to a material change of use, and that some actual use is required. However, Lord Mance, at paragraph 29 of *Welwyn Hatfield v SSCLG* [2011] UKSC 15, did not share the doubt on this point expressed in *Backer*. Too much stress had, he thought, been placed on the need for actual use, with its connotations of familiar domestic activities carried on daily.

In dealing with a provision which speaks of "change of use of any building to use as a single dwelling house" [or other statutory words to the same effect], it is more appropriate to look at the matter in the round and to ask what use the building has or of what use it is. Lord Mance considered it artificial to say that a building has or is of no use at all, or that its use is as anything other than a dwelling house, when its owner has just built it to live in and is about to move in within a few days' time, having probably also spent a good deal of that time planning the move.

In light of what Lord Mance said in *Welwyn Hatfield*, whilst the change of use cannot be said to have taken place until or unless the building has the necessary facilities to qualify it as a dwellinghouse under the rule in *Gravesham*, it is nevertheless clear, on the basis of both *Impey* and *Welwyn Hatfield*, that the actual use of the building as a dwelling need not actually have commenced, although it should perhaps be imminent, or imminently likely. In other words it should be immediately available or potentially available for residential occupation. If that point has been reached, then it would seem that the change of use can be said to have taken place, so that the development comprising that change of use can be regarded at that point both to have been 'begun', and to have been completed, for the purposes of compliance with any time limit imposed by the relevant Class in Part 3. This point is likely to be of particular importance in relation to the deadline imposed on development permitted under Class P (residential conversion of a building used for storage).

A further issue may arise in the case of development that involves the creation of more than one residential unit, where not all of the residential units have been occupied by the due date leaving one or more other units uncompleted by that date. This is most likely to arise in developments carried out under Class O, which sometimes involve the creation of a substantial number of new dwellings, and it is therefore discussed in *paragraph 7.5 of Chapter 7*.

1.4   *Temporary uses under Part 4*

Part 4 of the Second Schedule to the GPDO permits the temporary use of open land for various purposes (under Class B), the temporary use of certain buildings (under Classes C and D) and the temporary use of buildings or land for film-making (under Class E).

The physical extent of the change of use permitted by Part 4 varies in the case of each class of development. Class B refers to the use of "any land", which must be taken to be the whole of the relevant planning unit (but excluding any building on the land and any land within the curtilage of a building).

Classes C and D both refer to "a building and any land within its curtilage". The permitted development specified by these two Classes clearly extends only to the land within the curtilage of the building, which in some cases will not cover the whole of the relevant planning unit (as explained in *paragraph B.2.1* in *Appendix B*). In any such cases, the area of land which may be included in the permitted change of use is clearly restricted to that part of the property which falls within the area that can properly be defined as the 'curtilage' of the building.

Class E refers to "any land or buildings" and "such land". As in the case of Class B, this must be taken to refer to the whole of the relevant planning unit, and in this case it would embrace any building within that planning unit and any land within the curtilage of such a building, subject to the limit as to its area imposed by Class E.

The individual classes of development permitted by Part 4 of the Second Schedule to the GPDO are summarised in *Table 2* at the end of this Chapter, and the detailed provisions are explained in *Chapters 16, 17* and *18*.

The asterisk in the first column of *Table 2* against Classes E(a) and E(b) serve as a reminder that a prior approval application is required (as explained in the *Chapter 18*). With the exception of Class E, all the Classes of development in Part 4 also appeared in Part 4 in the 1995 Order.

The paragraph numbers in the last column on the right in *Table 2* refer to the paragraphs in the text of the relevant chapter that explain the provisions of Part 4 in detail.

1.5   *Caravan sites and recreational uses under Part 5*

Part 5 of the Second Schedule to the GPDO permits the temporary use of land as a caravan site (under Class A), and also permits the use of land (on a permanent basis) by members of certain organisations for camping and other recreational or instructional purposes (under Class C). The latter provision replaces the former Part 27 in the 1995 Order.

[Part 5, Class B relates to operational development, and is not within the scope of the present book.]

The change of use permitted by Class A of Part 5 applies to "land, other than a building". This must be taken to apply to the whole of the relevant planning unit (but excluding any building within that planning unit). On the other hand, it may include any part of the land that is within the curtilage of a building within the same planning unit.

Class C relates simply to "land", and therefore applies to the whole of the relevant planning unit, subject only to the following exclusions. In this case, development is not permitted if the 'land' in question is a building, nor is it permitted within the curtilage of a dwellinghouse, but development within the curtilage of any other building is not precluded.

As in other cases, the identification of the relevant planning unit is explained in *part B.1* of *Appendix B*, and the 'curtilage' of a dwellinghouse or other building may be identified by reference to the rules discussed in *part B.2* of *Appendix B*.

The individual classes of development permitted by Part 5 of the Second Schedule to the GPDO are summarised in *Table 3* at the end of this Chapter, and the detailed provisions are explained in *Chapters 19* and *20*.

With the exception of Class C, all the Classes of development in Part 5 also appeared in Part 5 in the 1995 Order. Class C formerly comprised Part 27 of the 1995 Order. The paragraph numbers in the last column on the right in *Table 3* refer to the paragraphs in the text of the relevant chapter that explain the provisions of Part 5 in detail.

1.6 *Saving provisions in respect of the 1995 Order*

Article 8 of the GPDO 2015 revokes all the statutory instruments listed in Schedule 4 of this Order, including the 1995 Order, and the amendment orders of 2013, 2014 and March 2015.

So far as the continuing effect of the provisions of the 1995 Order is concerned, section 16(1) of the Interpretation Act 1978 provides that where an Act repeals an enactment, the repeal does not (unless the contrary appears) affect the previous operation of the enactment repealed or anything done or suffered under that enactment. Although this section refers to Acts of Parliament, section 23(1) makes it clear that the provisions of the Interpretation Act also apply (unless the contrary intention appears) to subordinate legislation, including any such legislation made after the commencement of that Act, in the same way as they apply to Acts of Parliament.

Section 17(2)(b) also provides that where an Act repeals and re-enacts, with or without modification, a previous enactment (or piece of subordinate legislation - see section 23) then, unless the contrary intention appears, in so far as any thing done under the enactment so repealed could have been made or done under the provision re-enacted, it is to have effect as if made or done under that provision (i.e. under the re-enacted provision).

The effect of sections 16(1) and 17(2)(b) is therefore that if, for example, an Article 4 Direction was made under the 1995 Order, it will continue to have effect in respect of permitted development under the corresponding provisions of the 2015 Order, as if made under that Order. Similarly, it would seem that, under section 16(1), permitted development commenced before 15 April 2015 can be completed in accordance with the terms of the 1995 Order, and that the restrictions, limitations and conditions relating to that permitted development will continue to be those of the 1995 Order.

However, it would appear that the effect of section 17(2)(b) when applied to a prior approval given before 15 April 2015, but where the permitted development did not commence before that date, is that this should be treated as a prior approval granted under the 2015 Order, so that the permitted development in question will now be governed by the restrictions, limitations and conditions in the relevant Class of the 2015 Order.

In the same way, where a prior approval application, or an appeal against the refusal of prior approval, was made before 15 April 2015 but had not been determined by that date, it will now fall to be determined as if the application had been made under the 2015 Order, and it will be determined in accordance with the provisions of the 2015 Order. LPAs and the Planning Inspectorate have certainly been proceeding since 15 April 2015 on the basis that applications and appeals already 'in the pipeline' are to be processed and determined in this way.

It could reasonably be expected that a savings provision would in any event have been included in the new Order, and Article 8 does indeed contain such a provision. However, the saving in Article 8(2) is solely for the purposes of development specified in Article 6(2) of the March 2015 amendment order, namely in respect only of a temporary change of use, under Class C or Class D of Part 4, of premises used within Use Class A4 (drinking establishments) [see *Chapters 17* and *18*] , and certain demolition under what had been Part 31 in the 1995 Order (now replaced by Part 11 in the 2015 Order). There is nothing else in the 2015 Order itself that expressly preserves the effect of any of the provisions of the 1995 Order, which must therefore be governed solely by the Interpretation Act.

There remains, however, a slight element of doubt as to whether section 16 and/or section 17 of the Interpretation Act (read together with section 23) would have the effect of amalgamating those conditions which imposed limits on the cumulative amount of floorspace that can be converted under a particular Class in the 1995 Order or which limited the number of dwellings that could be created under that Class, with the corresponding conditions in the Classes of development which have replaced them in the 2015 Order. If one applies a purposive interpretation to the 1978 Act, it is reasonable to conclude that it was intended to have such an effect, and in practice LPAs and the Planning Inspectorate can be expected to apply these sections in the Interpretation Act to the operation of the 1995 GPDO and the 2015 GPDO in this way. It is unfortunate, however, that the opportunity was not taken in the 2015 Order to spell this out in clear terms.

Table 1: Changes of use permitted by Part 3

An asterisk in the first column indicates that a prior approval application is required.

The paragraph numbers in the last column on the right refer to the paragraphs in the text of the following chapters that explain the relevant provisions in detail.

Part 3 (2015) CLASS	Part 3 (1995) CLASS	FROM Use Class	TO Use Class	Para in text
A	(A)	A3, A4 or A5	A1	2.1.1
	(C)	A3, A4 or A5	A2	2.2.1
B	AA	A4 or A5	A3	3.1
*C(a)(i)	---	A1 or A2	A3	3.2.1
*C(a)(ii)	---	Betting or Loans	A3	3.2.1
*C(a)(iii)	---	Casino	A3	3.2.1
*C(b)(i)	---	----------	Ventilation/extraction for C(a)	3.2.1
*C(b)(ii)	---	----------	Rubbish storage for C(a)	3.2.1
D	(CA)	A1	A2	2.2.2
E(a)	D	A2	A1	2.1.2
E(b)	---	Betting or Loans	A1	2.1.2
F	---	Betting or Loans	A2	2.2.3
G(a)	F(a)	A1	A1 + flat(s)	2.3.1
G(b)	---	A1	A2 + flat(s)	2.3.3
G(c)(i)	F(b)	A2	A2 + flat(s)	2.3.4
G(c)(ii)	---	Betting or Loans	A2 + flat(s)	2.3.4
G(d)(i)	F(c)	A2	A1 + flat(s)	2.3.1
G(d)(ii)	---	Betting or Loans	A1 + flat(s)	2.3.1
G(e)	---	Betting or Loans	Betting or Loans + flat(s)	2.3.4
H(a)	G(a)	A1 + flat(s)	A1	2.3.2
H(b)	---	A1 + flat(s)	A2	2.3.5
H(c)(i)	G(b)	A2 + flat(s)	A2	2.3.6
H(c)(ii)	---	Betting or Loans + flat(s)	A2	2.3.6
H(d)(i)	G(c)	A2 + flat(s)	A1	2.3.2
H(d)(ii)	---	Betting or Loans + flat(s)	A1	2.3.2
H(e)	---	Betting or Loans + flat(s)	Betting or Loans	2.3.6
I(a)	B(a)	B2 or B8	B1	4.1
I(b)	B(b)	B1 or B2	B8	4.1
*J(a)	---	A1 or A2	D2	11.1
*J(b)	---	Betting or Loans	D2	11.1

Table 1 *(continued)*

Part 3 (2015) CLASS	Part 3 (1995) CLASS	FROM Use Class	TO Use Class	Para in text
K	*H*	Casino	D2	*4.5*
L(a)	*I(a)*	C4	C3	*5.1*
L(b)	*I(b)*	C3	C4	*5.1*
*M(a)(i)	*IA(a)(i)*	A1 or A2	C3	*5.2.1*
*M(a)(ii)	---	Betting or Loans	C3	*5.2.1*
*M(a)(iii)(aa)	---	C3 + Betting or Loans	C3	*5.2.1*
*M(a)(iii)(bb)	*IA(a)(ii)*	C3 + A1 or A2	C3	*5.2.1*
*M(b)	*IA(b)*	----------	Building operations for M(a)	*5.2.1*
*N(a)(i)	---	Amusements	C3	*6.1*
*N(a)(ii)	---	Casino	C3	*6.1*
*N(b)	---	----------	Building operations for N(a)	*6.1*
*O	*J*	B1(a)	C3	*7.1*
*P	---	B8	C3	*8.1*
*Q(a)	*MB(a)*	Agricultural building	C3	*9.1*
*Q(b)	*MB(b)*	----------	Building operations for Q(a)	*9.1*
(*) R	*M*	Agricultural building	Flexible use - A1, A2, A3, B1, B8, C1 or D2	*12.2.1*
*S	*MA*	Agricultural building	State-funded school or registered nursery	*10.2*
*T	*K*	B1, C1, C2, C2A or D2	State-funded school or registered nursery	*10.1.1*
U	*L*	Use permitted by Class T	Previous lawful use	*10.1.7*
V	*E*	Use under flexible PP	Other use under flexible PP	*12.1*

Table 2: Changes of use permitted by Part 4

An asterisk in the first column indicates that a prior approval application is required.

The paragraph numbers in the last column on the right refer to the paragraphs in the text of the following chapters that explain the relevant provisions in detail.

Part 4 (2015) CLASS	Part 4 (1995) CLASS	Permitted development	Para in text
(A)	(A)	(Temporary buildings and structures)	(19.9)
B	B	Temporary use of any land	16.1
C	C	Temporary use as a state-funded school	17.1.1
D	D	Temporary use of various business premises	17.2.1
* E(a)	---	Temporary use for film-making	18.1
* E(b)	---	Building operations for E(a)	18.1

Table 3: Changes of use permitted by Part 5

* The entries in Column 1 indicated by an asterisk refer to relevant paragraphs in Schedule 1 to the Caravan Sites and Control of Development Act 1960.

The paragraph numbers in the last column on the right refer to the paragraphs in the text of the following chapters that explain the relevant provisions in detail.

Part 5 CLASS	Permitted development	Para in text
A	Temporary use as a caravan site	19.1
(* para 1)	(- caravans within the curtilage of a dwellinghouse)	19.4
* para 2	- temporary caravan camping on a small site	19.5
* para 3	- temporary caravan camping on larger sites	19.6
* para 4	- sites occupied and supervised by exempted organisations	19.7
* para 5	- sites approved by exempted organisations	19.7
* para 6	- meetings organised by exempted organisations	19.7
* para 7	- temporary use of a caravan site by agricultural workers	19.8
* para 8	- temporary use of a caravan site by forestry workers	19.8
* para 9	- temporary use by workers on building and engineering sites	19.9
* para 10	- travelling showmen's sites	19.10
[B]	[excluded from this book]	-------
C	Use for camping and recreation by certain organisations	20.1

CHAPTER 2

CHANGES OF USE TO / FROM SHOPS OR 'RETAIL' SERVICES

2.0   Preliminary note

A distinction has always been drawn between those premises classified by the Use Classes Order as 'shops' (falling within Use Class A1) and premises used for the provision of financial and professional services or other services which it is appropriate to provide in a shopping area, often referred to colloquially as 'retail services' (falling within Use Class A2).

The description of the latter in the Use Classes Order specifically included betting offices as an example of 'other' services which were appropriate in a shopping area, but with effect from 15 April 2015, a betting office is now a *sui generis* use. Similarly, 'financial services' were not limited by any classification or description, and would therefore have included the type of use known as a 'Pay Day Loan Shop'. However, with effect from 15 April 2015, this too has become a *sui generis* use.

A 'Pay Day Loan Shop' is defined by Article 3(6) of the UCO as premises from which high-cost short-term credit is provided principally to visiting members of the public and includes premises from which such credit is provided in addition to other financial or professional services, and which would otherwise fall within Use Class A2 (financial and professional services). The reference to "high-cost short-term credit" in Article 3(6) has the meaning given in the edition of the Financial Conduct Authority's Handbook which came into effect on 1 April 2014 (following an amendment by the Authority in the Consumer Credit (Consequential and Supplementary Amendments) Instrument 2014).

Notwithstanding this, it should be borne in mind that a lawful use of premises within Use Class A2 that existed before 15 April 2015, or for which a planning permission was granted before that date (even if it was not implemented until after that date), still enables the premises to be used for the whole range of uses within that use class *as it existed before 15 April 2015*, including use as a betting office or as a pay day loan shop (unless prevented by a condition attached to the planning permission, as discussed in *paragraph A.5* in *Appendix A*).

Paragraph 22 of Circular 03/2005 confirmed that, unless otherwise indicated, a planning permission is interpreted on the basis of the Use Classes Order in force at the time the consent was given. [Circular 03/2005 was cancelled in March 2014, but the principles that it expounded continue to hold good, notwithstanding that it no longer bears the ministerial *imprimatur*.]

Circular 03/2005 referred specifically to "consent for an A3 use", but it is clear that this would also apply to Use Class A2 in the same way, and that it would apply equally to any permission which identifies the development solely by description (e.g. as a 'bank' or 'building society branch') without referring to the use class as such. In that case, the premises could only be used in the first place for the precise purpose described in the permission but, in the absence of any condition preventing it, any change of use within the pre-2015 version of Use Class A2, including use as a betting office or as a pay day loan shop, could then be made subsequently, and could still be made, by virtue of section 55(2)(f) of the 1990 Act.

There had long been resistance to the change of use of premises within Use Class A1 to uses falling within Use Class A2, although the GPDO has for many years allowed a change of use in the opposite direction, from A2 to A1 (subject to certain limitations). Now, however, there is significantly greater freedom for changes of use from Use Class A1 ('shop') to A2 (financial or professional services) and also to A3 (café or restaurant). Following the removal of betting offices and pay day loan shops from Use Class A2, the GPDO also permits changes of use from either of these two *sui generis* uses to A1, A2 or A3 (although not *vice versa*).

The detailed provisions relating to these permitted changes of use are explained in this chapter.

2.1 Changes of use to and from use as a shop

The various changes of use permitted by Part 3 are complicated by the inclusion among them of changes of use to and from a shop (or premises used for financial or professional services) and up to two flats above those premises. The permitted changes of use to a use within Use Class A1 not involving additional residential accommodation are described first in this chapter (in *paragraphs 2.1.1* to *2.1.3*), and the various changes of use to and from A1 involving both a shop and a flat or flats above are dealt with separately (in *part 2.3* of this chapter).

The former provision in Part 3 of the GPDO which permitted a change of use from a car showroom to a use within Use Class A1 (shops) was removed with effect from 21 April 2005 and so, since that date, such a change of use has required planning permission.

2.1.1 Change of use from a catering use to use as a shop

Class A permits a change of use from a use falling within Use Classes A3 (restaurants and cafés), A4 (drinking establishments) or A5 (hot food take-aways) to a use within Use Class A1.

These permitted changes of use were not originally subject to any restriction, limitation or condition (other than the obvious proviso, as in all cases, that these permitted development rights have not been removed in any of the ways discussed in *Appendix A*) but, with effect from 6 April 2015, there is a restriction on changes of use of a building currently within Use Class A4. (See *paragraph 3.1.3* in *Chapter 3*.)

Prior to 15 April 2015, these were 'ratchet' provisions; they originally oper-ated in one direction only, and did not permit a change of use from Use Class A1 to Classes A3, A4 or A5. However, as explained in *part 3.2* of *Chapter 3*, Class C(a)(i) now permits a change of use from Use Class A1 to Use Class A3 (although not to A4 or A5).

2.1.2   *Change of use from 'retail services' to use as a shop*

Class E(a) (formerly Class D in the 1995 Order) permits a change of use of any building with a display window at ground floor level from a use falling within Use Class A2 (financial and professional services) to a use falling within Use Class A1 (shops). In addition, **Class E(b)** now permits a change of use of such a building from use as a betting office or as a pay day loan shop to a use falling within Use Class A1.

These changes of use are not subject to any condition, but can only arise if the qualifying criterion that the building must have a display window at ground floor level is met. This permitted change of use originally operated in one direction only (from A2 to A1), but the converse change of use from A1 to A2 (but not to use as a betting office or as a pay day loan shop) is now permitted by Class D (see *paragraph 2.2.2* below).

The ground floor display window does not need to be a purpose-designed display window. It is a matter of fact and degree in each case. Any ground floor window could potentially fulfil this role, provided it is not too small, too high, too far back from the pavement, or too obscured by glazing bars to qualify. (See *N Cornwall DC v SSETR* [2002] EWHC 2318 Admin.)

2.1.3   *Change of use of agricultural building to use as a shop*

Class R (formerly Class M in the 1995 Order) allows the change of use of a building and any land within its curtilage (subject to various conditions and restrictions) from use as an agricultural building to a flexible use that may include Use Class A1. There is a 500 sq m floorspace limit, and prior approval is required if the change of use involves more than 150 sq m of floorspace. This is discussed in detail in *part 12.2* of *Chapter 12*.

2.1.4   *Change of use from a shop to other uses*

The changes of use from Use Class A1 to other uses that are permitted by Part 3 are separately dealt with in this and the following chapters, but for ease of reference they are also listed here.

Class C(a)(i) permits a change of use from A1 to A3 (see *part 3.2* of *Chapter 3*).

Class D permits a change of use from A1 to A2 (see *paragraph 2.2.2* below).

Class J(a) permits a change of use from A1 to D2 (see *Chapter 11*).

Class M(a)(i) (formerly Class IA(a)(i) in the 1995 Order) permits a change of use from A1 to C3 (see *part 5.2* of *Chapter 5*).

Class M(a)(iii)(bb) (formerly Class IA(a)(ii) in the 1995 Order) permits a change of use from a mixed use combining a dwellinghouse with a use falling within Use Class A1 to a use falling wholly within Use Class C3 (see *part 2.3* of this chapter).

2.2   Changes of use to or from 'retail services'

The various changes of use permitted by Part 3 are complicated by the inclusion among them of changes of use to and from premises used for financial or professional services (or as a shop) and up to two flats above those premises. The permitted changes of use to a use within Use Class A2 not involving additional residential accommodation are described below in *paragraphs 2.2.1* to *2.2.3*, and the various changes of use to and from A2, and also to and from use as a betting office or as a pay day loan shop, involving both those premises and a flat or flats above, are dealt with separately in *part 2.3* of this chapter.

2.2.1   Change of use from catering use to 'retail services'

Class A permits a change of use from a use falling within Use Classes A3 (restaurants and cafés), A4 (drinking establishments) or A5 (hot food take-aways) to a use within Use Class A2 (financial or professional services - colloquially referred to as 'retail services'). These permitted changes of use were not originally subject to any restriction, limitation or condition (other than the obvious proviso, as in all cases, that these permitted development rights have not been removed in any of the ways discussed in *Appendix A*) but, with effect from 6 April 2015, there is a restriction on changes of use of a building currently within Use Class A4. (See *paragraph 3.1.3* in *Chapter 3*.)

Prior to 15 April 2015, these were 'ratchet' provisions. They originally operated in one direction only, and did not permit a change of use from Use Class A2 to Use Classes A3, A4 or A5. However, as explained in *part 3.2* of *Chapter 3*, Class C(a)(i) now permits a change of use from Use Class A2 to A3 (although not to A4 or A5).

2.2.2   Change of use of shop to 'retail services'

Between 6 April 2014 and 14 April 2015 the former Class CA in the 1995 Order permitted the change of use of a building and any land within its curtilage from a use falling within Use Class A1 (shops) to use as a 'deposit-taker' falling within Use Class A2 (financial and professional services). This permitted development has now been extended by **Class D** in the 2015 Order to allow a change of use to any use falling within Use Class A2 without restriction. However, the removal of betting offices and pay day loan shops from Use Class A2 with effect from 15 April 2015 prevents a change of use to either of these *sui generis* uses.

The development permitted by former Class CA related to "a building and any land within its curtilage". The wider permitted development under Class D is clearly intended to relate to the same unit, but there is a misprint in the printed copy of the 2015 Order, which will no doubt be corrected in due course, where the words "and any land" have been inadvertently omitted in Class D. The term 'curtilage' as used in Class D is not defined or limited, and must therefore be construed in accordance with its ordinary or natural meaning. (See *Appendix B, paragraph B.2.1.*)

In contrast to the former Class CA, there is no restriction in Class D preventing this change of use where the site is or forms part of a site of special scientific interest, a safety hazard area or a military explosives storage area, or if the site is, or contains, a scheduled monument. This restriction in the former Class CA would appear to have been anomalous and does not appear in Class D.

Similarly, the somewhat pettifogging conditions in the former Class CA of the 1995 Order have not been carried over into the new Class D. This change of use is therefore entirely free of conditions or restrictions.

2.2.3   Change of use of betting office / pay day loan shop to 'retail services'

Consequent on the removal of betting offices and pay day loan shops from Use Class A2, **Class F** now permits a change of use of such premises from use as a betting office or as a pay day loan shop to a use falling within Use Class A2 (financial or professional services, colloquially known as 'retail services'). This change of use is entirely free of conditions or restrictions.

2.2.4   Change of use of agricultural building to 'retail services'

Class R (formerly Class M in the 1995 Order) allows the change of use of a building and any land within its curtilage (subject to various conditions and restrictions) from use as an agricultural building to a flexible use that may include Use Class A2 (financial or professional services , colloquially known as 'retail services') but not a betting office or pay day loan shop. There is a 500 sq m floorspace limit, and prior approval is required if the change of use involves more than 150 sq m of floorspace. This is discussed in detail in *part 12.2* of *Chapter 12*.

2.2.5   Changes of use from 'retail' services to other uses

The changes of use from Use Class A2 to other uses that are permitted by Part 3 are separately dealt with in this and the following chapters, but for ease of reference they are also listed here. They are now supplemented by similar changes of use from use as a betting office or as a pay day loan shop to various other uses.

Class C(a)(i) permits a change of use from A2 to A3 (see *part 3.2* of *Chapter 3*).

Class C(a)(ii) permits a change of use from use as a betting office or as a pay day loan shop to A3 (also dealt with in *part 3.2* of *Chapter 3*).

Class E(a) (formerly Class D in the 1995 Order) permits a change of use from A2 to A1 (see *paragraph 2.1.2.* above).

Class E(b) permits a change of use from use as a betting office or as a pay day loan shop to A1 (also dealt with in *paragraph 2.1.2.* above).

Class J(a) permits a change of use from A2 to D2 (see *Chapter 11*).

Class M(a)(i) (formerly Class IA(a)(i) in the 1995 Order) permits a change of use from A2 to C3 (see *part 5.2* of *Chapter 5*).

Class M(a)(ii) permits a change of use from use as a betting office or as a pay day loan shop to C3 (also dealt with in *part 5.2* of *Chapter 5*).

Class M(a)(iii)(aa) permits a change of use from a mixed use combining a dwellinghouse with use as a betting office or as a pay day loan shop to a use falling wholly within Use Class C3. (This too is dealt with in *part 5.2* of *Chapter 5*.)

Class M(a)(iii)(bb) (formerly Class IA(a)(ii) in the 1995 Order) permits a change of use from a mixed use combining a dwellinghouse with a use falling within Use Class A2 to a use falling wholly within Use Class C3 (see again *part 5.2* of *Chapter 5*).

2.3   Flats above shops or 'retail services'

In an effort to increase the availability of residential accommodation in town centres and other retail centres, the government amended the GPDO some years ago to allow premises above shops or financial or professional services to be converted for residential use, initially limited to one flat but now (since 1 October 2012) up to two flats.

The re-conversion of such flats to form part of the shop premises or for the accommodation of the financial or professional services below them is also permitted by the GPDO, but only if those premises were used for that purpose immediately before their conversion to a flat or flats.

Following the removal of betting offices and pay day loan shops from Use

Class A2 with effect from 15 April 2015, the GPDO makes similar provision for a flat or flats to be created above such premises, and for the reconversion of such flats to their previous use as part of a betting office or pay day loan shop.

Bearing in mind that the GPDO permits not only a change of use from Use Class A2 to A1, but now also from A1 to A2, the changes of use that are now permitted by the GPDO include a combination of these uses with up to two flats, or a change of use between these two use classes involving the reconversion of such flats in connection with that change of use.

These various changes of use are permitted by Classes G and H in Part 3 of the GPDO, and are subject to the conditions and restrictions set out in paragraphs G.1 and H.1 respectively. In the following paragraphs the development permitted is described first, and the conditions and restrictions that apply to these changes of use are then dealt with in *paragraphs 2.3.7* and *2.3.8*.

2.3.1   *Change of use to shop plus flat(s)*

Class G(a) (formerly Class F(a) in the 1995 Order) permits the change of use of a building from a use for any purpose within Use Class A1 (shops) to a mixed use comprising any purpose within Use Class A1 and use as up to two flats.

Where that building has a display window at ground floor level (as to which, see *paragraph 2.1.2* above), **Class G(d)(i)** (formerly Class F(c) in the 1995 Order) permits a change of use from a use for any purpose within Use Class A2 (financial and professional services) to a mixed use comprising any purpose within Use Class A1 (shops) and up to two flats.

Class G(d)(ii) permits a similar change of use from use as a betting office or as a pay day loan shop to a mixed use comprising any purpose within Use Class A1 (shops) and up to two flats.

The conditions applying to changes of use under Class G are explained in *paragraph 2.3.7* below, where attention is also drawn to the judgment in *Valentino Plus Limited v SSCLG*.

2.3.2   *Reversion of part residential use to shop*

Class H(a) (formerly Class G(a) in the 1995 Order) permits the change of the use of a building from a mixed use comprising any purpose within Use Class A1 and up to two flats to a use for any purpose within Use Class A1 alone.

Where that building has a display window at ground floor level (as to which, see *paragraph 2.1.2* above), **Class H(d)(i)** (formerly Class G(c) in the 1995 Order) permits a change of use from a mixed use comprising any purpose within Use Class A2 (financial and professional services) and up to two flats to a use for any purpose within Use Class A1 (shops) alone.

Class H(d)(ii) permits a similar change of use from mixed use as a betting office or as a pay day loan shop and up to two flats to a use for any purpose within Use Class A1 (shops).

The changes of use permitted by Class H are subject to the exclusions set out in paragraph H.1, which are explained in *paragraph 2.3.8* below.

2.3.3   Change of use of shop to 'retail services' plus flat(s)

Class G(b) permits a change of use of a building from a use for any purpose within Use Class A1 (shops) to a mixed use comprising any purpose within Use Class A2 (financial or professional services, colloquially known as 'retail services') and use as up to two flats.

This change of use is subject to the conditions set out in paragraph G.1, which are explained in *paragraph 2.3.7* below, where attention is also drawn to the judgment in *Valentino Plus Limited v SSCLG*.

2.3.4   Partial residential conversion from 'retail services'

Class G(c)(i) (formerly Class F(b) in the 1995 Order) permits a change of use of a building from a use for any purpose within Use Class A2 (financial and professional services) to a mixed use comprising any purpose within Class A2 and use as up to two flats.

Class G(c)(ii) permits a similar change of use from use as a betting office or as a pay day loan shop to a mixed use comprising any purpose within Use Class A2 and up to two flats.

Class G(e) permits a similar change of use from use as a betting office or as a pay day loan shop to a mixed use comprising use as a betting office or as a pay day loan shop and up to two flats.

The changes of use permitted by Class G(c)(i) and G(c)(ii) are subject to the conditions set out in paragraph G.1, which are discussed in *paragraph 2.3.7* below, where attention is also drawn to the judgment in *Valentino Plus Limited v SSCLG*.

2.3.5   Change of use of shop and flat(s) to 'retail services'

Class H(b) permits a change of the use of a building from a mixed use comprising any purpose within Use Class A1 and up to two flats to a use for any purpose within Use Class A2 (financial and professional services, colloquially known as 'retail services').

This change of use is subject to the exclusions set out in paragraph H.1, which are explained in *paragraph 2.3.8* below.

2.3.6 Reversion of part residential use to 'retail services'

Class H(c)(i) (formerly Class G(b) in the 1995 Order) permits a change of the use of a building from a mixed use comprising any purpose within Use Class A2 (financial or professional services) and up to two flats to a use for any purpose within Class A2 alone.

Class H(c)(ii) permits a similar change of use from a mixed use as either a betting office or a pay day loan shop and up to two flats to a use within Use Class A2 alone.

Class H(e) permits a similar change of use from a mixed use as either a betting office or a pay day loan shop and up to two flats to use solely as a betting office or as a pay day loan shop.

These changes of use are subject to the exclusions set out in paragraph H.1, which are explained in *paragraph 2.3.8* below.

2.3.7 Conditions applying to changes of use under Class G

Paragraph G.1 provides that development permitted by Class G is subject to the following conditions:

(a) Some or all of the parts of the building used for any purposes within Use Class A1 or A2 (or as a betting office or pay day loan shop) must be situated on a floor below the lowest part of the building used as a flat;

(b) Where the development consists of a change of use of any building with a display window at ground floor level, the ground floor must not be used in whole or in part as a flat; and

(c) A flat must not be used otherwise than as a dwelling (whether or not as a sole or main residence) by a single person or by people living together as a family, or by not more than six residents living together as a single household (including a household where care is provided for residents).

[The reference to a household where care is provided for residents means personal care for people in need of such care by reason of old age, disablement, past or present dependence on alcohol or drugs or past or present mental disorder (paragraph G.2). It therefore includes a use within Use Class C3(b).]

The restriction of the use of each flat to use as a dwelling by a single person or by people living together as a family, or by not more than six residents living together as a single household, has the effect of restricting the use to one that falls wholly within Use Class C3 (including Class C3(c)). This condition therefore prevents the use of the building as a house in multiple occupation ('HMO' or 'HiMO' - now Use Class C4), even by way of a further change of use under Part 3.

These conditions prevent the creation of a basement flat below the shop, office premises, betting office or pay day loan shop. They also preclude the creation of a flat or flats on any floor below an upper floor of the building on which financial, professional or other services are situated. Nor can a flat be created on the ground floor where the building has a ground floor display window. In that case, the flat (or flats) must be on the floor or floors above the shop, office premises, betting office or pay day loan shop.

As confirmed by the High Court in *Valentino Plus Limited v SSCLG* [2015] EWHC 19 (Admin), the use of the premises resulting from the change of use permitted by Class G (formerly Class F) will not in reality be a mixed use because, having regard to the rule in *Burdle* (see *Appendix B, paragraph B.1.2.*), the change of use will result in the creation of separate planning units, namely the shop plus a separate flat (or two separate flats). Class G does not imply that the flat(s) need remain in the same ownership or occupation as the shop, office premises, betting office or pay day loan shop or be physically or functionally connected with them in any way.

2.3.8   *Development not permitted by Class H*

Paragraph H.1 provides that neither of the changes of use permitted by Class H can take place unless each part of the building used as a flat was, immediately prior to being used for that purpose, used for any purpose within Use Class A1 or A2, or (where applicable) as a betting office or pay day loan shop. In other words, the premises must already have been in use for the relevant purpose before the flat or flats was/were created or put to residential use, and so Class H is simply intended as the converse of Class G, so as to allow the change of use permitted by Class G to be reversed. The drafting is not as clear as it could be, but there is clearly no intention here to allow a change of use of, for example, a shop plus flat above to use as a betting office or as a pay day loan shop.

CHAPTER 3

CHANGES OF USE TO AND FROM CATERING USES

3.1 *Change of use of pub, bar or hot food take-away to café or restaurant*

Class B (formerly Class AA in the 1995 Order) permits the change of use of a building from a use falling within Use Class A4 (drinking establishments) or A5 (hot food take-aways) to a use falling within Use Class A3 (restaurants and cafés). It should be noted, however, that there is no permitted development right for a change of use from Use Class A5 to Class A4. These are 'ratchet' provisions. They operate in one direction only; they do not permit a change of use from Use Class A3 to Classes A4 or A5.

These permitted changes of use were not originally subject to any restriction, limitation or condition (other than the obvious proviso, as in all cases, that these permitted development rights have not been removed in any of the ways discussed in *Appendix A*), but there are now restrictions (introduced on 6 April 2015) on changing the use of a building currently within Use Class A4. (See *paragraph 3.1.3* below.)

3.1.1 *Change of use involving a pre-2005 A3 use*

There are two points that should be borne in mind when considering a change of use under Class B. First, the right to use catering premises which were granted planning permission before 21 April 2005 still extends to the whole range of uses covered by the pre-2005 version of Use Class A3 (subject only to any express exclusions or limitations contained in that or any subsequent planning permission).

This was confirmed by paragraph 22 of Circular 03/2005 which explained that, unless otherwise indicated, a planning permission is interpreted on the basis of the Use Classes Order in force at the time the consent was given. [Circular 03/2005 was cancelled in March 2014, but the principles that it explained continue to hold good, notwithstanding that it no longer bears the ministerial *imprimatur*.]

In its pre-2005 form, Use Class A3 comprised "*Use for the sale of food or drink for consumption on the premises or of hot food for consumption off the premises.*" This version of Class A3 covered all types of catering establishment, including pubs, wine bars, cafés/restaurants and hot food take-aways. No material change of use was involved in changing between any of these (although conditions attached to a planning permission could prevent such changes). Thus in the case of a planning permission issued before 21 April 2005, there is no need to resort to the GPDO in order to make such a change of use.

3.1.2   *Change of use involving a post-2005 A3 use*

The second point that is relevant when considering Class B is that whilst the new Use Class A3 (which came into effect on 21 April 2005) no longer embraces a use that is purely for the sale of drink for consumption on the premises (now covered by Use Class A4), it still includes "the sale of food *and* drink". Thus the current version of Use Class A3 embraces a range of uses in which the sale of drink for consumption on the premises may still be a substantial part of the business.

Paragraph 12 of Circular 03/2005 pointed out that it is the primary purpose of the use which must be considered, but a use will still fall within the current version of Use Class A3 if the primary use is clearly "use for the sale of food *and* drink for consumption on the premises"; it is not simply a question of whether the sale of food or the sale of drink comprises more than 50% of the business. A primary/ancillary relationship between uses is not dependent on the proportion or ratio of one use to the other, either in terms of turnover, or in terms of the floorspace devoted to the respective elements of these uses, but is dependent on their functional relationship. (See *Main v SSE* (1998) P. & C. R. 300; [1999] J.P.L. 195.)

The sale of food for consumption on the premises is likely to be ancillary to the sale of drink only if it is functionally dependent on the sale of drink. If it represents a substantial part of the business (which it may well do in many licensed premises nowadays) it is likely to be an independent element of the use in its own right, even if it represents less than 50% of the total turnover of the business. In the absence of the UCO, this might well have been regarded as a 'mixed use', but bearing in mind that the definition in Use Class A3 refers to the sale of both food *and* drink, any business consisting of a substantial element of both types of sale, without the sale of food necessarily being functionally dependent on the sale of drink (i.e. without any primary/ ancillary relationship between these two uses), would nevertheless appear to come within the current version of Class A3.

It would therefore appear that the amended wording of Use Class A3 is still wide enough to cover many public houses and wine bars where the service of food is a substantial part of the business in circumstances in which it cannot realistically be said to be purely ancillary to the sale of drink. Such premises would therefore appear to come within the current Use Class A3 rather than A4. In the same way, a licensed restaurant or café which sells drinks as a separate element of its business might still fall within Use Class A3, rather than A4, unless the sale of food for consumption on the premises is so limited as to be functionally dependent on, and therefore ancillary to, the sale of drink. This might allow significant expansion of the 'drinks' side of the business (at the bar) while remaining within Use Class A3, assuming that the bar is not both physically and functionally separate from the restaurant, and provided that the sale of food for consumption on the premises remains sufficiently substantial not to be merely ancillary to the sale of drink.

For these reasons, the author would respectfully disagree with the suggestion, formerly printed in paragraph 12 of Circular 03/2005, that in the case of premises which incorporate a restaurant use as well as a pub or bar use, it is necessary to determine whether the existing primary use of the premises is as a restaurant (A3), or as a drinking establishment (A4), or a mixed use. The paragraph went on to state that this would depend on such matters as "whether customers come primarily to eat, or drink, or both - it is the main purpose of that use that is to be considered". This assertion would appear to have been significantly at variance with the true legal position, which is explained above.

Thus in the circumstances described above, a use involving the sale of liquor and other drinks on the premises which already embraces, as a significant element of its use, the sale of hot food for consumption on the premises may already fall within the current Use Class A3 and thus can increase the proportion of the business devoted to the service of food without resort to the permitted development allowed by Part 3, Class B. The restriction and condition now contained in Class B (see *paragraph 3.1.3* below) would not therefore apply to any such change, provided that the sale of hot food for consumption on the premises was already a significant element of the business before 6 April 2015.

3.1.3   Restrictions on changes of use from Use Class A4

With effect from 6 April 2015, there is a restriction on the changes of use permitted by Part 3, Classes A and B, in respect of a building used within Use Class A4 (drinking establishments), where that building has been either nominated or designated as an "asset of community value" ('ACV'). Furthermore, even where the building has not been either nominated or designated as an asset of community value, the development permitted by those two classes of Part 3 is subject to the prior condition mentioned below.

A public house (as well as many other types of property) may be designated by the LPA as an ACV, on the application of the parish council or a recognised community interest group under Part 5, Chapter 3 of the Localism Act 2011, as supplemented by the Assets of Community Value (England) Regulations 2012 (S.I. 2012 No. 2421) (which came into effect on 21 September 2012). Public houses seem to be the type of property most commonly designated under the Act, representing slightly more than one-third of designated ACVs, with a very high proportion of nominations (not far short of 90%) having led successfully to the designation of pubs as assets of community value.

The primary effect of an ACV designation (which lies beyond the scope of this book) is a moratorium on the disposal of the property. However, in addition, there is now a restriction on the changes of use that are permitted by Part 3, Class A (change of use to a use within Use Class A1 - shop, or Use Class A2 - financial or professional services) and Class B (change of use to a use within Use Class A3 - for the sale of food and drink for consumption on the premises, i.e. a restaurant or café).

The restriction applies where the building is used for a purpose falling within Use Class A4 (drinking establishments) and either it has been designated as an ACV, or the LPA has notified the developer that it has been nominated as an ACV (i.e. proposed for designation) under section 89(2) of the Localism Act 2011.

In the case of a building which is already a designated ACV, the restriction lasts for a period of 5 years, beginning with the date on which the building was entered on the list of assets of community value. The restriction no longer applies where the building has been removed from that list under Regulation 2(c) of the Assets of Community Value (England) Regulations 2012 following a successful appeal against its designation, or because the local authority no longer considers the land to be land of community value, or where the building has been removed from that list under section 92(4)(a) of the Localism Act 2011 following the local authority's decision on a review that the land concerned should not have been included in the local authority's list of assets of community value. In those cases, the restriction applies during the period from the date on which the building was entered on the list of assets of community value to the date on which it was removed from that list.

In the case of a building that has been nominated as an ACV, but which has not yet been designated as such, the restriction lasts from the date on which the LPA notifies the developer of the nomination, to the date on which the building is entered on the list of assets of community value, or a list of land nominated by unsuccessful community nominations under section 93 of the Localism Act 2011. It follows that if the nomination results in the designation of the building as an ACV, the 5-year restriction mentioned above will then apply immediately, so that the restriction on the change of use will continue without a break, subject only to its possible termination by the subsequent removal of the building from the list of ACVs.

In the case of a building which is not an asset of community value but which is used for a purpose falling within Use Class A4 (drinking establishments) it is a condition that, before beginning the development, the developer must send a written request to the LPA as to whether the building has been nominated for designation as an ACV. This request must include the address of the building, the developer's contact address (and the developer's email address if the developer is content to receive communications electronically).

If the building is nominated for designation, whether before or after the date of the developer's request, the LPA must notify the developer as soon as is reasonably practicable after it is aware of the nomination, and upon that notification development is not permitted for the specified period mentioned above. Development under Classes A or B must not begin before the expiry of a period of 56 days following the date of the developer's request as to whether the building has been nominated for designation as an ACV and must be completed within a period of 1 year of the date of that request.

See *paragraph 1.3.2* in *Chapter 1* for a discussion of what constitutes the commencement and completion of development for the purposes of this condition.

It should be noted that even if a notification of the building's nomination for designation as an ACV is received after the expiry of the 56-day period (not to be confused with the 56-day period for the determination of any prior approval application), or after the LPA had earlier confirmed that no ACV nomination had been received, the restriction on the development permitted by Class A or Class B will nevertheless apply, unless the development has actually begun before the date on which notification is received from the LPA. It is therefore in a developer's interests to commence development as soon as possible after the expiry of this 56-day period, provided that no notification of an ACV nomination has been received from the LPA in the meantime.

If the use of the building had already changed from Use Class A4 to A3 (or to Use Class A2 or A1) before 6 April 2015, none of these restrictions or conditions applies to that building.

Consideration should also be given to the possibility that, if the use as a pub or wine bar began or became lawful before 21 April 2005, it may in any event be unnecessary to rely on Class B (as explained in *paragraph 3.1.1* above). Similarly, for the reasons explained in that paragraph, the new rules would not apply to a building used as a pub or wine bar within the scope of the previous version of Use Class A3, where planning permission was granted prior to that date.

In the case of a building that began to be used as a pub or wine bar within the scope of Use Class A4, or obtained planning permission for that use, after 20 April 2005, consideration should alternatively be given to the possibility that a change of use to a use within the scope of the current Use Class A3 may already have occurred (always provided that this happened before 6 April 2015) in the circumstances discussed in *paragraph 3.1.2* above.

3.2 Change of use from Use Class A1 or A2 (etc.) or Casino to Café or Restaurant

3.2.1 The development permitted

With effect from 15 April 2015, **Class C** permits a change of use from several other uses to use as a café or restaurant within Use Class A3. This permitted development falls into several sub-classes. **Class C(a)(i)** permits the change of use of a building from a use falling within Use Class A1 (shops) or A2 (financial and professional services); **Class C(a)(ii)** permits a change of use from use as a betting office or a pay day loan shop; and **Class C(a)(iii)** permits a change of use from use as a casino.

Building or other operations for the provision of facilities for ventilation and extraction (including the provision of an external flue) and for the storage of rubbish which are reasonably necessary for the use of the building as a café or restaurant are also permitted by **Class C(b)**. In contrast to similar operational development permitted under other classes in Part 3, there is no prohibition on the building or other operations that are permitted by Class C(b) resulting in the external dimensions of the building extending beyond the external dimensions of the existing building, but clearly this would be permissible only insofar as is strictly necessary for the purpose of providing ventilation or extraction and rubbish storage.

3.2.2 The qualifying use

Changes of use under Class C can be made if the building in question has an existing use within one or other of Use Classes A1 (shops) or A2 (financial and professional services) or if it is in use as a betting office, as a pay day loan shop or as a casino (all three of which are *sui generis* uses).

In this case, there is no qualifying date on or before which the building must have been in use for the purpose from which its use is to be changed, although the rule in *Kwik Save Discount Group Ltd v SSW* [1981] J.P.L. 198 should be borne in mind. (See *paragraph A.12* in *Appendix A.*)

3.2.3 Exclusions

Permitted development is excluded under Class C where the building is in a site of special scientific interest (SSSI), a safety hazard area or a military explosives storage area. Permitted development under Class C is also excluded where the building is a listed building or is within the curtilage of a listed building or where it is a scheduled monument.

So far as a building within the curtilage of a listed building is concerned, the relevant curtilage in this context (consistent with the interpretation of other legislative provisions prohibiting or restricting development within the curtilage of a listed building) must be taken to refer to the curtilage of the building at the time when it was first listed. (See *paragraph B.2.2* in *Appendix B* and the judgment in *R (Egerton) v Taunton Deane BC* cited in that paragraph.) The inclusion in the listing of any building attached to the listed building is also discussed at *paragraph B.2.3*.

However, in this case development is *not* excluded where the building is within a National Park, an Area of Outstanding Natural Beauty, a Conservation Area or the Broads or is within a World Heritage Site.

A "safety hazard area" is an area notified to the LPA by the Health and Safety Executive (the "HSE") for the purposes of paragraph (e) of the Table in Schedule 4 to the Development Management Procedure Order (or under the old General Development Procedure Order) or by the Office for Nuclear Regulation for the purposes of paragraph (f) of that Table.

A "military explosives storage area" is an area, including an aerodrome, depot or port, within which the storage of military explosives has been licensed by the Secretary of State for Defence, and identified on a safeguarding map provided to the LPA for the purposes of a direction made by the Secretary of State in exercise of powers conferred by article 33(1) of the DMPO (or under the old GDPO) (Article 2(1)).

There is at least one example of a change of use being prevented because the building was in a designated safety hazard area. An appeal in south-east London against the refusal of prior approval in respect of the proposed residential conversion of a small office unit under Class O was dismissed in August 2015 because it was within an HSE consultation zone. This is an absolute bar to permitted development. The appellant's argument that the nearby gasholders which had led to the designation are now empty and disused, so that they no longer represent a hazard, was unavailing.

3.2.4   Floorspace limit

The cumulative floor space of the existing building changing use under Class C must not exceed 150 sq m, and the change of use (together with any previous change of use under Class C) must not result in more than 150 sq m of floor space in the building having changed use under Class C.

3.2.5   Prior approval

Before beginning the development, the developer must apply to the local planning authority for a determination as to whether the prior approval of the authority will be required as to:

(a)   noise impacts of the development;

(b)   odour impacts of the development;

(c)   impacts of storage and handling of waste in relation to the development;

(d)   impact of the hours of opening of the development;

(e)   transport and highways impacts of the development;

(f)   whether it is undesirable for the building to change to a café or restaurant use because of the impact of the change of use on adequate provision of services of the sort that may be provided by a building falling within Use Class A1 (shops) or, as the case may be, Use Class A2 (financial and professional services) [i.e. depending on which of those two use classes applies to the current use of the building that is to be converted], but only where there is a reasonable prospect of the building being used to provide such services, or (where the building is located in a key shopping area) on the sustainability of that shopping area; and

(g)   the siting, design or external appearance of the facilities to be provided under Class C(b).

In contrast to the provisions relating to some other classes of permitted development under Part 3, there is no requirement in this case to take account of contamination risks or flooding risks in relation to the building.

The determination of the prior approval application in relation to these criteria, and other material considerations that are to be taken into account (under paragraph W), is discussed in *part 14.4* of *Chapter 14*.

A question has arisen in the past as to whether a prior approval application in respect of the permitted operational development may be made (and therefore considered and determined) separately from the prior approval application for the change of use. However, amendments to the GPDO incorporated in the 2015 Order have made it clear that an application for the change of use alone can no longer be made separately from the application in respect of the prior approval in respect of any necessary operational development, unless no such works will be required.

Thus paragraph C.2(2) provides that where the development proposed is development under both Class C(a) and Class C(b), an application is required as to whether the prior approval of the LPA will be required as to all of items (a) to (g) above, whereas if the application is made under Class C(a) only, where no building operations are proposed because they are not required in order to facilitate the change of use, then there is no need to address item (g). It will, however, be a fairly rare case where no provision is required for ventilation and extraction or for rubbish storage.

3.2.6   Commencement

It is a condition that the development permitted by Class C(a) and Class C(b) respectively must begin within a period of three years beginning with the date on which any prior approval is granted for that development, or beginning with the expiry of the 56-day period referred to in paragraph W(11)(c) without the local planning authority notifying the developer as to whether prior approval for that development is given or refused, whichever is the earlier (see *paragraph 14.10* in *Chapter 14*).

See *paragraph 1.3.2* in *Chapter 1* for a discussion of what constitutes the commencement of development for the purposes of this condition.

3.3   Other changes of use to café or restaurant

There is one other provision that allows a change of use from other uses outside the scope of the catering use classes to Use Class A3. This is **Class R** (formerly Class M in the 1995 Order), which allows the change of use of a building and any land within its curtilage (subject to various conditions and restrictions) from use as an agricultural building to a flexible use that may include Use Class A3. This is discussed in detail in *part 12.2* of *Chapter 12*.

3.4   Changes of use from catering uses to other uses

The only change of use from Use Classes A3, A4 or A5 to other uses outside the scope of the catering use classes that is permitted by Part 3 is **Class A**, which permits a change of use to a use within Use Classes A1 or A2. These changes of use are explained in *Chapter 2*, in *paragraphs 2.1.1* and *2.2.1* respectively.

CHAPTER 4

CHANGES OF USE TO AND FROM OTHER COMMERCIAL AND INSTITUTIONAL USES

4.1   Changes of use to and from a business, industrial or storage use

Class I(a) (formerly Class B(a) in the 1995 Order) permits a change of use of a building from any use falling within Use Class B2 (general industrial) or B8 (storage and distribution) to a use for any purpose falling within Use Class B1 (business), and **Class I(b)** (formerly Class B(b) in the 1995 Order) permits a change of use of a building from any use falling within Use Class B1 or B2 to a use for any purpose falling within Use Class B8.

Where the change of use is to or from a use falling within Use Class B8, paragraph I.1 restricts this change of use to no more than 500 sq m of floorspace in the building. (This floorspace limit was increased from 235 sq m with effect from 30 May 2013.) There is no limit as to floorspace in respect of a change of use from Use Class B2 to Class B1.

These permitted development rights do not allow the change of use of any floorspace from Use Class B1 to Class B2, but Article 3(4) of the Use Classes Order should be borne in mind, which provides that where land on a single site or on adjacent sites used as part of a single undertaking is used for purposes consisting of or including purposes falling within use classes B1 and B2, those classes may be treated as a single class in considering the use of that land for the purposes of the UCO, provided that the area used for a purpose falling within Use Class B2 is not substantially increased as a result.

Young v SSE [1983] A.C. 662 is an example of a change of use from Use Class B2 to Class B1 having taken place merely by virtue of the installation of equipment which eliminated emissions that had previously emanated from the premises, even though such a change of use had not been intended by the owners (with the result that the operations that could be conducted on the premises were thereafter constrained by the parameters of Use Class B1, rather than Class B2).

Class R (formerly Class M in the 1995 Order) permits the change of use of a building and any land within its curtilage (subject to various conditions and restrictions) from use as an agricultural building to a flexible use that may include Use Class B1 or Class B8. There is a 500 sq m floorspace limit, and prior approval is required if the change of use involves more than 150 sq m of floorspace. This provision is examined in detail in *part 12.2* of *Chapter 12*.

Turning to permitted changes of use of premises currently in use within Classes B1, B2 or B8 to uses within other use classes, **Class O** (formerly Class J in the 1995 Order) permits the change of use of a building and any land within its curtilage used as an office within Use Class B1(a) to residential use within Use Class C3 (dwellinghouses). This is subject to a prior approval process, and is currently excluded in certain areas specified in the GPDO, as well as by Article 4 Directions made by some authorities (see *paragraph A.8* in *Appendix A*). This permitted development does not include any works to the exterior of the building in order to facilitate the residential use of the premises. The detailed provisions relating to this permitted change of use, including forthcoming amendments, are examined in *Chapter 7*.

With effect from 15 April 2015, **Class P** permits the change of use of a building and any land within its curtilage from a use falling within Use Class B8 (storage, or distribution centre) to residential use within Use Class C3 (dwellinghouses). This is subject to a prior approval process. This permitted development does not allow any works to be carried out to the exterior of the building in order to facilitate the residential use of the premises. The detailed provisions relating to this permitted change of use are examined in *Chapter 8*.

This permitted development right will last for a period of only three years from the date on which it came into effect, so that a use permitted by this provision must be completed by 15 April, 2018. Although a similar deadline in respect of Class O (which would have expired on 30 May 2016) is to be lifted, no proposal has been made to extend the deadline in respect of Class P.

Class T (formerly Class K in the 1995 Order) permits the change of use of a building and any land within its curtilage from use within various use classes, including Use Class B1 (but not B2 or B8) to use as a state-funded school or as a registered nursery. This is subject to a prior approval process. There is also a right under **Class U** (formerly Class L in the 1995 Order) to revert to the previous lawful use of the land, without requiring any prior approval, where a permitted change of use to a state-funded school or registered nursery has taken place. These provisions are examined in detail in *part 10.1* of *Chapter 10*.

4.2 *Changes of use to and from use as a hotel or guest-house, etc.*

Class R (formerly Class M in the 1995 Order) permits the change of use of a building and any land within its curtilage (subject to various conditions and restrictions) from use as an agricultural building to a flexible use that may include Use Class C1 (use as a hotel or as a boarding or guest house, etc.). This provision is examined in detail in *part 12.2* of *Chapter 12*.

The only other change of use relating to Use Class C1 permitted under Part 3 of the Second Schedule to the General Permitted Development Order is under **Class T** (formerly Class K in the 1995 Order), which permits the change of use of a building and any land within its curtilage from a use falling within (inter alia) Use Class C1 (hotels) to use as a state-funded school, or to use as a registered nursery. This is subject to a prior approval process. Class U (formerly Class L in the 1995 Order) permits a change of use back to the previous lawful use of the land (without prior approval) where a permitted change of use to a state-funded school or registered nursery has taken place. These provisions are explained in detail in *part 10.1* of *Chapter 10*.

4.3 Changes of use to and from use as a residential institution

There is a right under **Class T** (formerly Class K in the 1995 Order) to change the use of various buildings, including premises falling within Use Class C2 (residential institutions, such as hospitals, nursing homes, residential schools and colleges and residential care homes) to use as a state-funded school or as a registered nursery. This is subject to a prior approval process. There is also a right under **Class U** (formerly Class L in the 1995 Order) to revert to the previous lawful use of the land, without requiring any prior approval, where a permitted change of use to a state-funded school or registered nursery has taken place. These provisions are examined in detail in *part 10.1* of *Chapter 10*.

4.4 Changes of use to and from Use Class C2A

There is a right under **Class T** (formerly Class K in the 1995 Order) to change the use of various buildings, including premises falling within Use Class C2A (secure residential institutions) to use as a state-funded school or to use as a registered nursery. This is subject to a prior approval process. There is also a right under **Class U** (formerly Class L in the 1995 Order) to revert to the previous lawful use of the land, without requiring any prior approval, where a permitted change of use to a state-funded school or registered nursery has taken place. These provisions are examined in detail in *part 10.1* of *Chapter 10*.

4.5 Change of use from Casino or Amusements to other uses

Class C(a)(iii) permits the change of use of a building from use as a Casino (a *sui generis* use) to use as a café or restaurant within Use Class A3. This change of use is subject to a prior approval application, and is explained in detail in *part 3.2* of *Chapter 3*.

Class N(a)(i) permits the residential conversion of a building used as an Amusement Centre or Amusement Arcade (a *sui generis* use). This change of use is subject to a prior approval application, and is explained in detail in *Chapter 6*.

Class N(a)(ii) permits the residential conversion of a building used as a Casino, and is also explained in *Chapter 6*. This too is subject to a prior approval application.

Class K (formerly Class H in the 1995 Order) permits the change of use of a building from use as a Casino to a use falling within Use Class D2 (Assembly and leisure). There are no conditions or restrictions relating to this permitted change of use.

4.6   *Temporary changes of use*

In addition to the changes of use described in this chapter, Part 4, Class D, of the Second Schedule to the GPDO permits a change of use, for up to two years, of a building and any land within its curtilage from a use falling within Use Classes A1 (shops), A2 (financial and professional services), A3 (restaurants and cafés), A4 (drinking establishments), A5 (hot food take-aways), B1 (business), D1 (non-residential institutions) or D2 (assembly and leisure) to a flexible use falling within either Use Class A1 (shops), A2 (financial and professional services), A3 (restaurants and cafés) or B1 (business). This provision is explained in detail in *part 17.2* of *Chapter 17*.

4.7   *Changes of use between flexible uses*

Class V in Part 3 (formerly Class E in the 1995 Order) permits development consisting of a change of the use of a building or other land from a flexible use authorised by a planning permission, to another use which that permission would have authorised when it was granted. These provisions are explained in *part 12.1* of *Chapter 12*.

CHAPTER 5

CHANGES OF USE TO AND FROM RESIDENTIAL USE

5.0 Preliminary note

This and the next four chapters deal with various residential conversion that are now permitted by Part 3 of the Second Schedule to the GPDO.

This chapter deals first (in *paragraph 5.1*) with the permitted development right originally introduced in 2010 which allows a change of use from a house in multiple occupation (within Use Class C4) to use as a single private dwelling (within Use Class C3), and *vice versa*.

The remainder of the chapter (*part 5.2*) then deals with residential conversion of a shop (A1) or of premises used for financial or professional services (A2), as well as from use as a betting office or as a pay day loan shop (the two *sui generis* uses recently separated from Use Class A2), including the incorporation of up to two existing flats (if any) above. Change of use from two other 'town centre' *sui generis* uses - as an amusement arcade or centre and as a casino, which would otherwise have come within Use Class D2 - then follows in *Chapter 6*.

The residential conversion of offices (used within Use Class B1(a)) is dealt with in *Chapter 7*, followed by the residential conversion from a storage or distribution centre use (within Use Class B8) in *Chapter 8*.

Finally, residential conversion of an agricultural building (a use falling wholly outside the statutory definitions in section 55, by virtue of section 55(2)(e) of the 1990 Act) is discussed in *Chapter 9*.

However, there are no permitted development rights under Part 3 for the residential conversion of any building whose use falls within the various catering uses within Use Classes A3, A4 and A5, within Use Class B2 (general industrial use), within Use Class C1 (use as a hotel or as a boarding or guest house), within Use Class C2 (use for the provision of residential accommodation and care to people in need of care, use as a hospital or nursing home, or use as a residential school, college or training centre), within Use Class C2A (use for the provision of secure residential accommodation of the types listed in that use class), within Use Class D1 (comprising various non-residential institutions used for the purposes listed in that use class) or within Use Class D2 (various assembly and leisure uses, as listed in that use class). The residential conversion of a building or part of a building in use for any of the uses listed above will therefore require planning permission.

At the time of writing there are no permitted development rights under Part

3 for the residential conversion of any building whose use falls within Use Class B1(b) (use for research and development) or B1(c) (light industrial use), but the government announced in October 2015 that they propose in future to allow the residential conversion of light industrial premises. At the time of going to press, further details were awaited.

One other point that should be borne in mind is that the definition of a "dwellinghouse" in Article 2(1) of the 2015 GPDO (which until 5 April 2014 entirely excluded any building containing one or more flats, and also a flat contained in such a building) no longer excludes buildings that contain flats, or any flat in such a building, from the definition of a dwellinghouse for the purposes of Part 3 of the Second Schedule to the GPDO (a "flat" being a separate and self-contained set of premises constructed or adapted for use for the purpose of a dwelling and forming part of a building from some other part of which it is divided horizontally). Bearing in mind that a "building" includes any part of a building, the relevant Classes of Part 3 that permit residential conversions therefore permit the change of use of the whole or any part of a building to use as a flat or flats.

5.1   Changes of use between single dwelling and house in multiple occupation

Prior to 2010, there were no provisions in the General Permitted Development Order which allowed a change of use to or from Use Class C3 (dwellinghouses). It was the introduction with effect from 6 April 2010 of Use Class C4 (houses in multiple occupation, previously a *sui generis* use), that prompted the addition to Part 3 of the Second Schedule to the GPDO of what was then Class I, now **Class L(a)** in the 2015 Order, which permits a change of use from Use Class C4 to use within Use Class C3. The incoming coalition government then amended Class I with effect from 1 October 2010, now **Class L(b)** in the 2015 Order, to allow in addition a change of use from Use Class C3 to an HMO within Use Class C4. This not only allows a change of use from C4 to C3 to be reversed but now allows complete freedom to change the use of a building at any time from Use Class C3 to C4 or *vice versa*.

In the 1995 Order, these either-way changes of use were not subject to any restriction, limitation or condition (other than the obvious proviso, as in all cases, that these permitted development rights had not been removed in any of the ways discussed in *Appendix A*), provided that they complied with the very detailed and prescriptive definitions of these two use classes, which were inserted in the Use Classes Order in April 2010. However, Class L in the 2015 Order is now subject to the proviso that development is not permitted by Class L if it would result in what had been a single dwellinghouse used as an HMO (within Use Class C4) being used as two or more separate dwellinghouses falling within Use Class C3, or *vice versa* (i.e. excluding from this permitted development the use of what had been a single dwellinghouse, used as such within Use Class C3, as two or more separate HMOs within Use Class C4, or the use of what had been a single HMO, used as such within Use Class C4, as two or more separate dwellings within Use Class C3).

It should be noted that the provisions in the Housing Act 2004 which apply to houses in multiple occupation make it important to determine whether a particular use falls within Use Class C3 or Class C4, and whether a change of use from C3 to C4 (or *vice versa*) has occurred.

There are no other permitted development rights that allow the change of use of a dwelling from Use Class C3 to any other use except C4, and none which allows any other change of use to or from Use Class C4. However, significant further provisions permitting changes of use of various other buildings and premises to residential use within Use Class C3 were introduced in 2013 and 2014, and were further extended in 2015. These most recent changes are all subject to a prior approval process, as explained below.

5.2 Residential conversion of a shop or from financial or professional services

5.2.1 The development permitted

Class M(a)(i) (formerly Class IA(a)(i) in the 1995 Order) permits the change of use of a building from a use falling within Use Class A1 (shops) or A2 (financial and professional services) to a use falling within Use Class C3 (dwellinghouses). Similarly, **Class M(a)(ii)** permits the residential conversion of a betting office or pay day loan shop; **Class M(a)(iii)(aa)** permits the residential conversion of a building from a mixed use as a dwellinghouse and as a betting office or pay day loan shop; and **Class M(a)(iii)(bb)** (formerly Class IA(a)(ii) in the 1995 Order) permits the residential conversion of a building from a mixed use as a dwellinghouse and as a use falling within Use Class A1 or A2, whether that mixed use was granted permission under Class G of Part 3 (formerly Part F in the 1995 Order) or otherwise.

It is a condition of Class M(a) that a building which has changed use under this class is to be used only as a dwellinghouse within the meaning of Use Class C3 and for no other purpose, except to the extent that the other purpose is ancillary to its primary use as a dwellinghouse.

Building operations that are reasonably necessary to convert the building to a use falling within Use Class C3 are also permitted by **Class M(b)** (formerly Class IA(b) in the 1995 Order), but this operational development must not result in the external dimensions of the building extending beyond the external dimensions of the existing building at any given point. In addition to the works permitted under Class M(b) being restricted to what is reasonably necessary for the building to function as a dwellinghouse, any partial demolition must also be limited to the extent reasonably necessary to carry out the building operations that are permitted. Works that amount to substantial demolition and reconstruction or replacement of the existing fabric would go beyond what is permitted. This is explained in more detail in *paragraph 9.7* in *Chapter 9* in relation to Class Q(b) (works in connection with the residential conversion of an agricultural building), but is equally applicable to development under Class M(b).

A launderette is a *sui generis* use and is not therefore included in the permitted development for the residential conversion of shops. However, in October 2015, the government announced that the residential conversion of launderettes is to become permitted development, and they will presumably be added to Class M, and be subject to the same provisions that relate to both Classes M(a) and M(b). This provision is expected to be incorporated in the amendments to the GPDO which are due to be made within the next six months, probably coming into effect on 31 May 2016.

5.2.2   The qualifying use

Development is not permitted by Class M where the building was not used for one of the uses referred to in Class M(a) on 20 March 2013 or, in the case of a building which was in use before that date but was not in use on that date, when it was last in use; nor can a change of use be made under Class M where permission to use the building for a use falling within Use Class A1 (shops) or A2 (financial and professional services) has been granted only by Part 3 itself as permitted development.

The requirement regarding the use of the building on or before 20 March 2013 incorporates some redrafting compared with the wording in the 1995 Order. The words used in the 1995 Order seemed to imply that the words *"before that date"* were to be understood in that sentence, but the redrafting has made this explicit. If this were not so, it might theoretically have been possible for one of the uses listed in Class M(a) to commence after 20 March 2013, so that the building would still qualify as being last used for that purpose at any time before the prior approval application is made. This was certainly not what was intended, and the redrafting has resolved the latent ambiguity in the original wording.

Whilst there is no explicit requirement that one of the specified uses in Class M(a) must have continued *after* 20 March 2013, it seems clear that the use (or at least the right, in planning terms, to use the building for that purpose) must continue until the change of use is made under Class M(a), for the reasons explained in *paragraph A.3* in *Appendix A*.

Class M(a)(iii)(bb) is stated to apply whether the mixed use was granted permission under Class G of Part 3 [or by the former Class F in the 1995 Order] or otherwise but, as noted in *paragraph 2.3.7* in *Chapter 2*, the use of the premises resulting from a change of use permitted by Class G (formerly Class F in the 1995 Order) will not in reality be a mixed use because, having regard to the rule in *Burdle* (see *Appendix B, paragraph B.1.2*), the change of use will result in the creation of separate planning units, namely the shop plus a separate flat (or two separate flats). This was confirmed by the High Court in *Valentino Plus Limited v SSCLG* [2015] EWHC 19 (Admin).

It would therefore seem that, notwithstanding the reference to Class G in the text of Class M(a)(iii), the change of use permitted by M(a)(iii) can only apply in the unlikely event that the residential element of the use is genuinely part of a mixed use, i.e. where the residential use is not both physically and functionally separate from the commercial use of the building. It follows that Class M(a)(iii) cannot apply where the 'dwellinghouse' referred to is in fact a separate self-contained flat, because this is not a mixed use.

Residential conversion of the shop or business premises under Class M(a)(i) or M(a)(ii) (as the case may be) would still be possible in these circumstances, but if there is also a dwelling in the building which is a separate planning unit, and which is not therefore part of a genuine mixed use, it would not seem to be possible to incorporate this existing dwelling in the proposed residential conversion of the commercial premises. The law relating to the amalgamation of two or more existing dwellings lies beyond the scope of this book, but the judgment in *Richmond upon Thames LBC v SSETR* [2001] J.P.L. 84 suggests that there may be circumstances in which this could be regarded as development requiring planning permission.

5.2.3 *Exclusions*

Permitted development is excluded under Class M where the building is within a Conservation Area, an Area of Outstanding Natural Beauty, the Broads, a National Park or a World Heritage Site (formerly known in the 1995 Order as 'Article 1(5) land', but now identified in the 2015 Order as 'Article 2(3) land'). It is also excluded where the building is in a site of special scientific interest (SSSI), a safety hazard area or a military explosives storage area. The definitions of a "safety hazard area" and a "military explosives storage area" are quoted at the end of *paragraph 3.2.3* in *Chapter 3*.

Finally, permitted development under Class M is also excluded where the building is a scheduled monument or is a listed building (although this exclusion does not specifically extend to a building within the curtilage of a listed building, where the curtilage building is not itself listed).

So far as a building which is within the curtilage of a listed building is concerned (which is not specifically disqualified from residential conversion under Class M), it should be noted that, by section 1(5) of the Listed Buildings Act, any structure fixed to a listed building forms part of the listed building. The effect of this provision is discussed in *paragraph B.2.3* of *Appendix B*, where the decisions in *Debenhams plc v Westminster LBC* and *Richardson Development Ltd v Birmingham City Council* are considered.

Section 1(5) also provides that any structure within the curtilage of the building which, although not fixed to the building, forms part of the land and has done so since before July 1, 1948 is treated as part of the listed building. Thus the disqualification under Class M would apply to a building within the curtilage of a listed building, unless this curtilage building was built after 1 July 1948.

It should be noted, however, that the relevant curtilage in this context (consistent with the interpretation of other legislative provisions prohibiting or restricting development within the curtilage of a listed building) is the curtilage of the building at the time when it was first listed. (See *paragraph B.2.2* in *Appendix B* and the judgment in *R (Egerton) v Taunton Deane BC* cited in that paragraph.) It will therefore be necessary in cases where this issue arises to identify the curtilage of the building at that time, bearing in mind that the curtilage of a building can change significantly from time to time (as confirmed by *Sumption v Greenwich LBC* [2007] EWHC 2776 (Admin) - see *paragraph B.2.4* in *Appendix B*).

5.2.4   Floorspace limit

The cumulative floor space of the existing building changing use under Class M must not exceed 150 sq m, and the change of use (together with any previous change of use under Class M) must not result in more than 150 sq m of floor space in the building having changed use under Class M but, subject to this cumulative limit not being exceeded, the creation of more than one dwelling in the building is not precluded. It should be borne in mind that where the relevant development is outside any such limitations, even marginally, neither the change of use nor any part of the proposed operational development can be permitted development, and the whole development will require planning permission.

As discussed in *paragraph 1.6* of *Chapter 1*, it would seem that the cumulative floorspace limit under the former Class IA in the 1995 Order must be counted with the development now permitted under Class M in the 2015 Order for the purposes of the cumulative limit imposed by this Class in reckoning the limit of floorspace that may be converted under Class M.

Although there is a cumulative floorspace limit, as stated above, there is no other limit as to the size of dwelling that can be created. Certain development plans stipulate the minimum size of flats (for example, in one case, 37 sq m for a studio flat, 50 sq m for a 1-bed 3-person flat etc.), but this has no application to a development under Part 3 of the GPDO. This has been confirmed by an appeal decision on a prior approval application in respect of Class O, which is referred to in *paragraph 7.1* of *Chapter 7*.

As explained in *paragraph 14.5* of *Chapter 14*, the power of the LPA to impose conditions on their prior approval in respect of the proposed change of use does not extend to issues (such as the minimum size of each dwelling) falling outside the scope of the specified matters in respect of which prior approval is being given (transport and highways impacts, contamination risks, flooding risks, and retail impact in the case of Class M(a), and also the design or external appearance of the building in the case of Class M(b)).

5.2.5   *Limits on building operations*

Compared with the corresponding provisions relating to Class Q(b) (see *paragraph 9.7* in *Chapter 9*), the restrictions on the building operations that can be carried out under Class M(b) are somewhat less prescriptive. Thus, there is no reference in paragraph M.1 to those building operations being confined to the installation or replacement of windows, doors, roofs, or exterior walls, or water, drainage, electricity, gas or other services, to the extent reasonably necessary for the building to function as a dwellinghouse, as is the case under Class Q, although, as noted in *paragraph 5.2.1* above, the development must not result in the external dimensions of the building extending beyond the external dimensions of the existing building at any given point. Paragraph M.1 however, provides that development under Class M(b) is not permitted if the development consists of demolition (other than partial demolition which is reasonably necessary to convert the building to residential use).

Substantial demolition of the building and its effective replacement would therefore be outside the scope of the development that is permitted by Class M(b). This is discussed in respect of development under Class Q(b) in *paragraph 9.7* in *Chapter 9*, but it clearly applies with equal force to building operations under Class M(b), and this is also a factor which will go to the question of its practicability, and so may be a material consideration in the determination of the prior approval application (as discussed in *paragraph 13.3* in *Chapter 13*).

The government amended their online Planning Practice Guidance on 5 March 2015 to make it clear that it is not the intention of these permitted development rights to include the construction of new structural elements for the building. Therefore it is only where the existing building is structurally strong enough to take the loading which comes with the external works to provide for residential use that the building would be considered to have the permitted development right. (This point is discussed in more detail in *paragraph 9.7* of *Chapter 9*.)

In practice, this issue is less likely to be a problem in relation to development under Class M than it may be under Class Q (residential conversion of an agricultural building), because a building that is to be converted under Class M will probably be of orthodox construction, and will be likely to have been built with substantial materials. Significant demolition and reconstruction is therefore less likely to be required in order to adapt the building for residential occupation and to comply with the Building Regulations.

5.2.6   *Prior approval*

Before beginning the development, the developer must apply to the local planning authority for a determination as to whether the prior approval of the authority will be required as to:

(a)   transport and highways impacts of the development;

(b)   contamination risks in relation to the building;

(c)   flooding risks in relation to the building;

(d)   whether it is undesirable for the building to change to a residential use because of the impact of the change of use on adequate provision of services of the sort that may be provided by a building falling within Use Class A1 (shops) or, as the case may be, Use Class A2 (financial and professional services) [i.e. depending on which of those two use classes applies to the current use of the building that is to be converted], but only where there is a reasonable prospect of the building being used to provide such services, or (where the building is located in a key shopping area) on the sustainability of that shopping area; and

(e)   the design or external appearance of the building.

The determination of the prior approval application in relation to these criteria, and other material considerations that are to be taken into account (under paragraph W), is discussed in *part 14.4* of *Chapter 14*.

A question has arisen in the past as to whether a prior approval application in respect of the permitted operational development may be made (and therefore considered and determined) separately from the prior approval application for the change of use. However, amendments to the GPDO incorporated in the 2015 Order have made it clear that an application for the change of use alone can no longer be made separately from the application in respect of the prior approval in respect of any necessary operational development, unless no such works will be required.

Thus paragraph M.2(2) provides that where the development proposed is development under both Class M(a) and Class M(b), an application is required as to whether the prior approval of the LPA will be required as to all of items (a) to (e) above, whereas if the application is made under Class M(a) only, where no building operations are proposed because they are not required in order to facilitate the change of use, then there is no need to address item (e).

5.2.7   *Commencement and completion*

It was a condition in the 1995 Order, applicable to both of what were then Classes IA(a) and IA(b), that the development must *begin* within a period of three years. However, there is no longer any requirement as to the date of commencement of the development, but the corresponding condition in paragraph M.2(3)(a) of the 2015 Order, applying to both Class M(a) and M(b), requires instead that development under either the first or, where applicable, both of these classes must be *completed* within a period of three years beginning with the date on which any prior approval is granted for that development, or beginning with the expiry of the 56-day period referred to in paragraph W(11)(c) without the local planning authority notifying the developer as to whether prior approval for that development is given or refused, whichever is the earlier (see *paragraph 14.10* in *Chapter 14*).

See *paragraph 1.3.2* in *Chapter 1* for a discussion of what constitutes the completion of development for the purposes of this condition.

5.2.8   *Exclusion of permitted development under Part 1*

It should be noted that the permitted development which can normally be carried out under Part 1 of the Second Schedule to the GPDO (relating to development within the curtilage of a dwellinghouse, as well as alteration or enlargement of the dwelling itself) is entirely excluded where a residential conversion has been carried out as permitted development under Part 3, Class M (residential conversion of various commercial premises).

Thus development is entirely excluded under Part 1, Class A (the enlargement, improvement or other alteration of the dwellinghouse), Class B (the enlargement of the dwellinghouse consisting of an addition or alteration to its roof), Class C (any other alteration to the roof of the dwellinghouse), Class D (the erection or construction of a porch outside any external door of the dwellinghouse), Class E (the provision within the curtilage of the dwellinghouse of any building or enclosure, swimming or other pool, or the maintenance, improvement or other alteration of such a building or enclosure; or the provision of a container used for domestic heating purposes for the storage of oil or liquid petroleum gas), Class F (the provision within the curtilage of the dwellinghouse of a hard surface for any purpose incidental to the enjoyment of the dwellinghouse as such; or the replacement in whole or in part of such a surface), Class G (the installation, alteration or replacement of a chimney, flue or soil and vent pipe on the dwellinghouse) and Class H (the installation, alteration or replacement of a microwave antenna on the dwellinghouse or within the curtilage of the dwellinghouse). Planning permission will therefore be required if it is subsequently proposed to carry out any of these developments at a dwelling that has been converted under Class M.

5.2.9   *Other permitted development that may be possible*

The provisions of Part 3 do not prohibit or limit in any way operations carried out under Part 2. These will not be relevant in some cases, but are discussed here in relation to the operations that may be carried out in connection with permitted changes of use generally, whether under Class M or under any of the other Classes in Part 3.

Part 2, Class A permits the erection, construction, maintenance, improvement or alteration of gates, fences, walls or other means of enclosure (subject to certain height limits).

Part 2, Class B permits the formation, laying out and construction of a means of access to a highway *which is not a trunk road or a classified road*, where that access is required in connection with development permitted by any Class in Schedule 2. This would include all classes of development covered by Part 3, provided that this is "required" on an objective basis. "Required" means more than a simple desire on behalf of the applicant; it must in some sense be necessary. It follows that in order to qualify under Class B of Part 2, the access must be formed at or about the same time as the change of use under Part 3.

Permitted development under Class B of Part 2 is, however, subject to the proviso in Article 3(6) of the GPDO that this does not authorise any development which creates an obstruction to the view of persons using any highway used by vehicular traffic, so as to be likely to cause danger to such persons, as well as repeating that it does not authorise any development which requires or involves the formation, laying out or material widening of a means of access to a trunk road or classified road.

A 'classified road' is not confined to 'A' Class and 'B' class roads, but also includes Class C roads (otherwise known as 'Classified Unnumbered roads'), which are not identified as such on maps. This last point may be a trap for the unwary. A Classified Unnumbered road will be of lower significance and be of primarily local importance, but will perform a more important function than an unclassified road, and must be identified by the local highway authority and approved by the Secretary of State. The local highway authority is responsible for recording the classification of roads in their area, but records of the classification of roads may be incomplete in some areas in the case of classifications made before 2012.

There is nothing in the wording of Part 2 which suggests that the formation of an access to a highway under Part 2, Class B must be confined only within the planning unit on which the other permitted development for which the access is required (in this case under Part 3) is being carried out. Although the Court of Appeal did not adjudicate on the point in *Shepherd v SSETR* (1998) 76 P. & C. R. 74, it seems to have been accepted in that case that ownership of the land over which the access is to be formed is not an issue. Similarly, there is no constraint as to the length of the access, which is not therefore confined solely to the actual point of access with the highway. The heading to Part 2, which refers to "minor operations", cannot in itself be taken to limit the scope of the operational development that is permitted by the various Classes in Part 2.

On the other hand, it is clear from the judgment in *James v SSW* (1998) 76 P. & C. R. 62 that Part 2, Class B, by reference to its actual wording, is intended to apply only to an access directly onto the highway, and does not permit the formation of an access which gives only indirect access to a highway (for example, connecting to another driveway in order to reach the road). The court upheld the Inspector's conclusion in that case that a separation in excess of 30 metres between the access works and the highway itself meant that they did not constitute the formation of a means of access to the highway within the meaning of Part 2, Class B.

Apart from the exclusions mentioned above, development under Part 2, Class B is not subject to any other conditions, restrictions or limitations, and it does not require prior approval. However, in any case where a new or improved access (including, for example a new visibility splay) cannot be formed as permitted development under Class B of Part 2 (due to any of the exclusions mentioned above), a separate planning application will be required.

Also under Part 2, exterior painting of any building is permitted by Class C, and Classes D and E permit (subject to certain limitations and conditions) the installation, alteration or replacement, within an area lawfully used for off-street parking, of an electrical outlet mounted on a wall for recharging electric vehicles, or an upstand with an electrical outlet mounted on it for recharging electric vehicles. Class F permits the installation of CCTV cameras on any building for security (but this too is subject to certain limitations and conditions).

Permitted development under Part 2 is not confined to dwellinghouses, nor is it confined to the curtilage of a building. No notice to the LPA or prior approval application is required in respect of any development under Part 2.

CHAPTER 6

RESIDENTIAL CONVERSION OF AMUSEMENT ARCADE OR CENTRE OR CASINO

6.1 The development permitted

Class N(a)(i) permits the change of use of a building and any land within its curtilage from use as an amusement arcade or centre to a use falling within Use Class C3 (dwellinghouses). Similarly, **Class N(a)(ii)** permits the residential conversion of a casino.

Building operations that are reasonably necessary to convert the building to a use falling within Use Class C3 are also permitted by **Class N(b)**, but there is no limitation or condition in this case that prevents this operational development resulting in the external dimensions of the building extending beyond the external dimensions of the existing building. There are, nevertheless, strict limitations on the works that can be carried out, and these are explained in *paragraph 6.5* below. There is also a requirement to make an application to the LPA in respect of the prior approval of certain matters (see *paragraph 6.6* below).

Within the cumulative floorspace limit of 150 sq m mentioned in *paragraph 6.4* below, there is no maximum or minimum limit as to the number or size of any individual dwellings that can be created. Certain development plans stipulate a minimum size for flats (for example, in one case, 37 sq m for a studio flat, 50 sq m for a 1-bed 3-person flat etc.), but this has no application to a development under Part 3 of the GPDO. This has been confirmed by an appeal decision on a prior approval application in respect of Class O, which is referred to in *paragraph 7.1* in *Chapter 7*.

6.2 The qualifying use

Development is not permitted by Class N where the building was not used for one of the uses referred to in Class N(a) on 19 March 2014 or, in the case of a building which was in use before that date but was not in use on that date, when it was last in use.

Whilst there is no explicit requirement that the qualifying use as an amusement arcade or centre or as a casino must have continued *after* 19 March 2014, it seems clear that the use (or at least the right, in planning terms, to use the building for that purpose) must continue until the change of use is made under Class N(a), for the reasons explained in *paragraph A.3* in *Appendix A*.

6.3 Exclusions

Permitted development is excluded under Class N where the building is within a National Park, an Area of Outstanding Natural Beauty, or the Broads or is within a World Heritage Site. It is also excluded where the building is in a site of special scientific interest (SSSI), a safety hazard area or a military explosives storage area. The definitions of a "safety hazard area" and a "military explosives storage area" are quoted at the end of *paragraph 3.2.3* in *Chapter 3*.

Finally, permitted development under Class N is also excluded where the building is a listed building or is within the curtilage of a listed building or where the site is, or contains, a scheduled monument. (However, there is no prohibition in this case in respect of the conversion of a building in a Conservation Area.)

So far as a building within the curtilage of a listed building is concerned, the relevant curtilage in this context (consistent with the interpretation of other legislative provisions prohibiting or restricting development within the curtilage of a listed building) must be taken to refer to the curtilage of the building *at the time when it was first listed.* (See *paragraph B.2.2* in *Appendix B* and the judgment in *R (Egerton) v Taunton Deane BC* cited in that paragraph.) The inclusion in the listing of any building attached to the listed building is also discussed at *paragraph B.2.3.*

6.4 Floorspace limit

The cumulative floor space of the existing building changing use under Class N must not exceed 150 sq m, and the change of use (together with any previous change of use under Class N) must not result in more than 150 sq m of floor space in the building having changed use under Class N but, subject to this cumulative limit not being exceeded, the creation of more than one dwelling in the building is not precluded. It should be borne in mind, however, that where the relevant development is outside any such limitations, even marginally, neither the change of use nor any part of the proposed operational development can be permitted development, and the whole development will require planning permission.

As noted in *paragraph 6.1* above, there is no maximum or minimum limit as to the number or size of any individual dwellings that can be created within the cumulative floorspace limit of 150 sq m.

As explained in *paragraph 14.5* of *Chapter 14*, the power of the LPA to impose conditions on their prior approval in respect of the proposed change of use does not extend to issues (such as the minimum size of each dwelling) falling outside the scope of the specified matters in respect of which prior approval is being given (transport and highways impacts, contamination risks, flooding risks, plus the design or external appearance of the building in the case of Class N(b)).

6.5   Limits on building operations

The works permitted under Class N(b) are restricted to what is reasonably necessary for the building to function as a dwellinghouse, and any partial demolition must also be limited to the extent reasonably necessary to carry out the building operations that are permitted by this class. This imposes a practical constraint on the convertibility of some buildings. Works that amount to substantial demolition and reconstruction or replacement of the existing fabric would go beyond what is permitted.

In any event, the development under Class N(b) must not consist of building operations other than the installation or replacement of windows, doors, roofs, or exterior walls, or water, drainage, electricity, gas or other services, to the extent reasonably necessary for the building to function as a dwellinghouse, and partial demolition to the extent reasonably necessary to carry out the building operations listed there.

The government amended their online Planning Practice Guidance on 5 March 2015 to make it clear that it is not the intention of these permitted development rights to include the construction of new structural elements for the building. Therefore it is only where the existing building is structurally strong enough to take the loading which comes with the external works to provide for residential use that the building would be considered to have the permitted development right. (This point is discussed in more detail in *paragraph 9.7* of *Chapter 9*.)

6.6   Prior approval

Before beginning the development, the developer must apply to the local planning authority for a determination as to whether the prior approval of the authority will be required as to:

(a)   transport and highways impacts of the development;

(b)   contamination risks in relation to the building;

(c)   flooding risks in relation to the building; and

(d)   the design or external appearance of the building.

The determination of the prior approval application in relation to these criteria, and other material considerations that are to be taken into account (under paragraph W), is discussed in *part 14.4* of *Chapter 14*.

A question has arisen in the past as to whether a prior approval application in respect of the permitted operational development may be made (and therefore considered and determined) separately from the prior approval application for the change of use. However, amendments to the GPDO incorporated in the 2015 Order have made it clear that an application for the change of use alone can no longer be made separately from the application in respect of the approval of any necessary operational development, unless no such works will be required.

Thus paragraph N.2(2) provides that where the development proposed is development under both Class N(a) and Class N(b), an application is required as to whether the prior approval of the LPA will be required as to all of items (a) to (d) above, whereas if the application is made under Class N(a) only, where no building operations are proposed because they are not required in order to facilitate the change of use, then there is no need to address item (d).

6.7   Commencement and completion

There is no condition as to the date by which development under Class N must begin, but paragraph N.2(3) makes it a condition in respect of development both under Class N(a) and under Class N(b) that the development must be *completed* within a period of three years starting with the date on which any prior approval is granted for that development, or starting with the expiry of the 56-day period referred to in paragraph W(11)(c) without the local planning authority notifying the developer as to whether prior approval for that development is given or refused, whichever is the earlier (see *paragraph 14.10* in *Chapter 14*).

See *paragraph 1.3.2* in *Chapter 1* for a discussion of what constitutes the completion of development for the purposes of this condition.

6.8   Exclusion of other permitted development

It should be noted that the permitted development which can normally be carried out under Part 1 of the Second Schedule to the GPDO (relating to development within the curtilage of a dwellinghouse, as well as alteration or enlargement of the house itself) is entirely excluded where a residential conversion has been carried out as permitted development under Part 3, Class N.

Thus development is entirely excluded under Part 1, Class A (the enlargement, improvement or other alteration of the dwellinghouse), Class B (the enlargement of the dwellinghouse consisting of an addition or alteration to its roof), Class C (any other alteration to the roof of the dwellinghouse), Class D (the erection or construction of a porch outside any external door of the dwellinghouse), Class E (the provision within the curtilage of the dwellinghouse of any building or enclosure, swimming or other pool, or the maintenance, improvement or other alteration of such a building or enclosure; or the provision of a container used for domestic heating purposes for the storage of oil or liquid petroleum gas), Class F (the provision within the curtilage of the dwellinghouse of a hard surface for any purpose incidental to the enjoyment of the dwellinghouse as such; or the replacement in whole or in part of such a surface), Class G (the installation, alteration or replacement of a chimney, flue or soil and vent pipe on the dwellinghouse) and Class H (the installation, alteration or replacement of a microwave antenna on the dwellinghouse or within the curtilage of the dwellinghouse). Planning permission will therefore be required if it is subsequently proposed to carry out any of these developments at a dwelling that has been converted under Class N.

On the other hand, various minor operations are permitted under Part 2. These are briefly summarised in *paragraph 5.2.9* in *Chapter 5,* where the formation or laying out of an access to a highway is also discussed.

CHAPTER 7

RESIDENTIAL CONVERSION OF COMMERCIAL OFFICES

7.1 The development permitted

Class O (formerly Class J in the 1995 Order) permits the change of use of a building and any land within its curtilage from a use falling within Use Class B1(a) (offices) to a use falling within Use Class C3 (dwellinghouses). This is subject to various restrictions, qualifications and conditions, which are discussed in the following paragraphs, including a requirement to make an application to the LPA in respect of the prior approval of certain matters. This development was originally subject to a completion deadline of 30 May 2016, but the deadline is now to be lifted, and replaced by a three-year time limit for completion. (See *paragraph 7.7* below.)

The development permitted by Class O does not at present include any building operations in connection with the residential conversion of the building. However, a planning appeal in south-west London decided in August 2015 demonstrates that, upon prior approval being granted for the residential conversion of offices under Class O, a subsequent planning application (before the residential conversion under the GPDO has been completed) seeking permission for the extension of the building to provide additional residential units is not ruled out. In this appeal, planning permission was granted for four extra flats by adding another storey to the building.

It would seem that, in principle, a planning application for such additional development could be submitted at the same time as a prior approval application for the residential conversion of the existing premises, but determination of such a planning application is likely to be dependent on the outcome of the prior approval application under the GPDO, and the planning application itself would have to be considered in accordance with section 70 of the 1990 Act and section 38(6) of the 2004 Act (i.e. in accordance with the development plan, and taking into account other relevant considerations). The grant of prior approval for the residential conversion under the GPDO would not necessarily lead to a grant of planning permission for additional development.

On 13 October 2015, the government announced that this permitted development right is to be extended to allow the demolition of office buildings and new building for residential use. At the time of going to press, further details are awaited. These changes will be incorporated in an amendment to the GPDO to be made within the next six months and, in the case of Class O, will come into effect on 31 May 2016.

There is no cumulative floorspace limit in respect of the size of office building (or of office buildings within the same planning unit) that can be converted, nor is there any maximum or minimum limit as to the number or size of any individual dwellings that can be created. Certain development plans stipulate a minimum size for flats (for example, in one case, 37 sq m for a studio flat, 50 sq m for a 1-bed 3-person flat etc.), but this has no application to a development under Part 3 of the GPDO.

This has been confirmed by an appeal decision in April 2015, in London, where an assertion by the LPA that the proposed residential units were too small to be classified as 'dwellinghouses' was rejected. The proposed dwellings were self-contained, and were between 18 sq m and 22 sq m in floor area. The proposed accommodation comprised a living space (which would include a fold-away bed), kitchenette, shower and toilet and domestic storage.

The Inspector pointed out that no minimum size is specified by Use Class C3. The proposed dwellings would meet the test in *Gravesham B.C. v SSE* (1984) P. & C. R. 142, because the building would, as a question of fact, be constructed or adapted for use as a dwellinghouse as normally understood, that is to say, as a building that provides for the main activities of, and ordinarily affords the facilities required for, day-to-day private domestic existence. The proposed residential conversion therefore complied with the terms of Class O.

A similar appeal in West London in June 2015, where 63 units of about 24 sq m each were proposed, was also allowed. Each of the proposed dwellings would have a self-contained toilet/shower unit, and an open plan living area, including cooking facilities and an area for sleeping (with a stowaway bed) and storage. In resisting this proposal, the LPA relied on floorspace standards prescribed by the London Plan, but whilst the proposed dwellings did not meet those standards, they would nevertheless provide the facilities for day-to-day living (a reference to *Gravesham* again). They therefore qualified as permitted development under Class O.

As explained in *paragraph 14.5* of *Chapter 14*, the power of the LPA to impose conditions on their prior approval in respect of the proposed change of use does not extend to issues (such as the minimum size of each dwelling) falling outside the scope of the specified matters in respect of which prior approval is being given (transport and highways impacts, contamination risks and flooding risks in this case).

7.2   Qualifying office use

The building will only qualify for conversion under Class O if it was used as an office falling within Use Class B1(a) (offices) on 29 May 2013 or, in the case of a building which was in use before that date but was not in use on that date, when it was last in use. The words *"before that date"* did not appear in the text of the 1995 Order, but were apparently to be implied by the context. If this had not been so, it might theoretically have been possible for an office use to commence on or after 30 May 2013, so that the building would still qualify as being last used for that purpose at any time before the prior approval application was made. This was certainly not what was intended, and the rewording of this provision in the 2015 Order has removed this latent ambiguity.

Whilst there is no explicit requirement that the qualifying office use must have continued *after* 29 May 2013, it seems clear that the use (or at least the right, in planning terms, to use the building for that purpose) must continue until the change of use is made under Class O, for the reasons explained in *paragraph A.3* in *Appendix A*.

One point that should be borne in mind is that this change of use can be carried out only where the planning unit in question is solely used as an office within Use Class B1(a). If the use of the planning unit comprises a mixed use, of which an office use is only one element, this represents a *sui generis* use, and the building (or the part of the building) in respect of which the change of use is proposed, will not qualify for residential conversion under the terms of Class O. In the case of development under Class O, the same disqualification would seem to apply even where other elements in the use of the planning unit fall within other parts of same Use Class (i.e. B1(b) use for research and development of products or processes, or B1(c) light industrial use). However, this might possibly change when the residential conversion of buildings in light industrial use becomes permitted development under the further amendments to the GPDO that are now proposed.

Where the use of a property as a whole comprises several distinct functions including an office use, it will be necessary to apply the rule in *Burdle* (see *paragraph B.1.2* in *Appendix B*) to determine whether the building or the part of the building in office use genuinely comprises a separate planning unit, or whether it is in truth merely part of a larger planning unit, to the use of which the office use is ancillary or with which it forms part of a mixed use.

This was confirmed by an appeal decision in February 2015, in the case of a proposed residential conversion of an office building in Yorkshire comprising 2,100 sq m of floorspace. The proposed change of use would have created 27 residential units, but an appeal against the refusal of a prior approval application was dismissed because the office building was part of a larger planning unit which was in general industrial use within Use Class B2. It had been argued on behalf of the appellant that the office building was a separate planning unit, but the Inspector accepted the council's contention that the office use was purely ancillary to the primary use of the site as a whole as a large-scale general industrial use. The use of the office building therefore fell within Use Class B2, not B1(a).

A similar conclusion was reached in another appeal in Yorkshire in September 2015. In that case the alleged office use was ancillary to a larger *sui generis* use of the site (which had been a council highways depot). The Inspector clearly applied the rule in *Burdle* (see above) in determining this issue.

The onus is on the applicant to establish that the building was in actual use as an office before 30 May 2013. An appeal in south London against the refusal of prior approval for the residential conversion of an office to provide three dwellings was dismissed in August 2015 because, whilst a demand for non-domestic rates was produced, the Inspector was not satisfied that there was sufficient evidence that the building had actually been occupied as an office prior to the qualifying date.

On the other hand, an appeal in Cheshire, involving the conversion of a large office building to create 448 residential units, was allowed despite the building having been removed from the rating list some time before 30 May 2013, following its having ceased to be used as offices. The essential point here was that the building had undoubtedly been in use within Use Class B1(a) earlier than the qualifying date and, although the office use had ceased before that date, it had not been abandoned; nor had the building subsequently been put to any other use. It therefore qualified for residential conversion under the terms of Class O.

These various appeals demonstrate that whether the building meets the criteria within Class O is a matter of fact and degree in each case, and applicants must be able to produce sufficient evidence of compliance with these criteria to satisfy an LPA (or an inspector on appeal) that the statutory requirements are met.

7.3   Exclusions

Development is not permitted by Class O where the building is in certain local authority areas that are exempted from its provisions by Article 2(5) of the GPDO. These will be found in Part 3 of Schedule 1 to the GPDO. They include the Central Activities Zone and Tech City, London (in the City of London), and parts of various London Boroughs including the whole of Kensington and Chelsea. Elsewhere, they include two areas in the centre of Manchester, and specified areas in the Vale of White Horse, Stevenage, Sevenoaks, Ashford and East Hants. These exempted areas will remain in being until 30 May 2019, but will then lose their exemption. It is expected that LPAs will make appropriate Article 4 Directions in the meantime, so as to continue the exclusion of permitted development for the residential conversion of offices in most of these areas.

Permitted development is also excluded where the site is or forms part of a safety hazard area or is or forms part of a military explosives storage area. The definitions of a "safety hazard area" and a "military explosives storage area" are quoted at the end of *paragraph 3.2.3* in *Chapter 3*.

Residential conversion is also excluded if the building is a listed building or is within the curtilage of a listed building, or if it is or contains a scheduled monument. (However, there is no prohibition in respect of development under Class O in National Parks, Areas of Outstanding Natural Beauty, Conservation Areas, World Heritage Sites or SSSIs.)

So far as a building within the curtilage of a listed building is concerned, the relevant curtilage in this context (consistent with the interpretation of other legislative provisions prohibiting or restricting development within the curtilage of a listed building) must be taken to refer to the curtilage of the building *at the time when it was first listed*. (See *paragraph B.2.2* in *Appendix B* and the judgment in *R (Egerton) v Taunton Deane BC* cited in that paragraph.) The inclusion in the listing of any building attached to the listed building is also discussed at *paragraph B.2.3*.

Unlike the changes of use permitted by Classes M, N and Q, the development permitted by Class O does not at present include any building operations in connection with the residential conversion of the building. Any such works will therefore require planning permission, unless they are exempt from the definition of development by virtue of section 55(2)(a) of the 1990 Act, because they affect only the interior of the building, or do not materially affect the external appearance of the building. Following the proposed amendments to the GPDO (which, in the case of Class O, are expected to take effect from 31 May 2016), the development permitted by Class O will include the demolition of existing buildings and other operational development. However, at the time of going to press, no details have yet been announced. In the meantime, as noted in *paragraph 7.1*, there is nothing to prevent a planning application for associated operational development being submitted at the same time as a prior approval application under Class O.

7.4 Prior approval

A change of use under Class O is permitted subject to the condition that before beginning the development, the developer must apply to the local planning authority for a determination as to whether the prior approval of the authority will be required as to:

(a) transport and highways impacts of the development;

(b) contamination risks on the site; and

(c) flooding risks on the site.

The determination of the prior approval application in relation to these criteria, and the other material considerations that are to be taken into account (under paragraph W), is discussed in *part 14.4* of *Chapter 14*.

When the proposed changes are made to Class O, additional matters requiring prior approval are likely to be added to the list above. These are discussed in *paragraph 7.7* below.

7.5   Commencement and completion

Paragraph O.1(c) provides that development under Class O is not permitted where the residential use of the building is begun after 30 May 2016, but this deadline is now to be lifted, and replaced by a three-year time limit for completion. (See *paragraph 7.7* below.)

As mentioned in *paragraph 1.3.2* in *Chapter 1*, even after the May 2016 deadline is lifted, some difficulty may arise where the change of use involves the creation of more than one dwelling, and where some of the dwellings created by that conversion are already in residential use when the three-year time limit for completion expires but others are not, so that the residential use of the whole building has not begun by that expiry date. It might be thought that the right to complete the conversion of any remaining residential units in the building would cease on the expiry of that three-year time limit, but this would undoubtedly produce an anomalous situation, since it is unlikely that it would be practicable for those parts of the building already in residential use by that date to revert to office use. At the very least, it would appear that the development should be considered complete so far as those units are concerned, bearing in mind that those dwellings already in separate use will thereby have become separate planning units, whose change of use has clearly met the deadline.

However, the position is far from certain with regard to any dwellings in the building whose conversion has not been completed within the three-year time limit and are not occupied or at least ready for immediate residential occupation by that date. Opinions differ on this point. It has variously been suggested that the completion and occupation of 15%, or alternatively 50%, of the dwelling units would suffice to secure the right to complete the residential conversion of the remaining units.

These arguments appear to be based on an assumption that the current wording of paragraph O.1(c) should be construed as referring to the residential use of *any part* of the building having been begun by that date, so that if some of the dwellings formed by the conversion of the building are already in residential use (or are ready for immediate residential occupation) by that date, it would be lawful to complete and occupy the remaining residential units in the building. It is, of course, possible that the amendment to the GPDO that will replace the May 2016 deadline with a three-year time limit may also contain provisions to clarify this point. (As to the point at which the change of use actually takes place, see *paragraph 1.3.2* in *Chapter 1*.)

On the other hand, there can certainly be no doubt that if no part of the building has been occupied by the expiry of the three-year time limit, or is at least ready for immediate residential occupation by that date, the development will no longer be permitted development under Class O, notwithstanding the LPA's prior approval in respect of the change of use and the commencement of the internal conversion works before that date. The residential conversion of the building would then require full planning permission, but if those works are well advanced by that time, there would seem to be little excuse for an LPA to refuse planning permission in such circumstances.

7.6   Permitted development within the curtilage under Part 1

In contrast to the position where a residential conversion has been carried out under Classes M, N, P or Q, permitted development under Part 1 (various developments within the curtilage of a dwellinghouse, as well as alteration or enlargement of the house itself) is not excluded following a residential conversion of an office building under Class O, but it should be borne in mind that Article 2(1) of the GPDO provides that "dwellinghouse" (except for the purposes of Part 3 of the Second Schedule - permitting various changes of use) does not include a building containing one or more flats, or a flat contained within such a building.

For the purposes of the GPDO, "flat" means a separate and self-contained set of premises constructed or adapted for use for the purpose of a dwelling and forming part of a building from some other part of which it is divided horizontally. Thus permitted development under Part 1 is excluded where a residential conversion under Class O creates one or more flats, but the development within the curtilage that is permitted by Part 1 can be carried out where a building converted under Class O does not contain a flat or flats.

It should also be borne in mind that various minor operations are also permitted under Part 2. These are briefly summarised in *paragraph 5.2.9* in *Chapter 5*, where the formation or laying out of an access to a highway is also discussed. As noted in *paragraph 7.1* above, a planning application for additional development can also be submitted.

7.7   Proposed changes to Class O

The government's "*Technical consultation on planning*" published in July 2014 included a proposal to extend or to make permanent those permitted development rights which were then due to expire in May 2016. Whilst most of these time limits have been extended as proposed, it was not until 12 October 2015 that the government confirmed that the deadline for the completion of the residential conversion offices under Class O is to be lifted, and replaced with a three-year completion condition.

The Government proposed to amend Class O with effect from May 2016, and indicated that these amendments would not come into force until the existing permitted development right was due to end on 30 May 2016. The amended permitted development under Class O would replace the existing right. It is understood that this remains the government's intention, so that a new Class O will entirely replace the existing provisions relating to the residential conversion of offices, and will come into effect on 31 May 2016.

The scope of the development permitted by Class O is also to be significantly extended, by allowing the demolition of existing buildings and new construction. This will no doubt be subject to strict limitations and conditions, the details of which had not been announced before this book went to press. The design or external appearance of the building will necessarily be one of the matters requiring prior approval.

It was originally the government's intention that the exemption of certain areas ('Article 2(5) land') which applies to the current permitted development right would not be extended to apply to the new permitted development right under Class O. However, ministers have been persuaded to retain this exemption for a period of three years, expiring on 30 May 2019. This will give LPAs the opportunity to make appropriate Article 4 Directions to replace the current exemption, and to give 12 months' notice of any such Direction, so as to avoid what could potentially be very large compensation claims if planning permission is subsequently refused for the residential conversion of offices that could have been carried out as permitted development in the absence of the Article 4 Direction, following the removal of the current exemptions under Article 2(5).

It was also proposed in the 2014 consultation paper that in addition to prior approval of the impact of the proposed development in relation to highways and transport, flooding and contamination, prior approval would also now be required in respect of the potential impact of the significant loss of the most strategically important office accommodation. However, in order to avoid this being used as an easy excuse by LPAs to refuse these prior approval applications, this would be tightly defined. The existing general exclusions would continue to apply (i.e. listed buildings and land within their curtilage, scheduled monuments, safety hazard areas and military explosive storage areas).

It is not clear, at the time of going to press, whether the government still intends to add this further item to the list of matters requiring prior approval under Class O but if they do so, the relevant provision would no doubt take a similar form to the existing provisions in Class M and Class P. The list of matters requiring prior approval might therefore include an extra item along these lines:

"(d) where the authority considers the building to which the development relates is located in an area that is strategically important for providing office accommodation within Class B1(a) (offices) of the Schedule to the Use Classes Order, whether it is undesirable for the building to change to a residential use because of the impact of the change of use on adequate provision of facilities of the sort that may be provided by a building falling within Use Class B1(a) (offices), but only where there is a reasonable prospect of the building being used to provide such facilities."

However, the precise drafting remains a matter of speculation.

CHAPTER 8

RESIDENTIAL CONVERSION OF 'STORAGE OR DISTRIBUTION CENTRE'

8.1 The development permitted

Class P permits the change of use of a building and any land within its curtilage from a use falling within Use Class B8 (storage or distribution centre) to a use falling within Use Class C3 (dwellinghouses). This is subject to various restrictions, qualifications and conditions, which are discussed in the following paragraphs, including a requirement to make an application to the LPA in respect of the prior approval of certain matters, and a time limit by which the residential use must be begun. This deadline is 15 April 2018 - see *paragraph 8.7* below.

The development permitted by Class P does not include any building operations in connection with the residential conversion of the building.

Subject to the overall size of building (in terms of floorspace) that may be converted (see *paragraph 8.5* below), there is no maximum or minimum limit as to the number or size of any individual dwellings that can be created. Certain development plans stipulate a minimum size for flats (for example, in one case, 37 sq m for a studio flat, 50 sq m for a 1-bed 3-person flat etc.), but this has no application to a development under Part 3 of the GPDO. This has been confirmed by an appeal decision on a prior approval application in respect of Class O, which is referred to in *paragraph 7.1* of *Chapter 7*.

8.2 Restricted curtilage

It should be particularly noted that an extremely restrictive definition of 'curtilage' is prescribed by paragraph P.3 for the purposes of Class P. This allows only a very small area of land adjacent to the building to be included in the permitted change of use. It is confined to:

(i)   the piece of land, whether enclosed or unenclosed, immediately beside or around the building in storage or distribution centre use, closely associated with and serving the purposes of that building; or

(ii)   an area of land immediately beside or around the building in storage or distribution centre use *no larger than the land area occupied by that building,*

whichever is the lesser.

A development that seeks to include more than this very limited amount of land in the residential conversion will not be permitted development under

Class P. Prior approval applications where a larger area of land has been included have been summarily rejected, and the rejection of the application has been upheld on appeal. If it is felt essential to incorporate a larger area of land in the development than is permitted under Class P, a planning application will have to be made, which will fall to be determined in accordance with all the policy considerations that apply to such developments.

The very restrictive curtilage that is permitted by Class P of Part 3 will make it impracticable in most cases to include within the prior approval application any access to a highway that may be required in connection with the proposed development. It should be borne in mind, however, that (subject to the terms of Part 2, Class B, which are discussed in *paragraph 5.2.9 of Chapter 5*), any access to a highway that needs to be formed in connection with the conversion of the building for its new purpose may in quite a few cases be permitted development under Part 2. Where the terms of Part 2, Class B do not allow the access to be formed as permitted development, however, a separate planning application may be required. In either case, the access itself should not be included in the prior approval application, although details of the highway access may be required as further information in connection with the consideration of any highways impacts of the development.

8.3   Qualifying storage use

The building will only qualify for conversion under Class P if it was used solely for a storage or distribution centre use on 19 March 2014 or, in the case of a building which was in use before that date but was not in use on that date, when it was last in use. Furthermore, in this case (in contrast to other similar residential conversions permitted by Part 3) development under Class P is not permitted if the building was not used solely for a storage or distribution centre use for a period of at least four years before the development under Class P begins.

There is a potential difficulty in construing the ambiguous drafting here, because a building that was not in use within Use Class B8 on 19 March 2014 would still qualify for conversion under Class P where this was its last use before that date, and yet paragraph P.1(b) requires continuous use for that purpose for a period of at least 4 years before the commencement of development under Class P (i.e. before the date on which the building is either occupied or is ready for immediate residential occupation). It is only possible to make sense of this additional stipulation (which is unique to Class P) if the prescribed 4-year period is construed to mean *at any time* "before the date development under Class P begins", but not necessarily *immediately* preceding that date.

If paragraphs P.1(a) and P.1(b) are construed together in this way, then there would appear to be three possible scenarios which would all qualify within these provisions:

(1)   the building was used for a purpose falling within Use Class B8 for at least 4 years immediately prior to the building either being occupied or being ready for immediate residential occupation (i.e. the date on which the development under Class P begins);

(2)   the building was used for a purpose falling within Use Class B8 for at least 4 years immediately prior to 19 March 2014; or

(3)   the building was used for a purpose falling within Use Class B8 for at least 4 years immediately prior to its last being used for that purpose before 19 March 2014.

In the second and third cases above, it seems clear that even if the actual use has not continued, the right in planning terms to use the building for that purpose must continue until the change of use is made under Class P, for the reasons explained in *paragraph A.3* in *Appendix A*.

Paragraph P.3 provides that, for the purposes of Class P, "a storage or distribution centre use" means a use falling within Use Class B8 (storage and distribution). This use class is not confined to a building which can be narrowly described as "a storage or distribution centre". It was established by the decision of the House of Lords in *Newbury DC v SSE* [1981] A.C. 578 (a case that dealt with the corresponding provision in the pre-1987 version of the UCO, which included use as a "repository") that any use that is primarily for storage is within this use class. Furthermore, it does not need to be a commercial use, although it must not be ancillary to some other use.

However, it should be noted that a "retail warehouse" has never fallen within Use Class B8. Such a use was formerly regarded as falling into Use Class A1 (as confirmed by former Circular 13/87, paragraph 23) but, as a result of an amendment of the UCO in 2005, a "retail warehouse" is now a *sui generis* use.

In addition to the need for the building to qualify under the criteria mentioned above, paragraph P.2(a) makes it a condition that the developer must submit a statement to the LPA, which must accompany the prior approval application (see *paragraph 8.6* below), setting out the evidence the developer relies upon to demonstrate that the building was used solely for a storage or distribution centre use on 19 March 2014 (or in the case of a building which was in use before that date, but was not in use in that date, when it was last in use) and for the period of at least 4 years before the date of commencement of the development under Class P. (See the discussion above, so far as this last point is concerned.)

It is clear that the residential conversion permitted by Class P can be carried out only where the planning unit in question is solely used for a purpose within Use Class B8. If the use of the planning unit comprises a mixed use, of which a storage use is only one element, this represents a *sui generis* use, and the building (or the part of the building) in respect of which the change of use is proposed, will not qualify under the terms of Class P.

Where the use of a property as a whole on which the building is located comprises several distinct functions including the use of the building in question for storage, it will be necessary to apply the rule in *Burdle* (see *paragraph B.1.2* in *Appendix B*) to determine whether the building or the part of the building in storage use genuinely comprises a separate planning unit, or whether it is in truth merely part of a larger planning unit, to the use of which the storage use is ancillary or with which it forms part of a mixed use.

The appeal decision in February 2015 referred to in *paragraph 7.2* of *Chapter 7*, relating to a proposed residential conversion of an office building, is equally applicable to a similar situation involving a storage use where the building in question is part of a larger planning unit which is in use for some wider use, such as Use Class B1 or B2. It had been argued on behalf of the appellant in that appeal that the office building was a separate planning unit, but the Inspector accepted the council's contention that the office use was purely ancillary to the primary use of the site as a whole as a large-scale general industrial use.

8.4   Exclusions

Permitted development under Class P is excluded where the site is or forms part of a safety hazard area or is or forms part of a military explosives storage area. The definitions of a "safety hazard area" and a "military explosives storage area" are quoted at the end of *paragraph 3.2.3* in *Chapter 3*.

Residential conversion is also excluded if the building is within an Area of Outstanding Natural Beauty, a National Park, a World Heritage Site, or the Broads or if it is, or forms part of an SSSI, or if the building is a listed building or is within the curtilage of a listed building or if it is, or contains, a scheduled monument. (However, there is no prohibition in this case in respect of the conversion of a building in a Conservation Area.)

So far as a building within the curtilage of a listed building is concerned, the relevant curtilage in this context (consistent with the interpretation of other legislative provisions prohibiting or restricting development within the curtilage of a listed building) must be taken to refer to the curtilage of the building *at the time when it was first listed*. (See *paragraph B.2.2* in *Appendix B* and the judgment in *R (Egerton) v Taunton Deane BC* cited in that paragraph.) The inclusion in the listing of any building attached to the listed building is also discussed at *paragraph B.2.3*.

Furthermore, development is not permitted by Class P if the site is occupied under an agricultural tenancy (a tenancy under the Agricultural Holdings Act 1986 or under the Agricultural Tenancies Act 1995), unless the express consent of both the landlord and the tenant has been obtained; nor is it permitted if, less than one year before the date development begins, an agricultural tenancy over the site has been terminated, and the termination was for the purpose of carrying out development under Class P, unless both the landlord and the tenant have agreed in writing that the site is no longer required for agricultural use. (There must be some doubt in any case as to whether a building genuinely falls within Use Class B8 if it is or has been subject to an agricultural tenancy!)

Unlike the change of use permitted by Classes M, N and Q, the development permitted by Class P does not include any building operations in connection with the residential conversion of the building. Any such works will therefore require planning permission, unless they are exempt from the definition of development by virtue of section 55(2)(a) of the 1990 Act, because they affect only the interior of the building, or do not materially affect the external appearance of the building.

There is, however, nothing to prevent a planning application for associated operational development being submitted at the same time as a prior approval application under Class P; and a planning application for additional windows, and possibly also alternative entrance doors, is likely to be unavoidable in most cases. Regulation 14(1A) of the 2012 Fees Regulations may apply in such a case. (See *paragraph 13.7* in *Chapter 13*.) Bearing in mind that planning permission for the change of use is granted by Article 3 (subject only to the prior approval required under Class P), it seems rather unlikely that any proper planning objection could be sustained in respect of such works, and LPAs could be at some risk as to costs on appeal if they were to refuse such an application.

8.5   Floorspace limit

Paragraph P.1(d) provides that the gross floorspace of the existing building must not exceed 500 sq m. If the building exceeds this floor area, no part of it will qualify for residential conversion under Class P. However, subject to this overall limit on the floor area of the existing building, there is no limit as to the floorspace within the building that can be converted to residential use.

Although there is an overall floorspace limit in respect of the size of the pre-existing building as stated above, there is no maximum or minimum limit as to the number or size of any individual dwellings that can be created. Certain development plans stipulate a minimum size for flats (for example, in one case, 37 sq m for a studio flat, 50 sq m for a 1-bed 3-person flat etc.), but this has no application to a development under Part 3 of the GPDO. This has been confirmed by an appeal decision on a prior approval application in respect of Class O, which is referred to in *paragraph 7.1* in *Chapter 7*.

As explained in *paragraph 14.5* of *Chapter 14*, the power of the LPA to impose conditions on their prior approval in respect of the proposed change of use does not extend to issues (such as the minimum size of each dwelling) falling outside the scope of the specified matters in respect of which prior approval is being given (impacts on air quality, transport and highways impacts, contamination risks, flooding risks, noise impacts and any impact on service provision).

8.6 Prior approval

A change of use under Class P is permitted subject to the condition that before beginning the development, the developer must apply to the local planning authority for a determination as to whether the prior approval of the authority will be required as to:

(i)   impacts of air quality on the intended occupiers of the development;

(ii)   transport and highways impacts of the development;

(iii)   contamination risks in relation to the building;

(iv)   flooding risks in relation to the building;

(v)   noise impacts of the development; and

(vi)   where the authority considers the building to which the development relates is located in an area that is important for providing storage or distribution services or industrial services or a mix of those services, whether the introduction of, or an increase in, a residential use of premises in the area would have an adverse impact on the sustainability of the provision of those services.

The terms used in sub-paragraph (vi) are defined in paragraph P.3. "Storage and distribution services" means services provided from premises with a storage or distribution centre use (i.e. a use within Use Class B8), and "industrial services" means services provided from premises with a light industrial or general industrial use (i.e. within Use Class B1(c) or B2).

The determination of the prior approval application in relation to these criteria, and the other material considerations that are to be taken into account (under paragraph W), is discussed in *part 14.4* of *Chapter 14*.

8.7 Commencement and completion

Paragraph P.1(c) provides that development under Class P is not permitted where the residential use of the building is begun after 15 April 2018. Bearing in mind that the change of use permitted by Class P must be made no later than that date, this permitted development is not subject to any condition as to the time within which the development must commence. See *paragraph 1.3.2* in *Chapter 1* for a discussion of what constitutes the completion of development for the purposes of this condition.

Following the removal of the completion deadline applying to development under Class O (residential conversion of offices), Class P will be the only Class of permitted development in Part 3 to which such a completion deadline applies. However, the changes to the GPDO announced in October 2015 did not refer to Class P, and the author is not currently aware of any proposal that this deadline should be extended or removed.

Some difficulty may arise where the change of use involves the creation of more than one dwelling, and where one or more of the dwellings created by that conversion are already in residential use (or are ready for immediate residential occupation) by 15 April 2018 but others are not, so that the residential use of the *whole* building has not begun by that expiry date. It might be thought that the right to complete the conversion of any remaining residential units in the building would cease on 15 April 2018, but this would undoubtedly produce an anomalous situation, since it is unlikely that it would be practicable for those parts of the building already in residential use by that date to revert to storage use. At the very least, it would appear that the development should be considered complete so far as the completed unit or units are concerned, bearing in mind that any dwelling already in separate use will thereby have become a separate planning unit, whose use has clearly met the deadline.

However, the position is far from certain with regard to any dwellings in the building whose conversion has not been completed by the deadline and/or which have not been occupied by that date. Opinions differ on this point. It has variously been suggested that the completion and occupation of 15%, or alternatively 50%, of the dwelling units would suffice to secure the right to complete the residential conversion of the remaining units. These arguments appear to be based on an assumption that the wording of paragraph P.1(c) should be construed as referring to the residential use of *any part* of the building having been begun by that date, so that if some of the dwellings formed by the conversion of the building are already in residential use by that date, it would be lawful to complete and occupy the remaining residential units in the building.

On the other hand, there can certainly be no doubt that if no part of the building has been occupied by 15 April 2018, or is at least ready for immediate residential occupation by that date, the development will not be permitted development under Class P, notwithstanding the LPA's prior approval in respect of the change of use and the commencement of the internal conversion works before that date. The residential conversion of the building would then require a full planning permission, but if those works are well advanced by that time, there would seem to be little excuse for an LPA to refuse planning permission in such circumstances.

8.8   *Exclusion of other permitted development*

It should be noted that the permitted development which can normally be carried out under Part 1 of the Second Schedule to the GPDO (relating to development within the curtilage of a dwellinghouse, as well as alteration or enlargement of the house itself) is entirely excluded where a residential conversion has been carried out as permitted development under Part 3, Class P.

Thus development is entirely excluded under Part 1, Class A (the enlargement, improvement or other alteration of the dwellinghouse), Class B (the enlargement of the dwellinghouse consisting of an addition or alteration to its roof), Class C (any other alteration to the roof of the dwellinghouse), Class D (the erection or construction of a porch outside any external door of the dwellinghouse), Class E (the provision within the curtilage of the dwellinghouse of any building or enclosure, swimming or other pool, or the maintenance, improvement or other alteration of such a building or enclosure; or the provision of a container used for domestic heating purposes for the storage of oil or liquid petroleum gas), Class F (the provision within the curtilage of the dwellinghouse of a hard surface for any purpose incidental to the enjoyment of the dwellinghouse as such; or the replacement in whole or in part of such a surface), Class G (the installation, alteration or replacement of a chimney, flue or soil and vent pipe on the dwellinghouse) and Class H (the installation, alteration or replacement of a microwave antenna on the dwellinghouse or within the curtilage of the dwellinghouse). Planning permission will therefore be required if it is subsequently proposed to carry out any of these developments at a dwelling that has been converted under Class P.

On the other hand, various minor operations are permitted under Part 2. These are briefly summarised in *paragraph 5.2.9* in *Chapter 5,* where the formation or laying out of an access to a highway is also discussed.

CHAPTER 9

RESIDENTIAL CONVERSION OF AN AGRICULTURAL BUILDING

9.1   The development permitted

Class Q(a) (formerly Class MB(a) in the 1995 Order) permits the change of use of a building and any land within its curtilage from use as an agricultural building to a use falling within Use Class C3 (dwellinghouses). Limited building operations reasonably necessary to convert the building to residential use are also permitted by **Class Q(b)** (formerly Class MB(b) in the 1995 Order). Both the change of use and any associated operational development are subject to a requirement to make an application to the LPA in respect of their prior approval of the matters mentioned in *paragraph 9.8* below.

9.2   Restricted curtilage

It should be particularly noted that an extremely restrictive definition of 'curtilage' is prescribed by paragraph X for the purposes of Class Q. This allows only a very small area of land adjacent to the agricultural building to be included in the permitted change of use. It is confined to:

(i)   the piece of land, whether enclosed or unenclosed, immediately beside or around the agricultural building, closely associated with and serving the purposes of the agricultural building, or

(ii)   an area of land immediately beside or around the agricultural building *no larger than the land area occupied by the agricultural building,*

whichever is the lesser.

A development that seeks to include more than this very limited amount of land in the residential conversion will not be permitted development under Class Q. Prior approval applications where a larger area of land has been included have been summarily rejected, and the rejection of the application has been upheld on appeal. If it is felt essential to incorporate a larger area of land in the development than is permitted under Class Q, a planning application will have to be made, which will fall to be determined in accordance with all the policy considerations that apply to such developments in the countryside.

Examples of appeals rejected on this basis have included an appeal in Somerset in April 2015 that included a barn, an enclosed yard in front of it and land to the rear and side. The cumulative area of land within the curtilage exceeded the area occupied by the building itself, so that the planned curtilage was too large for the proposed development to qualify for conversion under Class

Q, even if a walled yard was excluded from the calculation.

The very restrictive curtilage that is permitted by Class Q of Part 3 will make it impracticable in most cases to include within the prior approval application any access to a highway that may be required in connection with the proposed development. It should be borne in mind, however, that (subject to the terms of Part 2, Class B, which are discussed in *paragraph 5.2.9 of Chapter 5*), any access to a highway that needs to be formed in connection with the conversion of the building for its new purpose may in quite a few cases be permitted development under Part 2. Where the terms of Part 2, Class B do not allow the access to be formed as permitted development, however, a separate planning application may be required. In either case, the access itself should not be included in the prior approval application, although details of the highway access may be required as further information in connection with the consideration of any highways impacts of the development.

9.3 Qualifying agricultural use

Development is not permitted by Class Q where the site (i.e. the building and any land within its curtilage) was not used solely for an agricultural use, as part of an established agricultural unit, on 20 March 2013 or, in the case of a building which was in use before that date but was not in use on that date, when it was last in use. In the case of a site which was brought into use after 20 March 2013, the residential conversion of the building under Class Q may not begin within ten years of that agricultural use commencing.

An 'established agricultural unit' is defined by paragraph X of Part 3 as agricultural land occupied as a unit for the purposes of agriculture (in the case of Class Q) on or before 20 March 2013 or for ten years before the date the development begins. [The term 'agricultural unit' is further discussed in *paragraph B.1.3* in *Appendix B*.]

It is important to appreciate that the 10-year qualifying period applies only in respect of an agricultural use of the building that commences after 20 March 2013. No qualifying period is stipulated in respect of an agricultural use that commenced before that date. A comparatively short period of use before 20 March 2013 could potentially qualify as an established agricultural use for the purpose of Class Q, but the rule in *Kwik Save Discount Group Ltd v SSW* might apply in those circumstances, if the agricultural use lasted for somewhat less than a year. (See *paragraph A.12* in *Appendix A*.)

Whilst there is no explicit requirement that the qualifying use for agricultural purposes must have continued *after* 20 March 2013, it seems clear that the use must continue until the change of use is made under Class Q, for the reasons explained in *paragraph A.3* in *Appendix A*. Subsequent use for some other purpose or complete abandonment of the building might, as explained there, disqualify the building from residential conversion.

9.4   The definition of "agriculture" and "agricultural use"

An "agricultural building" is defined by paragraph X of Part 3 as a building used for agriculture and which is so used for the purposes of a trade or business, and excludes any dwellinghouse, and "agricultural use" refers to such uses. This definition therefore precludes the residential conversion of buildings that are used only for 'hobby' farming; the farming enterprise may not necessarily be profitable but must be commercial in nature. Non-agricultural use of the building, or an alleged agricultural use that is not carried out on a commercial basis, is a disqualification, as is a mixed use where agricultural use of the building has been combined with some other (non-agricultural) use.

"Agriculture" itself is not defined by the GPDO, and so the definition in section 336(1) of the 1990 Act prevails in the absence of any indication to the contrary; viz: "Agriculture" includes horticulture, fruit growing, seed growing, dairy farming, the breeding and keeping of livestock (including any creature kept for the production of food, wool, skins or fur, or for the purpose of its use in the farming of land), the use of land as grazing land, meadow land, osier land, market gardens and nursery grounds, and the use of land for woodlands where that use is ancillary to the farming of land for other agricultural purposes, and "agricultural" is to be construed accordingly. It is also relevant to note that the exclusion from the definition of development by section 55(2)(e) of the 1990 Act of the use of any land for the purpose of agriculture or forestry extends also to the use for any of those purposes of any [existing] building occupied with the land so used.

It is important for the purpose of establishing the qualifying use of an alleged 'agricultural building' to understand the limitations of what qualifies as "agriculture" or "agricultural use". Two issues may arise - first, whether or not certain activities constitute "the breeding and keeping of livestock" and, secondly, whether (and if so to what extent) the storage and packaging or processing of food is genuinely ancillary to an agricultural use (or whether it is in fact an industrial or storage use).

The reference in section 336(1) to the breeding of livestock does not include the breeding of horses except for use in farming (*Belmont Farm Ltd v MHLG* (1962) 13 P. & C. R. 417). So far as the keeping of livestock and/or the use of land as grazing land is concerned, the presence of horses on the land will only qualify as an agricultural use of the land if they are kept there as working horses actually used for farming the land (e.g. as plough horses, or as draught animals, etc.) or if they are there solely for the purpose of grazing that land, as distinct from their being kept there (*Sykes v SSE* [1981] J.P.L. 285).

The distinction may appear to be a fine one, but it is the underlying purpose that must be considered. Are the horses there simply to allow them to eat the grass (and for no other purpose)? If so, this is an agricultural use of the land. In the alternative, is the land being used primarily to provide accommodation for the horses? If they are present on the land primarily for their accommodation or for recreational use (even though they might graze the grass while they are present on the land), then this will not constitute an agricultural use of the land.

It follows that the status of the ancillary use of a building in connection with the presence of horses on the land will depend on the purpose of their presence there. The building can only be said to be in agricultural use if it is ancillary to the presence of horses on the land for purely agricultural purposes (i.e. as draught horses or plough horses - both very rare nowadays - or solely for grazing).

The problem as to whether certain activities constitute the breeding and keeping of livestock (including any creature kept for the production of food, wool, skins or fur, or for the purpose of its use in the farming of land) can also arise where the life forms being produced may fall outside this definition. This has arisen, for example, in relation to the breeding of worms (vermiculture). In *Powell v SSE* [1992] E.G.C.S 155, the High Court upheld an inspector's decision that the production of compost from rabbit droppings by vermiculture, was not an agricultural use of land but more akin to industry. The rabbit breeding itself was clearly agricultural, being "the breeding and keeping of livestock ... for food" (within the definition of 'agriculture' in section 336), but the argument that vermiculture was ancillary to that agricultural use was rejected.

A planning appeal decision in April 2005 (the parties to which were *Wickham Laboratories Ltd* and *Winchester City Council*, and which was reported at [2006] P.A.D. 7) serves as a reminder that where items, such as eggs, are produced other than as food or as a step towards the production of food, the use is not an agricultural use. In that case, fertile Specific Pathogen Free ('SPF') chicken's eggs were produced for use in the production of live viral vaccines. The appeal turned in fact on whether this was or was not an industrial (Class B1(c)) use, but it was held by the Inspector to be a *sui generis* use.

A second problem revolves around the question as to whether the storage or processing of food products can properly be said to be ancillary to an agricultural use. In this connection, it should be borne in mind that a subsidiary use can only be ancillary to a primary use carried on within the same planning unit (see *Westminster City Council v British Waterways Board* [1985] A.C. 676; [1984] 3 All E.R. 737). Notwithstanding this, the Inner House of the Scottish Court of Session held in *Farleyer Estate v Secretary of State for Scotland* [1992] P.L.R. 123 that the equivalent statutory definition in the Scottish legislation is wide enough to include the harvesting of the crop and its removal and storage. There would be little point in cultivating the crop unless the fruits of the operation in the form of the harvested produce were to be taken away for commercial purposes. Accordingly, the Court was satisfied that the removal and storage of the crop is part of the

primary agricultural (or forestry) use and falls within the statutory definition [within section 336 in the English legislation], so that it is not merely
ancillary to the primary agricultural use. In the Court's opinion it did not
matter that the area referred to in the Enforcement Notice was situated
some 1500 metres from where the crop was grown; what was important
was not the physical separation of the storage area from the area where the
crop was grown but the fact that the storage of the crop was part and parcel
of the same primary use.

Processing of agricultural produce on site (e.g. the pasteurisation and bottling
of milk, cheese-making and the manufacture of other dairy produce) has
sometimes been held not to be ancillary to the agricultural use of land and
buildings on an agricultural holding (see, for example, *Salvatore Cumbo v SSE*
[1992] J.P.L. 366), and 'as a matter of fact and degree' this may still be so in
many cases, particularly if additional produce is brought in from elsewhere
for processing. In *Cumbo*, the Inspector was satisfied that the production of
soft cheese from goat's milk produced on the holding would be outside the
realms of a wholly agricultural use, and would be in the nature of a mixed
farming and manufacturing use for which planning permission would be
necessary. This finding was upheld by the court.

However *Millington v SSE* [2000] J.P.L 297 established that some processing
of the product (in that case wine-making) is, in principle, capable of being
ancillary to the primary agricultural use of the planning unit. In that case, the
Court of Appeal had to consider whether wine-making could, having regard
to ordinary and reasonable practice, be regarded as ordinarily incidental to
the growing of the grapes (which in itself, as fruit-growing, is included in
the general term "agriculture"), and therefore ancillary to normal farming
activities, reasonably necessary to make the product marketable or dispos-
able for profit or, on the other hand, whether it had come to the stage where
the operations could not reasonably be said to be consequential on the agricultural operations of producing the crop. These are overlapping concepts
and they involve some evaluation of facts, but the view of Schiemann LJ was
that the making of wine, cider or apple juice on the scale with which the
court was concerned in that case is a perfectly normal activity for a farmer
engaged in growing grapes or apples. However, the facts are a matter for
the judgment of the decision-maker in each case.

Although it was a rating case, the decision of the House of Lords in *W & JB
Eastwood Ltd v Harrod (Valuation Officer)* [1971] A.C. 160 proposed a test
which may also be relevant in the planning context. Lord Reid pointed out
(at p.168):

*"It does not matter whether the uses which are made of the buildings are in
themselves agricultural operations. What does matter is whether those uses
are solely 'in connection with' agricultural operations on the agricultural
land…… Ordinary usage of the English language suggests that the buildings*

must be subsidiary or ancillary to the agricultural operations."

He continued (at p.169):

"The whole object of producing a crop on the agricultural land is to market it in one form or another, and I think that anything done in the farm buildings, including storage and treatment, must be held to be done in connection with the agricultural operations on the land. But here again there must be a limit. Everything is saleable at a price, so even storage for a time or very simple treatment is not strictly necessary. One must have regard to ordinary and reasonable practice. But there comes a stage when further operations cannot reasonably be said to be consequential on the agricultural operations of producing the crop."

The retail sale of farm produce may also be ancillary to an agricultural use, and so farm gate sales and even farm shops do not necessarily involve a material change in the use of land or buildings on an agricultural holding (see *Allen v SSE* [1990] J.P.L. 340), but the sale of goods not produced on this agricultural holding could take the use outside the scope of an ancillary use if the proportion of such sales and/or other factors undermine the functional primary/ancillary relationship of such a use. This may be a determining factor in deciding whether such a building qualifies for change of use under Class Q (or under Classes R or S).

Every determination as to whether an alleged agricultural use qualifies for permitted development under Class Q is bound to depend very much on its own facts, but an appeal decision in Suffolk in September 2015 provides an example of the issues that can arise. The LPA had argued that the building was not in use as part of an agricultural trade or business. However, it was established on inspection that four rooms in the building were used for packing eggs, for making and storing signs and other display materials for use at horticultural shows and as ancillary offices. Rabbit breeding also took place in another room in the building, and the evidence showed that these animals were being kept "for the production of food, wool, skins or fur" (within the statutory definition of agriculture). The Inspector concluded that most of the activities that had been carried on in the building were related to the management of the smallholding and so were agricultural, and the building did therefore qualify for residential conversion under Class Q.

9.5   Exclusions

Development is not permitted by Class Q if the site is occupied under an agricultural tenancy (a tenancy under the Agricultural Holdings Act 1986 or under the Agricultural Tenancies Act 1995), unless the express consent of both the landlord and the tenant has been obtained; nor is it permitted if, less than one year before the date development begins, an agricultural tenancy over the site has been terminated, and the termination was for the purpose of carrying out development under Class Q, unless both the landlord and the tenant have agreed in writing that the site is no longer required for agricultural use.

Development under Class Q is also precluded where permitted development has been carried out under Part 6, Classes A(a) or B(a) (works for the erection, extension or alteration of an agricultural building) on the established agricultural unit since 20 March 2013 or, where development under Class Q begins after 20 March 2023, within 10 years before the date when development under Class Q begins. [The words "whichever is the lesser" which appeared in Class MB in the 1995 Order are not repeated in the 2015 Order.]. This prevents the residential conversion of agricultural buildings erected as permitted development after 20 March 2013 until they are at least 10 years old, but it does not prevent the residential conversion of a newer agricultural building if it was erected before 20 March 2013. Nor does it prevent the residential conversion of a newer agricultural building, irrespective of the date of its erection, if it was built under a planning permission (unless prohibited by a condition in the planning permission - see *paragraph A.5 in Appendix A*).

Finally, development is not permitted by Class Q if the building is a listed building (although this exclusion does not specifically extend to a building within the curtilage of a listed building, where the curtilage building is not itself listed) and is not permitted if it is a scheduled monument, or is within a National Park, an Area of Outstanding Natural Beauty, a Conservation Area or the Broads or is within a World Heritage Site. Development is also excluded where the building is in a site of special scientific interest (SSSI), a safety hazard area or a military explosives storage area. The definitions of a "safety hazard area" and a "military explosives storage area" are quoted at the end of *paragraph 3.2.3* in *Chapter 3*.

So far as a building which is within the curtilage of a listed building is concerned (and which is not specifically disqualified from residential conversion under Class Q), readers should refer to the discussion in *paragraph 5.2.3* in *Chapter 5* regarding the effect of section 1(5) of the Listed Buildings Act in this context, which may still have the effect of disqualifying the building from change of use under Class Q.

9.6   Limits on numbers and floorspace

There would appear on the face of it to be some element of duplication between paragraph Q.1(b), which provides that the cumulative floor space of the existing building or buildings changing use under Class Q within an established agricultural unit must not exceed 450 sq m, and paragraph Q.1(h), which provides that the development (together with any previous development under Class Q) must not result in a building or buildings having more than 450 sq m of floor space in residential use.

The words "within an established agricultural unit" which appeared in paragraph MB.1(h) in the 1995 Order are not repeated in paragraph Q.1(h) in the 2015 Order, although it does not appear that any substantive amendment was intended by this omission. It is clear that 450 sq m is the absolute limit to development under this class. On the other hand, subject to this cumulative floorspace limit not being exceeded, there is no limit on the size of any one dwelling. However, the development must not result in the external dimensions of the building extending beyond the external dimensions of the existing building at any given point.

As discussed in *paragraph 1.6* of *Chapter 1*, it would seem that the cumulative floorspace limit under the former Class MB in the 1995 Order must be counted with the development now permitted under Class Q in the 2015 Order for the purposes of the cumulative limit imposed by this Class in reckoning the limit of floorspace that may be converted under Class Q.

Paragraph Q.1(c) provides that the cumulative number of separate dwellinghouses developed *under Class Q* within an established agricultural unit must not exceed three. The addition of the words in the 2015 Order which are printed here in italics resolves an ambiguity which caused difficulty in the interpretation of this provision under the 1995 Order.

The government originally sought to address this problem by amending their online Planning Practice Guidance on 5 March 2015 to make it clear that it was their intention that the total number of new homes (3 dwellinghouses) should not include existing residential properties within the established agricultural unit, unless they had also been created by permitted development under what was then Class MB.

This was intended to correct the effect of an appeal decision in which an inspector had held that the 3-dwelling limit applied to all such dwellings, and was not limited only to the number created under Class MB. The effect of that appeal decision was that any dwellings already in existence on the agricultural unit would count towards this total, so that if there were already three built under previous planning permissions, then no more could be created under Class MB.

The revised ministerial guidance in the government's online Planning Practice Guidance did not, however, resolve the difficulty posed by the drafting of the Order, because the interpretation of legislation does not depend on what ministers think it says or would like it to say, and the courts might not necessarily have agreed with the advice set out in the government's online practice guidance, if a local planning authority had sought to challenge this interpretation of the 3-dwelling limit in a future case. However, the redrafting of this provision in the 2015 Order has now entirely removed the ambiguity.

As in the case of the floorspace limit, it would seem (as discussed in *paragraph 1.6* of *Chapter 1*) that any dwellings on the agricultural holding which were converted under the former Class MB must be counted towards the cumulative limit of three dwellings that may be converted under Class Q.

Although there is a cumulative limit of 450 sq m of floorspace and a maximum number of three dwellings converted under Class Q, this does not imply that any one dwelling must not exceed 150 sq m. A single dwelling of 450 sq m could be created, or two of (say) 200 sq m and 250 sq m respectively (or one of 150 sq m and another of 300 sq m, and so on). In the same way, if three dwellings in total are built, whether simultaneously or in separate developments, the floor areas of the three dwellings may differ significantly, provided that their combined floorspace does not exceed a total of 450 sq m.

9.7   *Limits on building operations*

The definition of a "building" in Article 2(1) of the GPDO includes "any structure or erection" as well as any part of a building. This could in principle include various buildings and structures of unconventional, and perhaps in some cases rather insubstantial, construction. The well-known judicial authorities on what constitutes a building or structure are perfectly clear on this point (e.g. *Cardiff Rating Authority v Guest Keen Baldwin* [1949] 1 KB 385, *Skerritts of Nottingham v SSETR (No.2)* [2000] 2 P.L.R 102; [2000] J.P.L. 1025 and *R (Save Woolley Valley Action Group Ltd) v Bath and North East Somerset Council* [2012] EWHC 2161 (Admin)).

However, the works permitted under Class Q(b) are restricted to what is reasonably necessary for the building to function as a dwellinghouse, and any partial demolition must also be limited to the extent reasonably necessary to carry out the building operations that are permitted by this class. This imposes a practical constraint on the convertibility of some buildings. Works that amount to substantial demolition and reconstruction or replacement of the existing fabric would go beyond what is permitted.

The government amended their online Planning Practice Guidance on 5 March 2015, confirming that it is not the intention of what was then Class MB(b) (now Class Q(b)) to permit the construction of new structural elements for the building. Accordingly, it is only where the existing building is structurally strong enough to take the loading associated with the external works to adapt the building for residential use that certain building operations would be considered to come within Class Q(b).

In any event, the development under Class Q(b) must not consist of building operations other than the installation or replacement of windows, doors, roofs, or exterior walls, or water, drainage, electricity, gas or other services, to the extent reasonably necessary for the building to function as a dwellinghouse, and partial demolition to the extent reasonably necessary to carry out the building operations listed there. Furthermore, the development must not result in the external dimensions of the building extending beyond the external dimensions of the existing building at any given point.

The inclusion of roofs and walls in the list of items that can be installed or replaced as part of the building operations permitted by Class Q might be thought to allow scope for some significant rebuilding or replacement of the existing fabric, but an appeal decision in Bedfordshire, issued in February 2015, where the existing structures, and the materials from which they were constructed, were so insubstantial that the buildings would require almost complete demolition and reconstruction in order to meet the requirements of the Building Regulations, provides clear confirmation that the extent of the proposed building operations must not go beyond what is "reasonably necessary" for the building to function as a dwellinghouse, so that substantial demolition of the building and its effective replacement would be outside the scope of the development that is permitted. Not only would this clearly have gone beyond the extent of the works that were envisaged by the terms of what was then Class MB(b) [now Q(b)] as being "reasonably necessary" for the building to function as a dwellinghouse, but it was also sufficient in that case to disqualify the building from residential conversion under Class MB(a) [now Q(a)].

A further appeal decision in Nottinghamshire also illustrates this point. The Inspector in this case held that the proposed barn conversion would involve such major changes and reconstruction as to go beyond the scope of the development permitted by Class MB(b) [now Q(b)]. The building had a metal frame and walls comprising a single metal skin, plus an element of blockwork, and a roof of corrugated asbestos fibreboard. What was required to enable the adaptation of the building for residential use amounted to substantial demolition and reconstruction of the building, plus various physical alterations. This was quite clearly beyond the scope of the then Class MB(b).

Another example of a residential conversion under Class Q being rejected on structural grounds was provided by an appeal decision in Buckinghamshire in August 2015. In this case, the existing building comprised a steel frame clad with light corrugated sheet. The proposal was to replace this sheet with timber cladding, and a roof of slate. However, the Inspector doubted that the increased weight of the new materials could be carried by the existing steel frame, which was showing signs of rust. No structural report had been produced to confirm that the proposed conversion could be based on the existing steel frame, and so he concluded that the conversion could not be carried out within the limited structural parameters of the permitted development allowed by Class Q. A similar decision was reached on very similar grounds in an appeal in Hampshire in September 2015.

Notwithstanding these appeal decisions, and the government's online planning practice guidance (as revised in March 2015), there remains a potential conflict between their stated view that works involving significant structural changes fall outside the intended scope of permitted development under Part 3 and, on the other hand, such purely internal works as would in any event be lawful under the terms of section 55(2)(a) of the 1990 Act.

These might lawfully include additional strengthening or other alterations to the structure, such as mezzanine floors, new load-bearing walls, and the strengthening or even replacement of an existing internal frame, provided that they affect only the interior of the building or do not materially affect its external appearance.

Whilst it is clear from the wording in the GPDO that development is not permitted under Part 3 if it would consist of building operations other than (among other things) the installation or replacement of roofs, or exterior walls to the extent reasonably necessary for the building to function as a dwellinghouse, and partial demolition to the extent reasonably necessary to carry out those permitted building operations, this would not appear to preclude internal structural alterations which, as pointed out above, are not development within the meaning of the Act in any event. The statutory wording clearly does not permit wholesale demolition and reconstruction but, in the author's view, the scope for strengthening or even partial replacement of the internal structure of the building and other physical works may be somewhat wider than ministerial practice guidance and the cited appeal decisions would appear to suggest. This point has not yet, so far as the author is aware, been tested in the courts, but there may possibly be scope for disputing the stance that has so far been taken on this issue both by ministers and by the Planning Inspectorate.

It is clear, however, that the strict limitation on the works that may be carried out under Class Q(b), combined with the condition that they must not extend outside the envelope of the pre-existing building, does not allow the creation of any hard surface or other engineering works (such as the laying of gravel) to provide any hard surfaces within the curtilage for the purposes of parking, or the provision of a patio, etc.

Furthermore, as noted in *paragraph 9.9* below, such works cannot be carried out under Part 1 of the Second Schedule, because such development under that part of the Second Schedule to the GPDO is specifically excluded where use of the building as a dwellinghouse is permitted only by virtue of Class Q. Planning permission will therefore be required if it is desired to incorporate any such facilities in the development, and all the usual policy considerations relating to development in the countryside will apply to the determination of such an application.

On the other hand, these restrictions do not prevent any of the operational development that is permitted by Part 2 of the Second Schedule to the GPDO. (See *paragraph 5.2.9* in *Chapter 5*, where these permitted operations are summarised, and where the formation or laying out of an access to a highway is also discussed.)

9.8   Prior approval

The change of use permitted by Class Q(a) is subject to the condition that before beginning the development, the developer must apply to the local planning authority for a determination as to whether the prior approval of the authority will be required as to:

(a)   transport and highways impacts of the development,

(b)   noise impacts of the development;

(c)   contamination risks on the site;

(d)   flooding risks on the site;

(e)   whether the location or siting of the building makes it otherwise impractical or undesirable for the building to change from agricultural use to a residential use; and

(f)   the design or external appearance of the building.

The determination of the prior approval application in relation to these criteria, and other material considerations that are to be taken into account (under paragraph W), is discussed in *part 14.4* of *Chapter 14*.

The operational development permitted by Class Q(b) is also subject to the condition that before beginning the development, the developer must apply to the local planning authority for a determination as to whether the prior approval of the authority will be required as to the design or external appearance of the building. The provisions of paragraph W of Part 3 also apply with regard to this issue, as discussed in *paragraph 14.4.12* in *Chapter 14*.

A question has arisen in the past as to whether a prior approval application in respect of the permitted operational development may be made (and therefore considered and determined) separately from the prior approval application for the change of use. However, amendments to the GPDO incorporated in the 2015 Order have made it clear that an application for the change of use alone can no longer be made separately from the application in respect of the approval of any necessary operational development, unless no such works will be required.

Thus paragraph Q.2(2) provides that where the development proposed is development under both Class Q(a) and Class Q(b), an application must be made as to whether the prior approval of the LPA will be required as to all of items (a) to (f) above, whereas if the application is made under Class Q(a) only, where no building operations are proposed because they are not required in order to facilitate the change of use, then there is no need to address item (f).

9.9   Commencement and completion

It was a condition in the 1995 Order, applicable to both of what were then Classes MB(a) and MB(b), that the development must *begin* within a period of three years. However, there is no longer any requirement as to the date of commencement of the development, but the corresponding condition in paragraph Q.2(3) of the 2015 Order, applying to both Classes Q(a) and Q(b), requires that development under either the first or, where applicable, both of these classes must be *completed* within a period of three years beginning with the date on which any prior approval is granted for that development, or beginning with the expiry of the 56-day period referred to in paragraph W(11)(c) without the local planning authority notifying the developer as to whether prior approval for that development is given or refused, whichever is the earlier (see *paragraph 14.10* in *Chapter 14*).

See *paragraph 1.3.2* in *Chapter 1* for a discussion of what constitutes the completion of development for the purposes of this condition.

9.10   Exclusion of other permitted development

It should be noted that the permitted development which can normally be carried out under Part 1 of the Second Schedule to the GPDO (relating to development within the curtilage of a dwellinghouse, as well as alteration or enlargement of the house itself) is entirely excluded where a residential conversion has been carried out as permitted development under Part 3, Class Q.

Thus development is entirely excluded under Part 1, Class A (the enlargement, improvement or other alteration of the dwellinghouse), Class B (the enlargement of the dwellinghouse consisting of an addition or alteration to its roof), Class C (any other alteration to the roof of the dwellinghouse), Class D (the erection or construction of a porch outside any external door of the dwellinghouse), Class E (the provision within the curtilage of the dwellinghouse of any building or enclosure, swimming or other pool, or the maintenance, improvement or other alteration of such a building or enclosure; or the provision of a container used for domestic heating purposes for the storage of oil or liquid petroleum gas), Class F (the provision within the curtilage of the dwellinghouse of a hard surface for any purpose incidental to the enjoyment of the dwellinghouse as such; or the replacement in whole or in part of such a surface), Class G (the installation, alteration or replacement of a chimney, flue or soil and vent pipe on the dwellinghouse) and Class H (the installation, alteration or replacement of a microwave antenna on the dwellinghouse or within the curtilage of the dwellinghouse). Planning permission will therefore be required if it is subsequently proposed to carry out any of these developments at a dwelling that has been converted under Class Q

On the other hand, various minor operations are permitted under Part 2. (These are briefly summarised in *paragraph 5.2.9* in *Chapter 5*, where the formation or laying out of an access to a highway is also discussed.)

In addition, where a residential conversion has been carried out under Class Q, permitted development under Part 6 is excluded for a period of 10 years if it would consist of the erection or extension of any agricultural building on an established agricultural unit (as defined in paragraph X of Part 3 - see *paragraphs 9.3* and *9.4* above, and *paragraph B.1.3* in *Appendix B*). Farmers should bear this in mind before applying for prior approval in respect of a change of use under Class Q, as this will prevent any other buildings being erected on the farm or any buildings on the farm being extended for a period of 10 years (other than with planning permission, for which an application would have to be made in the usual way). The 10-year period runs from the date on which the change of use of a building on the agricultural holding to residential use takes place. Permitted development under Part 6, Classes A or B, comprising the erection, extension or alteration of an agricultural building anywhere else on that agricultural holding cannot be commenced until that 10-year period has expired.

CHAPTER 10

CHANGE OF USE TO USE AS A STATE-FUNDED SCHOOL OR REGISTERED NURSERY

10.1 Change of use of various commercial premises

10.1.1 The development permitted

Class T (formerly Class K in the 1995 Order) permits the change of use of a building and any land within its curtilage from a use falling within Use Classes B1 (business), C1 (hotels), C2 (residential institutions), C2A (secure residential institutions) or D2 (assembly and leisure) to use as a state-funded school, or to use as a registered nursery, but for no other purpose (including any other purpose falling within Use Class D1), except to the extent that the other purpose is ancillary to the primary use of the site as a state-funded school or as a registered nursery.

"State-funded school" means a school funded wholly or mainly from public funds, including an Academy school, an alternative provision Academy or a 16 to 19 Academy established under the Academies Act 2010, or a school maintained by a local authority, as defined in section 142(1) of the School Standards and Framework Act 1998. "Registered nursery" means non-domestic premises in respect of which a person is registered under Part 3 of the Childcare Act 2006 to provide early years provision (Paragraph X).

10.1.2 Exclusions

Development is not, however, permitted by Class T if the building is a listed building or is a scheduled monument (although the exclusion in respect of a listed building does not specifically extend to a building within its curtilage, where the curtilage building is not itself listed). Nor is it permitted where the site is or forms part of a military explosives storage area or a safety hazard area. The definitions of a "safety hazard area" and a "military explosives storage area" are quoted at the end of *paragraph 3.2.3* in *Chapter 3*.

So far as a building which is within the curtilage of a listed building is concerned (and which is not specifically disqualified from conversion under Class T), readers should refer to the discussion in *paragraph 5.2.3* in *Chapter 5* regarding the effect of section 1(5) of the Listed Buildings Act in this context, which may still have the effect of disqualifying the building from change of use under Class T.

Development under Class T is also excluded if the use of the site within

Class D2 (assembly and leisure) resulted from a permitted change of use under Part 3, Class J (change of use from use as a shop or for the provision of financial or professional services, or from use as a betting office or pay day loan shop).

The restrictive definition of "curtilage" in paragraph X applies for the purposes of Classes Q, R or S only. For the purposes of Class T, therefore, the generally accepted definition of the word discussed in *paragraph B.2.1 in Appendix B* should be applied.

10.1.3   Restrictions on further changes of use

The development permitted by Class T is subject to various conditions, the first of which (as outlined above) is that the site is to be used as a state-funded school, or as a registered nursery, and for no other purpose (including any other purpose falling within Use Class D1), except to the extent that the other purpose is ancillary to the primary use of the site as a state-funded school or as a registered nursery. This therefore excludes a change of use within this use class which could otherwise be carried out under section 55(2)(f) of the 1990 Act.

10.1.4   Prior approval

Before beginning the development, the developer must apply to the local planning authority for a determination as to whether the prior approval of the authority will be required as to:

(i)   transport and highways impacts of the development;

(ii)   noise impacts of the development; and

(iii)   contamination risks on the site.

(Note that flooding risk is not one of the issues that falls to be considered in respect of this class of development).

The provisions of paragraph W apply in relation to any such application, and readers should refer to *part 14.4* of *Chapter 14*, regarding the practical application of these provisions.

10.1.5   Operational development

The development permitted by Class T does not include any building operations in connection with the conversion of the building to use as a state-funded school or registered nursery. Any such works will therefore require planning permission, unless they are exempt from the definition of development by virtue of section 55(2)(a) of the 1990 Act, because they affect only the interior of the building, or do not materially affect the external appearance of the building. However, a planning application for any such 'associated operational development' will have the effect of extending the time for commencement of the development, as explained in *paragraph 10.1.6* below.

Once the change of use under Class T has taken place, Class M of Part 7 permits the extension or alteration of a school building (but not of a nursery). The cumulative gross floor space of any buildings erected, extended or altered is limited by paragraph M.1(a) to 25% of the gross floor space of the original school (defined by paragraph M.3 as any original building which is a school other than any building erected at any time under Class M itself), or 100 sq m, whichever is the lesser, provided that where two or more original buildings are within the same curtilage and are used for the same institution, they are to be treated as a single original building in making any measurement.

('Curtilage' is mentioned in several places in Classes M and N of Part 7, but this term is not defined for the purposes of Part 7, and so the generally accepted interpretation of this term applies – see *paragraph B.2.1* in *Appendix B.*)

No part of this additional development must be within 5 metres of a boundary of the curtilage of the premises (paragraph M.1(b)), and it must not use any land used as a playing field at any time in the past five years and remaining in use, if as a result of the development it could no longer be used as a playing field (paragraph M.1(c)). The height of any new building erected must not exceed 5 metres (paragraph M.1(d)), and the height of any extended or altered building must not exceed 5 metres if it is within 10 metres of a boundary of the curtilage of the premises or, in any other case, the height of the building being extended or altered (paragraph M.1(e)). Such development is not permitted within the curtilage of a listed building (paragraph M.1(f)), but this prohibition does not extend to a scheduled monument or its curtilage. Finally, such development is not permitted unless the predominant use of the existing buildings on the premises is for the provision of education (paragraph M.1(g)).

Development under Class M is subject to the condition that the development is within the curtilage of an existing school (paragraph M.2(a)), that the development is only used as part of, or for a purpose incidental to, the use of that school (paragraph M.2(b)), that any new building erected is, in the case of land within a conservation area, an area of outstanding natural beauty, a National Park, a World Heritage Site or the Broads, constructed using materials which have a similar external appearance to those used for the original school buildings (paragraph M.2(c)), and that any extension or alteration in such areas is constructed using materials which have a similar external appearance to those used for the building being extended or altered (paragraph M.2(d)).

Paragraph O of Part 7 confirms that in Part 7, "school" includes premises which have changed use under Class T of Part 3 to become a state-funded school or registered nursery, and so operational development can be carried out in this case under Part 7, Class M. However, this applies only to an "existing" school, so any such extension can only be made *after* the change of use permitted by Class T has actually taken place. Such an extension or alteration cannot take place in anticipation of the change of use.

In addition to this, Class N of Part 7 permits development consisting of the provision of a hard surface within the curtilage of any school (but not of a nursery), which is to be used for the purposes of that school, or the replacement in whole or in part of such a surface. The cumulative area of ground covered by a hard surface within the curtilage of the site (other than hard surfaces already existing on 6 April 2010) must not exceed 50 sq m (paragraph N.1(a)), and such development is not permitted if, as a result of the development, any land used as a playing field at any time in the five years before the development commenced and remaining in this use could no longer be used as a playing field (paragraph N.1(b)). However, such development is not permitted within the curtilage of a listed building (paragraph N.1(c)) but this prohibition does not extend to a scheduled monument or its curtilage.

The development permitted by Class N is subject to the condition that where there is a risk of groundwater contamination, the hard surface must *not* be made of porous materials (paragraph N(2)(a)). In all other cases, the hard surface must be made of porous materials, or provision must be made to direct run-off water from the hard surface to a permeable or porous area or surface within the curtilage of the school premises (paragraph N(2)(b)).

As noted above, paragraph O of Part 7 confirms that in Part 7, "school" includes premises which have changed use under Class T of Part 3 to become a state-funded school or registered nursery, and so operational development can be carried out in this case under Part 7, Class N, but only where the premises *have* (already) changed use under Class T, so any hard surface can only be provided *after* the change of use permitted by Class T has actually taken place. Such a hard surface cannot therefore be laid in anticipation of the change of use. In any event, before this occurs, the premises cannot properly be described as a 'school', and a planning application would have to be made for 'associated operational development' instead.

It should also be borne in mind that various other forms of operational development are permitted under Part 2. These include the formation or laying out of an access to a highway, as discussed in *paragraph 5.2.9* in *Chapter 5*, and they also include in Class A the erection, construction, maintenance, improvement or alteration of a gate, fence, wall or other means of enclosure up to 2 metres high at a school, even where this adjoins a highway used by vehicular traffic (provided that any part of it which is more than 1 metre above ground level does not create an obstruction to the view of highway users so as to cause danger to them). Although it was not perhaps strictly necessary, paragraph A.2 of Part 2 makes it clear that this provision includes premises which have changed use under Class T of Part 3 to become a state-funded school or registered nursery.

10.1.6 Commencement and completion

It is a condition, under paragraph T.2(2), that development under this class must begin within a period of three years starting with the date on which any prior approval is granted for that development, or starting with the expiry of the 56-day period referred to in paragraph W(11)(c) without the local planning authority notifying the developer as to whether prior approval for that development is given or refused, whichever is the earlier (see *paragraph 14.10* in *Chapter 14*).

See *paragraph 1.3.2* in *Chapter 1* for a discussion of what constitutes the commencement of development for the purposes of this condition.

The 3-year commencement deadline is extended by paragraph T.2(3) where, in relation to a particular development under Class T, planning permission is granted before the end of the 3-year period referred to in paragraph T.2(2) on an application in respect of associated operational development (defined as building or other operations in relation to the same building or land which are reasonably necessary to use the building or land for the use proposed under Class T). In this case, development under Class T must begin within the period of 3 years starting with the date on which such planning permission is granted.

If the application for planning permission for associated development were to be made, say, more than 2 years after the prior approval date, this could have the effect of extending the time limit for starting the development to more than 5 years from the prior approval date in respect of the change of use, compared with the 3-year commencement deadline originally imposed. However, it would be unwise to leave it too close to the end of the 3-year period before applying for planning permission for the associated works, in case the grant of planning permission is delayed, and the original 3-year deadline for the commencement of development is missed.

There is no time limit in this case for the completion of the development.

10.1.7 Change of use back to previous use

Class U (formerly Class L in the 1995 Order) permits the change of use of land from a use permitted by Class T (above) to the previous lawful use of the land. This is not subject to any conditions. The essential point is that the change of use permitted by Class U is strictly confined to land which is in use for one of the two purposes permitted by Class T, and this applies only where that use is the result of a change of use that was permitted by Class T itself, and not resulting from any other permission.

The position in this regard may, to some extent, be analogous with the effect of section 57 of the 1990 Act. For example, it is arguable that the right to resume the previous lawful use will not last indefinitely. If there is an extended period of disuse after the land has ceased to be used as a school or nursery, it is possible that the right to resume the previous lawful use may thereby have been lost. (See *Bramall v SSCLG* [2011] EWHC 1531 (Admin).) However, bearing in mind that a change of use to a use under Class T can only be made if the pre-existing use was lawful (see *paragraph A.4* in *Appendix A*), the problem identified in *Young v SSE* [1983] 3 W.L.R. 382; [1983] 2 A.C. 662, where the immediately preceding use was in fact unlawful, will not arise in relation to the change of use back to the pre-existing use that is permitted by Class U.

Other than the limited permission granted by Class U, there are no permitted development rights that would allow the change of use of a school or nursery to any other use. Nor are there any permitted development rights in Part 3 that would allow a change of use to or from any other use falling within Use Class D1.

10.2 Change of use of an agricultural building

10.2.1   The development permitted

Class S (formerly Class MA in the 1995 Order) permits the change of use of a building and any land within its curtilage from use as an agricultural building to use as a state-funded school or as a registered nursery, but for no other purpose (including any other purpose falling within Use Class D1), except to the extent that the other purpose is ancillary to the primary use of the site as a state-funded school or as a registered nursery. (For the definition of "state-funded school" and "registered nursery" see *paragraph 10.1.1* above.)

Bearing in mind that no building operations can be carried out under Class S, so that any works for the alteration of the building must necessarily be confined to works which affect only the interior of the building, or which do not materially affect the external appearance of the building, and which by virtue of section 55(2)(a) of the 1990 Act do not therefore amount to development, the scope for any element of rebuilding or structural alteration is clearly limited, and is likely to make the conversion of buildings and structures of unconventional or insubstantial, construction impracticable. (This point is discussed in more detail in *paragraph 9.7* of *Chapter 9*.)

10.2.2   Restricted curtilage

It should be particularly noted that an extremely restrictive definition of 'curtilage' is prescribed by paragraph X for the purposes of Class S. This allows only a very small area of land adjacent to the agricultural building to be included in the permitted change of use. It is confined to:

(i)   the piece of land, whether enclosed or unenclosed, immediately beside or around the agricultural building, closely associated with and serving the purposes of the agricultural building; or

(ii)   an area of land immediately beside or around the agricultural build-
       ing *no larger than the land area occupied by the agricultural building*;

whichever is the lesser.

In practical terms, this could be a problem for a proposed change of use to
a school (and possibly, although to a lesser extent, to use as a nursery), as it
allows very little space for a playground or other space for outdoor sport or
exercise. Planning permission will be required if it is desired to take any larger
area of land into the proposed development. (As to any engineering works
that may be required in order to form a playground or other hard surface
within the curtilage of the converted building, see *paragraph 10.2.9* below).

A development that seeks to include more than this very limited amount of
land in the conversion will not be permitted development under Class S. A
prior approval application where a larger area of land is included in order to
provide extra space for a playground or for sports and games is liable to be
summarily rejected. If it is felt essential to incorporate a larger area of land
in the development than is permitted under Class S, a planning application
will have to be made, which will fall to be determined in accordance with all
the policy considerations that apply to such developments in the countryside.

The very restrictive curtilage that is permitted by Class S of Part 3 will make
it impracticable in most cases to include within the prior approval application any access to a highway that may be required in connection with the
proposed development. It should be borne in mind, however, that (subject
to the terms of Part 2, Class B, which are discussed in *paragraph 5.2.9* of
Chapter 5), any access to a highway that needs to be formed in connection
with the conversion of the building for its new purpose may in quite a few
cases be permitted development under Part 2. Where the terms of Part 2,
Class B do not allow the access to be formed as permitted development,
however, a separate planning application may be required. In either case,
the access itself should not be included in the prior approval application,
although details of the highway access may be required as further information in connection with the consideration of any highways impacts of the
development.

10.2.3   *Qualifying agricultural use*

Development is not permitted by Class S where the site was not used solely
for an agricultural use, as part of an established agricultural unit, on 20
March 2013, or if the site was not in use on that date, when it was last in use.
If the site was brought into use after 20 March 2013, the conversion of the
building under Class S may not begin within ten years of that agricultural
use commencing.

Readers should refer to *paragraphs 9.3* and *9.4* in *Chapter 9* for the definitions of "agricultural building", "agriculture" and "agricultural use", and to

the note in *paragraph 9.7* as to the definition of a "building" for this purpose.

Whilst there is no explicit requirement that the qualifying use for agricultural purposes must have continued *after* 20 March 2013, it seems clear that the use must still subsist until the change of use is made under Class S, for the reasons explained in *paragraph A.3* in *Appendix A*. Subsequent use for some other purpose or complete abandonment of the building might, as explained there, disqualify the building from conversion under Class S.

A comparatively short period of use before 20 March 2013 could potentially qualify as an established agricultural use for the purpose of Class S, but the rule in *Kwik Save Discount Group Ltd v SSW* might apply in those circumstances, if the agricultural use lasted for somewhat less than a year. (See *paragraph A.12* in *Appendix A.*)

10.2.4   Exclusions

Development is not permitted by Class S if the site is occupied under an agricultural tenancy (a tenancy under the Agricultural Holdings Act 1986 or under the Agricultural Tenancies Act 1995), unless the express consent of both the landlord and the tenant has been obtained; nor is it permitted if, less than one year before the date development begins, an agricultural tenancy over the site has been terminated, and the termination was for the purpose of carrying out development under Class S, unless both the landlord and the tenant have agreed in writing that the site is no longer required for agricultural use.

Development under Class S is also precluded where permitted development has been carried out under Part 6, Classes A(a) or B(a) (works for the erection, extension or alteration of an agricultural building) on the established agricultural unit since 20 March 2013, or within 10 years before the date development under Class S begins, whichever is the lesser. This prevents the conversion of agricultural buildings erected as permitted development after 20 March 2013 until they are at least 10 years old, but it does not prevent the conversion of a newer agricultural building if it was erected before 20 March 2013. Nor does it prevent the conversion of a newer agricultural building, irrespective of the date of its erection, if it was built under a planning permission (unless prohibited by a condition in the planning permission - see *paragraph A.5* in *Appendix A*).

In contrast to a change of use under Class M or Class Q, conversion of an agricultural building under Class S is *not* precluded in a National Park, an Area of Outstanding Natural Beauty, the Broads, a Conservation Area or a World Heritage Site.

Development is not, however, permitted by Class S if the building is a listed building or is a scheduled monument (although the exclusion in respect of a listed building does not specifically extend to a building within its curtilage, where the curtilage building is not itself listed). Development under Class S is also excluded where the building is in a site of special scientific interest (SSSI), a safety hazard area or a military explosives storage area. The definitions of a "safety hazard area" and a "military explosives storage area" are quoted at the end of *paragraph 3.2.3* in *Chapter 3*.

So far as a building which is within the curtilage of a listed building is concerned (and which is not specifically disqualified from conversion under Class S), readers should refer to the discussion in *paragraph 5.2.3* in *Chapter 5* regarding the effect of section 1(5) of the Listed Buildings Act in this context, which may still have the effect of disqualifying the building from change of use under Class S.

10.2.5 Floorspace limit

Paragraph S.1(b) provides that the cumulative area of floor space within the existing building or buildings together with land within the curtilage of that building or those buildings changing use under Class S within an established agricultural unit must not exceed 500 sq m. As discussed in *paragraph 1.6* of *Chapter 1*, it would appear that any floorspace previously converted under the former Class MA in the 1995 Order must be counted towards the cumulative limit of floorspace that may be converted under Class S.

10.2.6 Prior approval

The change of use permitted by Class S is subject to the condition that before changing the use of the site, the developer must apply to the local planning authority for a determination as to whether the prior approval of the authority will be required as to:

(i)   transport and highways impacts of the development;

(ii)   noise impacts of the development;

(iii) contamination risks on the site;

(iv)   flooding risks on the site; or

(v)   whether the location or siting of the building makes it otherwise impractical or undesirable for the building to change from agricultural use to use as a state-funded school or as a registered nursery.

The determination of the prior approval application in relation to these criteria, and other material considerations that are to be taken into account (under paragraph W), is discussed in *part 14.4* of *Chapter 14*.

10.2.7 Commencement and completion

It is a condition, under paragraph S.2(2), that development under this class must begin within a period of three years starting with the date on which any prior approval is granted for that development, or starting with the expiry of the 56-day period referred to in paragraph W(11)(c) without the local planning authority notifying the developer as to whether prior approval for that development is given or refused, whichever is the earlier (see *paragraph 14.10* in *Chapter 14*).

(See *paragraph 1.3.2* in *Chapter 1* for a discussion of what constitutes the commencement of development for the purposes of this condition.)

The 3-year commencement deadline is extended by paragraph S.2(3) where, in relation to a particular development under Class S, planning permission is granted before the end of the 3-year period referred to in paragraph S.2(2) on an application in respect of associated operational development (defined as building or other operations in relation to the same building or land which are reasonably necessary to use the building or land for the use proposed under Class S). In this case, development under Class S must begin within the period of 3 years starting with the date on which such planning permission is granted.

If the application for planning permission for associated development were to be made, say, more than 2 years after the prior approval date, this could have the effect of extending the time limit for starting the development to more than 5 years from the prior approval date in respect of the change of use, compared with the 3-year commencement deadline originally imposed. However, it would be unwise to leave it too close to the end of the 3-year period before applying for planning permission for the associated works, in case the grant of planning permission is delayed, and the original 3-year deadline for the commencement of development is missed.

There is no time limit in this case for the completion of the development.

10.2.8   Restrictions on further changes of use

As noted above, the change of use permitted by Class S is subject to a condition that the site must not be used for any other purpose (including any other purpose falling within Use Class D1), except to the extent that the other purpose is ancillary to the primary use of the site as a state-funded school or as a registered nursery. This therefore excludes a change of use within this use class which could otherwise be carried out under section 55(2)(f) of the 1990 Act.

10.2.9   Operational development

Unlike the change of use permitted by Classes M, N and Q of Part 3, the development permitted by Class S does not include any building operations in connection with the conversion of the building or its curtilage to the new use. Any such works in connection with the change of use will therefore require planning permission, unless they are exempt from the definition of development by virtue of section 55(2)(a) of the 1990 Act, because they affect only the interior of the building, or do not materially affect the external appearance of the building. However, a planning application for any such 'associated operational development' will have the effect of extending the time for commencement of the development, as explained in *paragraph 10.2.7* above.

There was a provision in the former Class MA that after a change of use had been made under that class, the development that was permitted at that time by the former Part 41, Class B applied in the same way as it applied to an office building. This permitted the provision or replacement of a limited area of hard surface within the curtilage of the building. This provision has been replaced by Class N of Part 7. (See *paragraph 10.1.5* above for the permissible extent of such development and the exclusions and conditions that apply to it.)

('Curtilage' is mentioned in several places in Part 7, Class N, but this term is not defined for the purposes of Part 7, and so the generally accepted interpretation of this term applies – see *paragraph B.2.1* in *Appendix B*.)

As noted in *paragraph 10.1.5* above, development under Part 7, Class N can be carried out only where the premises *have* (already) changed use under Class S, so any hard surface can only be provided *after* the change of use permitted by Class S has actually taken place. In any event, before this occurs, the premises cannot properly be described as a 'school', and a planning application would have to be made for 'associated operational development' instead. Such a hard surface cannot therefore be laid in anticipation of the change of use.

Paragraph O of Part 7 confirms that in Part 7, "school" includes premises which have changed use under Class S of Part 3 to become a state-funded school or registered nursery *except in Class M* (extensions etc. for schools). Thus the development permitted by Class M of Part 7 is excluded in the case of a school created under Class S, and so no extensions or alterations can subsequently be carried out as permitted development in this case.

It should, on the other hand, be borne in mind that various other operations are permitted under Part 2. These are briefly summarised in *paragraph 5.2.9* of *Chapter 5*, and they include the formation or laying out of an access. They also include, in Class A, the erection, construction, maintenance, improvement or alteration of a gate, fence, wall or other means of enclosure up to 2 metres high at a school, even where this adjoins a highway used by vehicular traffic (provided that any part of it which is more than 1 metre above ground level does not create an obstruction to the view of highway users so as to cause danger to them). Although it was not perhaps strictly necessary, paragraph A.2 of Part 2 makes it clear that this provision includes premises which have changed use under Class S of Part 3 to become a state-funded school or registered nursery.

10.2.10 *Exclusion of permission for further agricultural buildings*

It should be noted that the where a change of use has been carried out under Class S, permitted development under Part 6 is excluded for a period of 10 years if it would consist of the erection or extension of any agricultural building on an established agricultural unit (as defined in paragraph X of Part 3 - see *paragraph 9.3* in *Chapter 9*, and *paragraph B.1.3* in *Appendix B*). Farmers should bear this in mind before allowing anyone to apply for prior approval in respect of a change of use under Class S, as this will prevent any other buildings being erected on the farm or any buildings on the farm being extended for a period of 10 years (other than with planning permission, for which an application would have to be made in the usual way). The 10-year period runs from the date on which the change of use of a building on the agricultural holding to use as a school or nursery takes place. Permitted development under Part 6, Classes A or B, comprising the erection, extension or alteration of an agricultural building anywhere else on that agricultural holding cannot be commenced until that 10-year period has expired.

CHAPTER 11

CHANGES OF USE TO AND FROM USE FOR ASSEMBLY AND LEISURE

11.1   The development permitted

Class J permits the change of use of a building from various retail or retail-related uses to a use within Use Class D2 (assembly and leisure). **Class J(a)** permits the change of use of a building from a use falling within Use Classes A1 (shops) or A2 (financial and professional services); **Class J(b)** permits a change of use from use as a betting office or a pay day loan shop. **Class K** (formerly Class H in the 1995 Order) similarly permits a change of use to Use Class D2 from use as a casino. The uses falling within Use Class D2 are summarised in *Appendix C* of this book. It should be noted that a number of leisure-related uses are in fact *sui generis*, and would not therefore fall within the scope of the uses to which the use of the building can be changed under Class J.

The change of use from use as a casino permitted by Class K is not subject to any restrictions or conditions. The paragraphs below therefore apply only to changes of use under Class J. A change of use from use as a casino to a use within Use Class D2 (assembly and leisure) can accordingly be made at will at any time - but this is, of course, a one-way only change; the use of the building cannot thereafter revert to use as a casino.

11.2   The qualifying use

Development is not permitted by Class J where the site was not used solely for one of the uses referred to in Class J(a) or J(b) on 5 December 2013, or if the site was not in use on that date, when it was last in use. If the site was brought into use after 5 December 2013, the conversion of the building under Class J may not begin within 5 years of that use commencing. However, this 5-year qualifying period applies only in respect of a use of the building that has commenced *after* 5 December 2013. No qualifying period is stipulated in respect of a use that commenced before that date. A comparatively short period of use before 5 December 2013 could potentially qualify for the purposes of Class J, but the rule in *Kwik Save Discount Group Ltd v SSW* might apply in those circumstances, if the previous use lasted for somewhat less than a year. (See *paragraph A.12* in *Appendix A*.)

Whilst there is no explicit requirement that the qualifying use must have continued *after* 5 December 2013, it seems clear that the use (or at least the right, in planning terms, to use the building for that purpose) must still subsist until the change of use is made under Class J, for the reasons explained in *paragraph A.3* in *Appendix A*. Subsequent use for some other purpose or complete abandonment of the building might, as explained there, disqualify the building from a change of use under Class J.

11.3   Exclusions

Permitted development is excluded under Class J where the building is within a Conservation Area, an Area of Outstanding Natural Beauty, the Broads, a National Park or a World Heritage Site (formerly known in the 1995 Order as 'Article 1(5) land', but now identified in the 2015 Order as 'Article 2(3) land'). It is also excluded where the building is in a site of special scientific interest (SSSI), a safety hazard area or a military explosives storage area. The definitions of a "safety hazard area" and a "military explosives storage area" are quoted at the end of *paragraph 3.2.3* in *Chapter 3*.

Permitted development under Class J is also excluded where the building is a listed building or is within the curtilage of a listed building or where it is a scheduled monument. So far as a building within the curtilage of a listed building is concerned, the relevant curtilage in this context (consistent with the interpretation of other legislative provisions prohibiting or restricting development within the curtilage of a listed building) must be taken to refer to the curtilage of the building *at the time when it was first listed*. (See *paragraph B.2.2* in *Appendix B* and the judgment in *R (Egerton) v Taunton Deane BC* cited in that paragraph.) The inclusion in the listing of any building attached to the listed building is also discussed at *paragraph B.2.3*.

11.4   Floorspace limit

The cumulative floor space of the existing building changing use under Class J must not exceed 200 sq m, and the change of use (together with any previous change of use under Class J) must not result in more than 200 sq m of floor space in the building having changed use under Class J.

11.5   Prior approval

Before beginning the development, the developer must apply to the local planning authority for a determination as to whether the prior approval of the authority will be required as to:

(a)   noise impacts if the development;

(b)   impact of the hours of opening of the development;

(c)   transport and highways impacts of the development;

(d)   whether it is undesirable for the building to change to a use falling within Use Class D2 because of the impact of the change of use on adequate provision of services of the sort that may be provided by a building falling within Use Class A1 (shops) or, as the case may be, Use Class A2 (financial and professional services) [i.e. depending on which of those two use classes applies to the current use of the building that is to be converted], but only where there is a reasonable prospect of the building being used to provide such services, or (where the building is located in a key shopping area) on the sustainability of that shopping area.

In contrast to the provisions relating to some other classes of permitted development under Part 3, there is no requirement in this case to take account of contamination risks or flooding risks in relation to the building.

The determination of the prior approval application in relation to these criteria, and other material considerations that are to be taken into account (under paragraph W), is discussed in *part 14.4* of *Chapter 14*.

11.6 Commencement and completion

It is a condition, under paragraph J.2(2), that development under this class must begin within a period of three years starting with the date on which any prior approval is granted for that development, or starting with the expiry of the 56-day period referred to in paragraph W(11)(c) without the local planning authority notifying the developer as to whether prior approval for that development is given or refused (see *paragraph 14.10* in *Chapter 14*), whichever is the earlier.

(See *paragraph 1.3.2* in *Chapter 1* for a discussion of what constitutes the commencement of development for the purposes of this condition.)

The 3-year commencement deadline is extended by paragraph J.2(3) where, in relation to a particular development under Class J, planning permission is granted before the end of the 3-year period referred to in paragraph J.2(2) on an application in respect of associated operational development (defined as building or other operations in relation to the same building or land which are reasonably necessary to use the building or land for the use proposed under Class J). In this case, development under Class J must begin within the period of 3 years starting with the date on which such planning permission is granted.

If the application for planning permission for associated development were to be made, say, more than 2 years after the prior approval date, this could have the effect of extending the time limit for starting the development to more than 5 years from the prior approval date in respect of the change of use, compared with the 3-year commencement deadline originally imposed. However, it would be unwise to leave it too close to the end of the 3-year period before applying for planning permission for the associated works, in case the grant of planning permission is delayed, and the original 3-year deadline for the commencement of development is missed.

There is no time limit in this case for the completion of the development.

11.7 Operational development

The development permitted by Class J does not include any building operations in connection with the conversion of the building or its curtilage to the new use. Any such works in connection with the change of use will therefore require planning permission, unless they are exempt from the definition of development by virtue of section 55(2)(a) of the 1990 Act, because they affect only the interior of the building, or do not materially affect the external appearance of the building.

However, a planning application for any such 'associated operational development' will have the effect of extending the time for commencement of the development, as explained in *paragraph 11.6* above.

It should also be borne in mind that various minor operations are permitted under Part 2. These are briefly summarised in *paragraph 5.2.9* in *Chapter 5*, where the formation or laying out of an access to a highway is also discussed.

11.8 Changes of use from use for assembly and leisure

The only permitted change of use from a use falling within Use Class D2 to another use is the change of use to a state-funded school or registered nursery permitted by **Class T**. This is dealt with in *part 10.1* of *Chapter 10*.

CHAPTER 12

FLEXIBLE USES

12.1 Changes of use within the terms of a flexible planning permission

In order to facilitate the grant of flexible planning permissions, so as to allow a planning permission to be implemented for alternative uses of a planning unit, and for changes of use then to be made between the alternative uses specified by the permission, **Class V** of Part 3 (formerly Class E in the 1995 Order) permits development consisting of a change of use of a building or other land from a use permitted by a planning permission granted on an application, to another use which that permission would have specifically authorised when it was granted.

The alternative uses to which the planning unit may be put must be specified in the planning permission, and any one of those uses can then be implemented (subject to the terms of the permission, including any conditions attached to the permission). Class V then allows the use to be changed to any one of the other uses authorised by the permission. Class V does not limit the permitted changes of use to a single change of use; there is nothing to prevent further changes of use within the scope of the planning permission (subject to the terms of the permission). In contrast to Class R, Class V does not require that any notice be given to the LPA when any of these permitted changes of use is made.

However, development is not permitted by Class V if the application for the flexible planning permission was made before 5 December 1988; nor is it permitted if the change of use would be carried out more than 10 years after the grant of planning permission. Thus, the flexibility in the planning permission will last for no more than 10 years, after which the use to which the planning unit is being put at that time cannot thereafter be changed, and the reference to an application made before 5 December 1988 is now otiose.

Consequent upon the amendment of the Use Classes Order with effect from 15 April 2015, an additional restriction has been added to Class V, stating that development is not permitted by Class V if the development would consist of a change of use of a building to use as a betting office or pay day loan shop.

For the avoidance of doubt, the right to use premises extends to the whole range of uses covered by the relevant Class in the Use Classes Order at the time when the planning permission which authorised that use was originally granted. (See paragraph 22 of former Circular 03/2005. That circular was cancelled in March 2014, but the principles that it explained continue to hold good, notwithstanding that it no longer bears the ministerial *imprimatur*.)

Bearing in mind that betting offices and pay day loan shops were only excluded from Use Class A2 (financial, professional or other services) with effect from 15 April 2015, the permissible uses under a flexible planning permission, if they included use within Use Class A2, included use as a betting office or as a pay day loan shop. It follows that if the use to which the premises were being put immediately before 15 April 2015 did in fact fall within Use Class A2, a change of use (within the former Use Class A2) to use as a betting office or pay day loan shop is still permissible (by virtue of section 55(2)(f) of the 1990 Act).

On the other hand, if the actual use of the premises immediately before 15 April 2015 fell within some other use class, even though a change of use to any use within the former Use Class A2 may have been permissible under the terms of the flexible planning permission, a change of use to use as a betting office or pay day loan shop is now specifically precluded by paragraph V.1(c).

The distinction between these two scenarios is that, in the former case, the change of use would be within one and the same use class, and would therefore be made by virtue of section 55(2)(f) of the 1990 Act, so that it would not constitute development at all, whereas a change of use involving a change of use from one use class to another, under the terms of the flexible planning permission, would be permitted development under Class V, and would therefore be subject to its terms, including paragraph V.1(c).

As indicated above, a change of use cannot be made under Class V if it would result in the breach of any condition, limitation or specification contained in that planning permission in relation to the use in question.

Unlike Class R (see *paragraph 12.2.9* below), Class V does *not* make any use to which the planning unit is put under the terms of a flexible planning permission and/or in accordance with Class V a *sui generis* use. Thus, if a planning unit whose use is governed by the flexible planning permission and by Class V is being put to a use falling within a use class which would qualify it for permitted development for the purposes of a particular Class within Part 3 which applies to that use class (or if it was being put to that use on or, as the case may be, before the qualifying date, where that is a necessary criterion, and it has not been put to any other use since that date) there would appear to be nothing to prevent that further change of use being made under that other class of Part 3. Similarly, there would be nothing to prevent any operational development that is permitted under the Second Schedule to the GPDO in respect of a building falling into the relevant qualifying use class. In both cases, this is of course subject to any terms of the original planning permission that might prevent this, and is also subject to the use falling wholly and exclusively into the relevant use class at the relevant time.

12.2   Change of use of an agricultural building to a flexible use

12.2.1   The development permitted

Class R (formerly Class M in the 1995 Order) permits a change of use of a building and any land within its curtilage from use as an agricultural building to a flexible use falling within any of Use Classes A1 (shops), A2 (financial and professional services), A3 (restaurants and cafés), B1 (business), B8 (storage or distribution), C1 (hotels) or D2 (assembly and leisure). For the purposes of Class R, "flexible use" means use of any building or land for a use falling within this list of uses and any change of use under the terms of this class between any use in that list.

Class R also provides that a site which has changed use under Class R may, subject to the conditions in paragraph R.3 (relating to notice being given to the LPA and, where required, making a prior approval application), subsequently change use to another use falling within one of the use classes comprising the flexible use.

Bearing in mind that no building operations can be carried out under Class R, so that any works for the alteration of the building must necessarily be confined to works which affect only the interior of the building, or which do not materially affect the external appearance of the building (and which by virtue of section 55(2)(a) of the 1990 Act do not therefore amount to development), the scope for any element of rebuilding or structural alteration will be very limited indeed, and cannot take place if it would in any way affect the external appearance of the building. This will make the conversion of buildings and structures of unconventional (and perhaps in some cases rather insubstantial) construction impracticable. (This point is discussed in more detail in *paragraph 9.7* of *Chapter 9.*)

12.2.2   Restricted curtilage

It should be particularly noted that an the extremely restrictive definition of 'curtilage' is prescribed by paragraph X for the purposes of Class R. This allows only a very small area of land adjacent to the agricultural building to be included in the permitted change of use. It is confined to:

(i)   the piece of land, whether enclosed or unenclosed, immediately beside or around the agricultural building, closely associated with and serving the purposes of the agricultural building; or

(ii)   an area of land immediately beside or around the agricultural building *no larger than the land area occupied by the agricultural building*,

whichever is the lesser.

A development that seeks to include more than this very limited amount of land in the change of use will not be permitted development under Class R. Prior approval applications under the former Class MB (now Class Q) where a larger area of land has been included have been summarily rejected, and the rejection of the application has been upheld on appeal. It would appear, therefore, that the same is likely to occur in relation to Class R. If it is felt essential to incorporate a larger area of land in the development than is permitted under Class R, a planning application will have to be made, which will fall to be determined in accordance with all the policy considerations that apply to such developments in the countryside.

The very restrictive curtilage that is permitted by Class R of Part 3 will make it impracticable in most cases to include within the prior approval application any access from the property to a highway that may be required in connection with the proposed development. It should be borne in mind, however, that (subject to the terms of Part 2, Class B, which are discussed in *paragraph 5.2.9* of *Chapter 5*), any access to a highway that needs to be formed in connection with the conversion of the building for its new purpose may in quite a few cases be permitted development under Part 2. Where the terms of Part 2, Class B do not allow the access to be formed as permitted development, however, a separate planning application may be required. In either case, the access itself should not be included in the prior approval application, although details of the highway access may be required as further information in connection with the consideration of any highways impacts of the development.

12.2.3   Qualifying agricultural use

Readers should refer to *paragraphs 9.3* and *9.4* in *Chapter 9* for the definitions of "agriculture" and "agricultural use", and to the note in *paragraph 9.7* as to the definition of a "building" for this purpose.

Development is not permitted by Class R where the site was not used solely for an agricultural use, as part of an established agricultural unit, on 3 July 2012, or if the site was not in use on that date, when it was last in use. If the site was brought into use after 3 July 2012, the conversion of the building under Class R may not begin within ten years of that agricultural use commencing.

The earlier qualifying date compared with classes Q and S should be noted. Subject to that point, readers should refer to *paragraphs 9.3* and *9.4* in *Chapter 9* for the definition of an 'established agricultural unit' and for a discussion of the interpretation of this qualifying criterion, substituting 3 July 2012 in place of 20 March 2013 wherever this date is mentioned in that paragraph.

12.2.4   Exclusions

It should be noted that the scope of the exclusions of development that can be carried out under Class R is much less extensive than it is in the case of Classes Q and S.

Development is not permitted by Class R if the building is a listed building or is a scheduled monument (although the exclusion in respect of a listed building does not specifically extend to a building within its curtilage, where the curtilage building is not itself listed). It is also excluded in a safety hazard area or a military explosives storage area. The definitions of a "safety hazard area" and a "military explosives storage area" are quoted at the end of *paragraph 3.2.3* in *Chapter 3*.

So far as a building which is within the curtilage of a listed building is concerned (and which is not specifically disqualified from conversion under Class R), readers should refer to the discussion in *paragraph 5.2.3* in *Chapter 5* regarding the effect of section 1(5) of the Listed Buildings Act in this context, which may still have the effect of disqualifying the building from change of use under Class R.

In contrast to Classes Q and S, development is not excluded by Class R where the site is or has been occupied under an agricultural tenancy. Nor is development precluded under Class R where any permitted development has been carried out under Part 6, again in contradistinction to Classes Q and S.

Furthermore (again, in contrast to Classes Q and S), Class R does not prevent development within 'Article 2(3) land' (National Parks, AONBs, Conservation Areas, etc.). Nor is development under Class R excluded where the building is in a site of special scientific interest (SSSI).

12.2.5   Limits on floorspace

Paragraph R.1(b) provides that development is not permitted by Class R if the cumulative floorspace of buildings which have changed use under Class R within an established agricultural unit exceeds 500 sq m.

As discussed in *paragraph 1.6* of *Chapter 1*, it would seem that any floorspace converted under the former Class M in the 1995 Order must be counted with the development now permitted under Class R in the 2015 Order for the purposes of the cumulative limit imposed by this Class in reckoning the limit of floorspace that may now be converted under Class R.

In addition to this limit, there is a requirement for prior approval in respect of certain matters by the local planning authority where the cumulative floorspace of the building or buildings within an established agricultural unit which have changed use under Class R exceeds 150 sq m. Here again (subject to the comments in *paragraph 1.6* of *Chapter 1*), it would appear that any floorspace converted under the former Class M must be taken into account in determining whether the limit of 150 sq m has been reached, so as to require a prior approval application for the conversion of the additional floorspace above that figure. This is discussed in *paragraph 12.2.7* below.

The drafting of these provisions (in paragraphs R.1(b), R.3(1)(a) and R.3(1) (b)) raises a potential problem of interpretation. They refer, in the past tense, to the cumulative floorspace of buildings which *have* changed use under Class R. This could be taken to refer to the cumulative floorspace in the buildings that have *already* changed use before the change of use which is now intended takes place.

If interpreted literally, this could allow the total converted floorspace to exceed the stated limits. Provided the converted floorspace that has *already* been converted to permitted uses under Class R does not exceed the relevant cumulative limit, then it would appear that a further change of use which would take the cumulative floorspace over the stated limit would not be precluded. In fact, a literal interpretation of these provisions could potentially allow the conversion of an unlimited amount of floorspace, without the need for any prior approval. This cannot have been what was intended, and it seems extremely unlikely that this interpretation would be accepted by local planning authorities, or by planning inspectors or the courts. It is, however, an unfortunate example of the ambiguous drafting of this legislation.

There is no limit under Class R on the number of individual planning units or the number of uses that may be created within an established agricultural unit, subject only to the cumulative floorspace limit not being exceeded. The drafting of Class R appears to assume that any one of such changes of use will itself be to a single use. A change of use to two or more separate uses (i.e. by creating separate planning units) is not, however, ruled out, although a change of use of a single planning unit to a mixed use would not be to a use within any of those use classes but would be a change of use to a *sui generis* use (and is not therefore permitted by Class R), bearing in mind that a mixed use is always a *sui generis* use and cannot simultaneously be within more than one use class.

12.2.6 Exclusion of building operations

Unlike the change of use permitted by Class Q, the development permitted by Class R does not include any building operations in connection with the conversion of the building. Any such works will therefore require planning permission, unless they are exempt from the definition of development by virtue of section 55(2)(a) of the 1990 Act, because they affect only the interior of the building, or do not materially affect the external appearance of the building. As noted in *paragraph 10.2.1* of *Chapter 10*, this does in practice limit the extent of any structural alterations that can be carried out in order to adapt the building for its new use.

There was a provision in the former Class M that after a change of use had been made under that class, the development that was permitted at that time by the former Part 41, Class B applied in the same way as it applied to an office building. This permitted the provision or replacement of a limited area of hard surface within the curtilage of the building. However, there is no longer any such provision in Class R, and so any operational development of this nature will now require planning permission. However, a planning application for any such 'associated operational development' will have the effect of extending the time for commencement of the development, as explained in *paragraph 12.2.8* below.

As noted in *paragraph 12.2.9* below, any other permitted development that is dependent on the building being within a specified use class is excluded in this case, because the use of the building after a change of use permitted by Class R is to be regarded as a *sui generis* use. However, it should be borne in mind that various minor operations are nevertheless permitted under Part 2. These are briefly summarised in *paragraph 5.2.9* in *Chapter 5*, where the formation or laying out of an access to a highway is also discussed.

12.2.7   Prior approval

A prior approval application is not required where the cumulative floorspace of the building or buildings which have changed use under Class R within an established agricultural unit does not exceed 150 sq m (although, as explained in *paragraph 12.2.5* above, any development carried out under the former Class M should be counted towards this total). However, in these cases the developer must, before changing the use of the site under Class R, and before any subsequent change of use to another use falling within one of the use classes comprising the flexible use, notify the local planning authority of the date the site will begin to be used for any of the flexible uses, and also the nature of the use or uses, and must also provide the authority with a plan indicating the site and which buildings have changed use.

In those cases where the cumulative floorspace of the building or buildings which have changed use under Class R within an established agricultural unit (taking into account, as explained in *paragraph 12.2.5*, any floorspace converted under the former Class M) exceeds 150 sq m but does not exceed the absolute floorspace limit of 500 sq m, the developer must apply to the local planning authority for a determination as to whether the prior approval of the authority will be required as to:

(i)   transport and highways impacts of the development;

(ii)   noise impacts of the development;

(iii)   contamination risks on the site; and

(iv)   flooding risks on the site.

Readers should refer to *paragraph 12.2.5* above for a discussion of the potential interpretational problem in connection with the floorspace limits specified in relation to the requirement for a prior approval application.

The determination of the prior approval application in relation to these criteria, and the other material considerations that are to be taken into account (under paragraph W), is discussed in *part 14.4* of *Chapter 14*. However, it should be noted that the scope of these criteria is not so wide as it is in the case of Classes Q and S and that, in particular, the practicability or desirability of a change from agricultural use to a use permitted by Class R by reference to the location or siting of the building will *not* be relevant to the determination of a prior approval application under Class R. The LPA's discretion in determining a prior approval application under Class R is therefore strictly limited to the four criteria listed in paragraph R.3(1)(b) (as discussed in *Chapter 14*, at *paragraphs 14.4.1, 14.4.2, 14.4.7* and *14.4.9*).

12.2.8 Commencement and completion

There was no time limit in the former Class M for the commencement or completion of the development. That is still the case with regard to a development where the cumulative floorspace of the buildings which have changed use under Class R does not exceed 150 sq m.

However, where the cumulative floorspace that has changed use under this Class, (taking into account, as explained in *paragraph 12.2.5*, any floorspace converted under the former Class M) exceeds that limit, and is therefore subject to the requirement to make an application in respect of prior approval of the matters specified in paragraph R.3(1)(b), it is now a condition, under paragraph R.3(2), that development under this class must begin within a period of three years starting with the date on which any prior approval is granted for that development, or starting with the expiry of the 56-day period referred to in paragraph W(11)(c) without the local planning authority notifying the developer as to whether prior approval for that development is given or refused (see *paragraph 14.10* in *Chapter 14*), whichever is the earlier.

(See *paragraph 1.3.2* in *Chapter 1* for a discussion of what constitutes the commencement of development for the purposes of this condition.)

The 3-year commencement deadline is extended by paragraph R.3(3) where, in relation to a particular development under Class R, planning permission is granted before the end of the 3-year period referred to in paragraph R.3(2) on an application in respect of associated operational development (defined as building or other operations in relation to the same building or land which are reasonably necessary to use the building or land for the use proposed under Class R). In this case, development under Class R must begin within the period of 3 years starting with the date on which such planning permission is granted.

If the application for planning permission for associated development were to be made, say, more than 2 years after the prior approval date, this could have the effect of extending the time limit for starting the development to more than 5 years from the prior approval date in respect of the change of use, compared with the 3-year commencement deadline originally imposed. However, it would be unwise to leave it too close to the end of the 3-year period before applying for planning permission for the associated works, in case the grant of planning permission is delayed, and the original 3-year deadline for the commencement of development is missed.

There is no time limit in this case for the completion of the development.

12.2.9   *Exclusion of other permitted development*

In contrast to development under Classes Q and S, development under Class R does not prevent further permitted development on the agricultural holding under Part 6.

However, the building or buildings that have been the subject of a change of use under Class R will in future have no permitted development rights which depend on the class of use to which the building is then put, other than those granted by Class R itself, because paragraph R.2(b) provides that for the purposes of the Use Classes Order and of the GPDO, after a site has changed use under Class R the site it is to be treated as having a *sui generis* use. Not only does this have the effect of excluding the operational development permitted by Part 3 in respect of some of the uses listed in Class R, but it will also prevent any further changes of use (outside the scope of Class R) that might apply, now or in the future, to any of those use classes.

Notwithstanding this, as noted at the end of *paragraph 12.2.6* above, Part 2 of the Second Schedule grants permitted development rights which are unaffected by this provision in Class R. The permitted development rights under Part 2 are entirely independent of the use of the building, and at the time when the change of use is being carried out, the formation or laying out of an access to a highway is not ruled out either, subject to the considerations discussed in *paragraph 5.2.9* of *Chapter 5*.

CHAPTER 13

PRIOR APPROVAL APPLICATIONS

13.0   Introductory note

The development permitted by Classes C, J, M, N, P, Q, S and T (and also Class R in certain cases) is conditional upon the submission of an application to the local planning authority for a determination as to whether the prior approval of the authority will be required in relation to various matters that are specified in respect of each of those Classes of development. These matters vary as between one Class and another, and are discussed separately in *part 14.4* of *Chapter 14*.

The effect of this requirement is that these Classes of permitted development can only proceed if the local planning authority determines that their prior approval will not be required, or if they give their approval in respect of the matters that they are required to consider. To that extent, these classes of development are not really permitted development in the sense in which that term was originally used and understood, but are subject in effect to the grant of a new type of consent, which requires less formality in its submission and processing than a planning application made under Part III of the 1990 Act, and is intended (at least in theory) to be a lighter form of development management, but one which still allows local planning authorities to determine, within strictly defined parameters, whether the proposed change of use should be allowed to take place or not.

It should be borne in mind in this connection that compliance with the prior approval procedure is an absolute requirement. Where a prior approval application is required, any development carried out before the applicant is notified by the LPA that prior approval is not required, or that approval is given (or before the expiry of the 56-day period following the application - see *paragraph 14.10* in *Chapter 14* and *paragraph 15.6* in *Chapter 15*) cannot be permitted development, even if it might otherwise qualify under the relevant criteria. Retrospective authorisation of such a development can only be achieved by a full planning permission; late application is simply not possible under Part 3 of the Second Schedule to the GPDO.

13.1   The nature of a prior approval application

A prior approval application under Part 3 is not a planning application, and is not therefore governed by the provisions of sections 62, 65 and 69 in the 1990 Act or by any of the other provisions in Part III of the Act relating to the submission and determination of planning applications, nor is it governed by any of the provisions of the Development Management Procedure Order 2015, which apply solely to planning applications.

Section 4(1) of the Growth and Infrastructure Act 2013 inserted sub-section 60(2A) into Part III of the 1990 Act to supplement the provisions relating to permission granted by a development order. This provides the statutory basis for the prior approval procedure in relation to permitted changes of use. But, apart from prescribing the provisions that may be made in a development order in this regard, the sub-section is purely an enabling section which does not contain any substantive provisions regarding the submission and determination of prior approval applications. These are left entirely to be dealt with by the GPDO itself.

Paragraph W in Part 3 of the Second Schedule to the GPDO sets out the requirements for a prior approval application under those Classes of development within Part 3 to which it applies, and the manner in which such an application is to be processed by the LPA. The provisions of paragraph W (as supplemented by certain definitions in paragraph X of Part 3) therefore represent the entire body of procedural rules that applies to these applications. Local planning authorities are consequently somewhat more limited in their freedom of action in processing and determining these prior approval applications compared with planning applications made under Part III of the 1990 Act.

Lest there be any doubt about the position, it should be clearly understood that planning permission for the development is granted automatically by Article 3 of the GPDO, not by the local planning authority. It is simply a condition of this permission that before beginning the development, the developer must apply to the LPA for a determination by them as to whether the prior approval of the authority will be required in respect of certain specified matters relating to the proposed development.

In determining this prior approval application, the LPA is not granting planning permission; they are simply deciding whether their prior approval in respect of certain aspects of the development is required and, if so, whether that approval is granted or refused. They are not even approving the permitted development itself. For example, under Class O (residential conversion of an office building), all the LPA is considering, until the GPDO is changed in 2016, is whether the prior approval of the authority will be required as to transport and highways impacts of the development, contamination risks on the site, and flooding risks on the site; no more than that.

The planning permission granted by Article 3 of the GPDO is the type of permission identified by section 58(1)(a) of the 1990 Act (a planning permission granted by a development order), as distinct from the type of planning permission identified by section 58(1)(b) (a planning permission granted by the local planning authority on application to the authority in accordance with a development order).

The reference, in section 58(1)(b), to the latter being "on application to the authority" relates solely to an application for planning permission (and not for any other type of approval or consent), and the reference in section 58(1)(b) to its being "in accordance with a development order" relates to the Development Management Procedure Order 2015 (which is a 'development order' within the meaning of the Act), but *not* in that case to the General Permitted Development Order.

13.2   Form of application

No form is prescribed for a prior approval application, although a form is provided on the Planning Portal website which can be downloaded and used for this purpose. Various local planning authorities have also devised their own application forms. Some of these may be more demanding than the requirements of paragraph W would justify, but the LPA is in no position to insist on the use of such an application form, nor to demand compliance with any requirements outside the scope of paragraph W. In particular, the national and local validation checklists, which have been published in accordance with the DMPO for use with planning applications, have no application to prior approval applications under the GPDO.

These points were confirmed by the Court of Appeal in *Murrell v SSCLG* [2010] EWCA Civ 1367 (as to which see *paragraph 15.1* in *Chapter 15*).

There is no requirement for an ownership certificate, nor does notice have to be served on the owner by an applicant who is not the owner of the building in question. In fact, anybody can make a prior approval application, without having to name the owner. It follows that a prior approval application may be made by an agent in their own name, and there is no obligation on the agent to state the name of their principal, or even to reveal the fact that they are making the application as an agent. There is no requirement that the application should be signed or authenticated in any way, although the means by which the application is communicated to the LPA must naturally make it clear that this is a prior approval application in accordance with the relevant Class in Part 3.

Actual delivery of the application to the LPA is discussed in *Chapter 15*, at the end of *paragraph 15.2*.

13.3   Application in respect of building or other operations

Where development is to be carried out under Class C (change of use from use as a shop or for financial, professional or other services to use as a café or restaurant), Class M (residential conversion of a shop or a building used for financial, professional or other services), Class N (residential conversion of an amusement arcade or centre, or of a casino) or Class Q (residential conversion of an agricultural building), prior approval is required in respect of both the change of use itself and also in respect of any building or other operations reasonably necessary to adapt the building for its new use.

The original wording of the statutory provisions in the 1995 Order seemed to indicate that an application in respect of building works could be made as a separate application. Paragraph W(2)(a), however, now provides that the written description of the development accompanying the prior approval application, in the case of development proposed under Class, C, M, N or Q, *must include any building or other operations*. In other words, a combined application must now be made for both the change of use and for any building or other operations, unless no such operational development is considered by the applicant to be necessary in order to convert the building for its new use.

This provision (which came into effect with the new Order on 15 April 2015) therefore overrides an appeal decision in Cornwall, in January 2015, in which an inspector allowed an appeal under what was then Class MB(a), where the application had been submitted for prior approval in respect of a change of use only. The Inspector accepted the applicant's statement that an application under Class MB(b) in respect of the building operations necessary to convert the building to residential use would be submitted at a later date.

This appeal decision could not easily be reconciled with two other roughly contemporaneous appeal decisions which determined that the prior approval application in respect of the proposed change of use could not be determined in the absence of an application for the necessary building operations which would be involved. Such conflicts are now resolved by the new requirement, and it is now a requirement when making a prior approval application in respect of a proposed change of use under Classes C, M, N or Q to include details of any necessary building operations at the same time (unless the building works to adapt the building will affect only the interior of the building, or will not materially affect its external appearance).

13.4   *Written description of the development*

Under the terms of paragraph W(2), the prior approval application must be accompanied by a written description of the proposed development. If a printed application form is used, this will no doubt include the identification of the building by reference to its postal address (and post code), which will be further identified by the submitted plan, although where the change of use relates to an agricultural building the identification of the building to be converted may need to be more precise. Where more than one dwelling is to be created, the number of units must necessarily be stated.

The description of the development itself can be framed in terms of its description in the relevant Class of Part 3, although the provisions of paragraph W(3) (see *paragraph 14.2* in *Chapter 14*) make it advisable to provide sufficient information to enable the LPA to establish whether the proposed development complies with the conditions, limitations or restrictions that are applicable to the development in question, as set out in the relevant Class of Part 3.

Similarly, in view of the provisions in paragraph W(3), where built development is to be carried out under Classes M(b) or Q(b), the written description of the proposed development will need to be supplemented by additional information sufficient to enable the LPA to establish that the development meets the particular criteria for that class of development and, in the case of Class Q(b), that the conversion can be carried out within the limitation imposed by paragraph Q.1(i)*(i)* and *(ii)*.

13.5   Plans and other drawings

Paragraph W(2) requires that the prior approval application must also be accompanied by a plan indicating the site and showing the proposed development, but it does not call for a complete set of drawings, such as elevations, sections, etc. The applicant is not required to supply multiple copies of the plan; one copy of the plan will suffice (although it might be helpful to the LPA to provide a couple of additional copies).

For the change of use of a shop or of a building used for financial, professional or other services to a use within Use Class D2 (assembly and leisure) under Class J, or for a residential conversion under Class O (from use as an office under Use Class B1(a)) to create not more than one single dwelling, or under Classes S or T (to convert a building to use as a school, or nursery), a site plan alone may well suffice, with the red line being drawn round the boundary of the new planning unit (the building and any land within its curtilage) and clearly indicating the building in question within the site.

The very restrictive definition of "curtilage" for the purposes of Classes P, Q, R and S should also be borne in mind, and care should be taken to ensure that no more land than is strictly permissible is included within the red line in the case of a conversion under any of those four Classes. The inclusion of too much land within the curtilage will disqualify the conversion as permitted development under those Classes, and invalidate the prior approval application.

This will make it impracticable in most cases to include within the prior approval application any access from the property to a highway that may be required in connection with the proposed development. It should be borne in mind, however, that (subject to the terms of Part 2, Class B, which are discussed in *paragraph 5.2.9* of *Chapter 5*), any access to a highway that needs to be formed in connection with the conversion of the building for its new purpose may in quite a few cases be permitted development under Part 2. Where the terms of Part 2, Class B do not allow the access to be formed as permitted development, however, a separate planning application may be required. In either case, the access itself should not be included in the prior approval application, although details of the highway access may be required as further information in connection with the consideration of any highways impacts of the development.

Where two or more dwellings are to be created within the building, there does not appear to be any reason in principle why the internal division or divisions within the building, and therefore the size of each individual dwelling, need necessarily be shown on the plan, bearing in mind that the size of each dwelling unit is of no concern to the LPA (as confirmed by several appeal decisions, including those referred to at the end of *paragraph 7.1* in *Chapter 7*). It may nevertheless be advisable, in order to avoid unnecessary argument, to show the internal divisions between the dwellings. There is, however, no requirement to show the internal arrangements of the proposed dwelling or dwellings.

The practical requirement for additional drawings where building or other operations are proposed is considered below (in *paragraph 13.5.1*). However, bearing in mind that permitted development under Classes J, O, R, S and T does not extend to any operational development, any building works will necessarily be confined to works for the alteration of the building which affect only the interior of the building, or which do not materially affect the external appearance of the building, and which by virtue of section 55(2)(a) of the 1990 Act do not therefore amount to development. Accordingly, there is no requirement to produce drawings of these works to the LPA.

The question of the practicability of the conversion and the extent of the works required to adapt the building for its new use should not therefore arise in relation to development under Classes J, O, and T, in contrast to the position under Class Q, and possibly under Class R or Class S. Compliance with the Building Regulations, on the other hand, should not be overlooked, which will clearly require rather more information relating to the physical details of the conversion, but this will be entirely separate from the prior approval application under the GPDO.

13.5.1   *Drawings of proposed building works*

Whilst paragraph W requires only the submission of a *plan* indicating the site and showing the proposed development, there are bound to be cases where such a plan, even when read with the written description of the proposed development, will not be adequate to explain what is proposed, and there would appear to be an inescapable practical requirement to produce drawings of any proposed building operations to supplement the written description and site plan, so as properly to explain the proposed works, particularly bearing in mind that the external appearance of the converted building is one of the issues to be considered in these cases.

There have been several appeal decisions, particularly with regard to the former Class MB (now Class Q), where appeals have been dismissed because the information provided with regard to proposed building operations was inadequate to enable the decision-maker to determine whether the proposed development complied with the conditions, limitations or restrictions specified as being applicable to that class of development.

It should be borne in mind in this connection that it is not the intention of the permitted development right under Part 3 to include the construction of new structural elements for the building. It follows that it is only where the existing building is structurally strong enough to take the loading which comes with the external works to provide for the new use that the building would be considered to have the permitted development right. (This point is discussed in more detail in *paragraph 9.7* of *Chapter 9*.)

The extent of the proposed building operations must not go beyond what is "reasonably necessary" for the building to fulfil its new function (for example, as a dwellinghouse), so that substantial demolition of the building and its effective replacement would be outside the scope of the development that is permitted by Part 3. The decision-maker will therefore be concerned to ensure that the proposed works do not go beyond what is permissible, and drawings of the proposed works may well be needed in order to confirm this.

13.6   Other information

The other information requirements for a prior approval application are mainly self-explanatory, but should not be overlooked or omitted if the application is to be a valid one. This information must include the applicant's contact address (and the applicant's email address if the applicant is content to receive communications electronically).

In those cases where the prior approval application relates (among other matters) to flooding risks [in practice *all* prior approval applications *with the exception of* those under Class C (conversion of retail premises or of a betting office, pay day loan shop or casino to use as a café or restaurant), Class J (change of use of retail premises or of a betting office or pay day loan shop to use for assembly or leisure) and Class T (change of use of business premises, hotels, etc. to use as a state-funded school or registered nursery)], paragraph W(2)(e) requires that a site-specific flood risk assessment must accompany the prior approval application where paragraph W(6) requires the Environment Agency to be consulted. This applies where the development is in an area within Flood Zone 2 or Flood Zone 3 (and also in an area within Flood Zone 1 which has critical drainage problems and which has been notified to the local planning authority by the Environment Agency).

Although the drafting is somewhat convoluted, it is clear that a flood risk assessment will never be required in respect of development under Classes C, J or T. In other cases, a flood risk assessment will only be required if one or other of the criteria in paragraph W(6) applies to the site in question. (However, as noted in *paragraph 18.3* of *Chapter 18*, it would seem that, on paper at least, a flood risk assessment is automatically required in respect of development under Part 4, Class E - temporary use for film-making.)

Whilst there is no requirement in paragraph W for the submission of additional information beyond that specified in paragraph W(2), the possibility that the LPA may refuse the prior approval application under paragraph W(3) (b), on the grounds that the developer has provided insufficient information to enable the authority to establish whether the proposed development complies with the conditions, limitations and restrictions that are applicable to that development (see *paragraph 14.2* in *Chapter 14*), suggests that there will be cases in which further information may have to be supplied to the LPA over and above the requirements in paragraph W(2), in order to demonstrate to them that the development does comply with the relevant conditions, limitations and restrictions.

It appears that one or two LPAs have refused to treat a prior approval application as valid without the submission of a CIL (Community Infrastructure Levy) pro forma. Whilst there will be some cases in which CIL may become payable, and where the applicant will sooner or later have to furnish the LPA with the requisite information for this purpose, it is not a requirement in connection with the submission of a prior approval application, and has no relevance whatsoever to the matters that the LPA has to consider in connection with a prior approval application under any of the Classes of permitted development in Part 3 of the Second Schedule to the GPDO. The submission or absence of a CIL pro forma does not therefore have any bearing on the determination of the application. Thus if the LPA were to demand a CIL pro forma, its absence cannot invalidate the prior approval application, nor can it justify its rejection under paragraph W(3) [see *paragraph 14.2* in *Chapter 14*]. It follows that the absence of a CIL pro forma cannot stop the 56-day period running (see *Chapter 15*), even if the LPA purports not to have 'validated' the application.

13.7   Application fees

The prior approval application must be accompanied by the correct fee. The fee payable where the application relates only to a change of use is £80. Where the application relates both to a change of use and to associated operational development to be carried out as permitted development in connection with that change of use, the combined fee is £172. [See the Town and Country Planning (Fees for Applications, Deemed Applications, Requests and Site Visits) (England) Regulations 2012, Reg.14(1)(za) and (zb)]. The local planning authority is not entitled to demand any other fees in connection with the prior approval application.

It has been noted in *paragraph 7.1* of *Chapter 7* that a prior approval application under the Second Schedule to the GPDO may be made in conjunction with a planning application for other development which falls outside the scope of the permitted development allowed under that Schedule. Regulation 14(1A) of the 2012 Fees Regulations provides that no application fee is required for the prior approval application where an application fee is paid for a planning application made in respect of proposals for development of a site which includes buildings or other land which are the subject of the prior approval application, provided that the application for planning permission is made on the same date and by or on behalf of the same applicant as the prior approval application.

The application fees payable in respect of prior approval applications are governed solely by Regulation 14. The provisions in Regulation 8 (which allow a 'free go' for a second planning application in certain circumstances) apply only to the fees payable under Regulation 3 in respect of applications for planning permission. There is no corresponding provision in respect of a second application for prior approval under the GPDO, and so where a second application for prior approval is submitted, for example in order to address some issue identified upon the refusal or withdrawal of a previous application, the relevant fee (£80 or £172) must always be paid in respect of this further application.

If a prior approval application is rejected as invalid, Regulation 14(3) of the Fees Regulations requires the LPA to refund any application fee that has been paid.

Difficulties have occasionally arisen over the payment of the application fee. The government's online planning practice guidance merely states that fees should be paid to the local planning authority at the time of submitting the application, and that the LPA will provide advice on how the payment should be made. However, several statutory instruments relating to various types of application under the planning legislation clearly envisage that an application fee may be paid by cheque, and provide for the consequences of the cheque being dishonoured on being presented for payment (for example Article 34(7) of the Development Management Procedure Order 2015, and paragraph 1(4) of Schedule 2 to the Infrastructure Planning (Changes to, and Revocation of, Development Consent Orders) Regulations 2011, among others).

Certain authorities have been known to refuse to accept a cheque in payment of the application fee, and the legal position is that no-one is obliged to accept payment by cheque. They are entitled to be paid in legal tender and can refuse payment in any other form. A cheque is not legal tender.

A question may arise as to whether the application fee has been paid where a cheque for the correct amount has been enclosed with the prior approval application, but the LPA has refused to accept payment by this means. The author is aware of one case in which an over-the-counter payment by cheque was refused, and the fee was then paid several days later by a means that was acceptable to the LPA. The LPA claimed that the 56-day period commenced on the day after receipt of that second tendered payment, and this was not disputed by the applicant. The author is not aware of this point having been taken on appeal in any other case, but in view of the strict legal position as to the ability of a payee to refuse payment by cheque, it is doubtful whether the 56-day period would begin to run in the event of the LPA declining to accept a cheque in payment of the application fee.

What is clear, however, is that if the LPA (in common with most authorities) does accept payment of the application fee by cheque, the fee is to be treated as being paid on the day on which the cheque is received, not when it is cleared. The only exception to this would arise in the event of the cheque being dishonoured upon its being presented to the bank for payment, in which case no fee will have been paid, and the application will be treated as not having been made until or unless proper payment is received subsequently.

A convenient alternative to payment by cheque is electronic payment. In this case, the payment will usually take the form of a BACS Direct Credit (also known as a "BACS transfer" or "Direct Deposit") or may be made by the "Faster Payments Service", which is intended to achieve "almost" real-time payments between banks within the UK. It may alternatively be possible in some cases to make the payment by means of a debit or credit card, either online or over the phone, if the council has arrangements in place to accept payment by this means.

To make a BACS transfer, the name of the council, the name of their bank, and the council's bank account number and sort code must be stated, as well as the same information in respect of the payer's bank account. The important question is – When precisely can payment be said to have been 'received' by the council? Is it upon receipt of the transfer instruction by the council's bank, or only when the payment clears? In the case of a standard BACS transfer, the payment will only be cleared on the third day from the day on which the BACS transfer instruction is given, having been processed by the banks during the second day. It is not until the third day that payment will be taken from the paying account and credited to the council's account.

Nevertheless, on the analogy of a payment by cheque (where it is the date of receipt of the cheque that is accepted as the date on which the fee is actually paid, unless the cheque is subsequently dishonoured on being presented for clearance through the bank), payment by BACS could reasonably be said to have been received by the council as soon as the BACS transfer instruction is received by their bank, even though the payment will not be cleared, and the funds actually transferred from the paying account to the receiving account until the third day.

Difficulties are less likely to arise if the "Faster Payments Service" is used. In this case the paying instruction will be actioned promptly by the paying bank, and clearance will usually be on the same day (usually, but not necessarily, within two hours, and it can be "within minutes"). Notwithstanding this, the author's attention has been drawn to a problem that has arisen in one case (which had not yet been resolved at the time of going to press) where, in order to avoid the consequences of their apparently failing to notify their determination of the prior approval application within the 56-day period, the LPA was claiming that although the fee payment was made on the Friday on which the application itself was also received, payment did not appear in their bank account until 7.00 p.m. that evening, so that having been received after their business hours it was to be treated as not having been received until the next working day, which was the following Monday.

In the author's view, the case referred to may ultimately turn on the precise time at which the payment instruction reached the council's bank (irrespective of the time then taken to process the payment). The email submitting the prior approval application was sent at 3.00 p.m. and it is understood that the payment instruction was transmitted to the applicant's bank at the same time, either online or by telephone. The LPA accepted that the application itself was received before the council offices closed at 4.00 p.m., but at the time of writing the precise time of receipt of the payment instruction by the council's bank (through the Faster Payments Service) had not yet been established.

In the case quoted, the LPA was relying on the provisions of Article 2(9) of the GPDO, namely that where the electronic communication is received by the recipient outside the recipient's business hours, it is taken to have been received on the next working day. By article 2(1) of the GPDO, "electronic communication" has the meaning given in section 15(1) of the Electronic Communications Act 2000. This (as amended by Schedule 17, paragraph 158, to the Communications Act 2003) refers to a "communication" transmitted by means of an electronic communications network, and the definition of "communication" in this section includes a communication effecting payment. It is perhaps worth noting that the electronic communication of the payment is not to the council itself, but to the council's bank, but as the bank is receiving that communication in effect as the council's agent, it is perhaps arguable that if the bank receives the payment instruction after the council's business hours, Article 2(9) could apply to the receipt of the payment instruction by the council's bank (but not to the time taken in the subsequent processing and clearance of the payment, for the reason discussed above).

Clearly the best way to avoid disputes of this sort arising is to ensure that the payment instruction is given to the applicant's bank in the morning, so as to be reasonably sure that payment by the Faster Payments Service will be completed that same day.

CHAPTER 14

PROCESSING AND DETERMINING THE PRIOR APPROVAL APPLICATION

14.1 *Request for further information*

In addition to the information that accompanies the prior approval application, the LPA may require the applicant (in accordance with paragraph W(9)) to submit such information as the authority may reasonably require in order to determine the application, which may include assessments of impacts or risks, statements setting out how those impacts or risks are to be mitigated and/or details of any proposed operational development. This request must necessarily be made after the prior approval application has been received by the LPA, and can be anticipated or forestalled by the applicant in most cases either by providing with the application itself such information as the LPA may reasonably be expected to need or by explaining why such information is unlikely to be needed.

It should, however, be noted that any request for further information must be confined to the matters that are specified for approval in relation to the Class of development in question (such as transport and highway impacts, contamination risks and so on). It is only in the case of a few specific Classes of development (such as Classes C, J, M and also P) that slightly wider issues may arise in relation to retail and other impacts, or (under Classes Q and S) as to whether the location or siting of the building makes it impractical or undesirable for the proposed change of use to take place; but in the last case, ministerial guidance has set a clear limit on the extent to which this issue may be a material consideration (see *paragraph 14.4.11* below).

Notwithstanding this point, there may still be additional matters on which the LPA may reasonably wish to be informed, particularly under Class Q or Class S, where the LPA is required to consider whether the location or siting of the building makes it impractical or undesirable for the building to change from agricultural use to a residential use (under Class Q) or to use as a state-funded school or registered nursery (under Class S). A bat survey, for example, may reasonably be required if there is a demonstrable ecological justification for it. Attention is drawn in *paragraph 14.4.11* below to an appeal against a refusal of prior approval in Shropshire which was dismissed in the absence of any bat survey having been provided.

Similarly, in view of the fact that transport and highways impacts are subject to approval in all those Classes in Part 3 requiring a prior approval application, it may be necessary to provide details of the proposed access to the highway, particularly in those cases where sight lines are potentially inadequate and where an improved visibility splay (or 'bell-mouth') may need to be formed at the junction with the highway. As explained in *paragraph 13.5* in *Chapter 13*, it will be impracticable in most cases to include within the prior approval application any access from the property to a highway that may be required in connection with the proposed development. If such an access needs to be formed or improved in connection with the conversion of the building for its new purpose it may in quite a few cases be permitted development under Part 2, but where the terms of Part 2, Class B do not allow the access to be formed as permitted development, a separate planning application may be required. Whilst, for the reason explained in *paragraph 13.5*, the access will not be included in the prior approval application in most cases, details of the highway access may nevertheless be required as further information in connection with the consideration of any highways impacts of the development.

A request for further information under paragraph W(9) would seem to be the appropriate way forward for the LPA, rather than rejecting the application out of hand under paragraph W(3). Clearly, however, if the applicant fails to provide such information promptly, the LPA would then be justified in rejecting the application under paragraph W(3). A request for further information does not in itself stop the clock in respect of the 56-day period (see *paragraph 15.1* in *Chapter 15*), although the LPA may seek the applicant's agreement to an extension of time (see *paragraph 15.3*). If the applicant does not agree to an extension of time, then the limited time which the LPA would have for determining the prior approval application may make it necessary for the LPA to reject the application in those circumstances, if there is a risk that they would otherwise run out of time.

14.2   Invalid applications

Under paragraph W(3), the local planning authority may refuse a prior approval application where, *in the opinion of the authority,* the proposed development does not comply with any conditions, limitations or restrictions specified in Part 3 as being applicable to the development in question, or where *in their opinion* the applicant has provided insufficient information to enable the authority to establish whether the proposed development complies with those conditions, limitations or restrictions.

Paragraph W(4) provides that for the purposes of section 78 (appeals) of the 1990 Act a rejection of the prior approval application based on paragraph W(3) is to be treated as a refusal of that prior approval application. It does therefore amount to a determination of that application, even if the LPA is objectively wrong as to the non-compliance of the development with the qualifying criteria under the relevant Class of Part 3. Consequently, the correctness or otherwise of the LPA's opinion can only be tested by way of an appeal against this decision under section 78 of the 1990 Act.

It should be noted that the adequacy of the information provided relates only to the issue as to whether it is reasonably sufficient to enable the authority to establish that the proposed development complies with the relevant conditions, limitations or restrictions, so as to qualify as permitted development under the Class in question. If the LPA purports to reject the application in relation to the adequacy of the information for other purposes, going outside the question of compliance with the qualifying criteria, this may perhaps call in question the validity of the decision.

If the LPA's opinion on this point strays outside these stated parameters, it might possibly be argued that the authority has not actually determined the application, which could raise the possibility that the 56-day period (discussed in *Chapter 15*) might continue running. In such cases, however, a notice or other written communication informing the applicant of the LPA's rejection of the prior approval application under paragraph W(3) is likely (in view of the provision contained in paragraph W(4)) to be regarded as a valid determination of the application, leaving an appeal under section 78 as the only course that would then be open to the applicant (unless the applicant chooses instead to make a planning application).

Where a prior approval application is rejected for either of the reasons specified by paragraph W(3), the LPA is not then obliged to go through the further steps in processing the application that are set out in paragraphs W(5) to (8) and (10) (including various consultations, etc.)

Local planning authorities should beware of purporting to reject applications as invalid for other reasons, such as those cited in *Murrell v SSCLG* [2010] EWCA Civ 1367 (as to which see *paragraph 15.1* in *Chapter 15*).

Quite apart from the rules relating to the rejection of invalid applications, it should be noted that under section 70A(5) an LPA has the same power to decline to determine repeated prior approval applications as it has in relation to repeated planning applications. This power applies where the LPA thinks there has been no significant change in the relevant considerations (i.e. in the development plan, so far as material to the application, or in any other material considerations) since one of the events specified in the conditions set out in sub-sections (3) and (4). [Sub-sections (2), (4A) and (4B) have no practical application in the context of a prior approval application.]

The power arises if either one of these conditions is satisfied:

– that in the period of two years before the renewed application, an appeal against the refusal or non-determination of a similar application has been dismissed; or

– that in that period the LPA has refused two or more similar applications, and either there has been no appeal against the refusal of those applications or any such appeal has been withdrawn.

The two-year period in the case of sub-section (3) runs from the dismissal of the appeal, and in the case of sub-section (4) it runs from the refusal of the latest of the similar applications.

An application is 'similar' to another application if (and only if) the LPA thinks that the development and the land to which the applications relate are the same or substantially the same (section 70A(8)).

In practice, the High Court has construed the LPA's powers under section 70A narrowly, emphasising that an LPA should refuse to entertain a repeat application in reliance on this power only where there has clearly been abuse of the planning system by the applicant in submitting repeated applications (see *R (Jeeves and Baker) v Gravesham BC* [2006] EWHC 1249). It is clear from this that a fresh prior approval application designed to address one or more issues that led to the rejection of a previous application or to the dismissal of an appeal cannot lawfully be rejected under section 70A.

Where this power is exercised, no right of appeal can arise against the LPA's decision under this section (provided they notify the applicant within the relevant time limit, which in the case of prior approval applications under the GPDO is 56 days), and such a decision can therefore be challenged only by way of Judicial Review. It is fair to say, however, that LPAs have not made a great deal of use of this power even in respect of planning applications, and many appear to be unaware that it can potentially extend to prior approval applications under the GPDO.

14.3 Consultations

Unless the local planning authority has rejected the application under paragraph W(3), they must carry out various consultations.

Where the application relates to prior approval as to transport and highways impacts of the development, and where in the opinion of the local planning authority the development is likely to result in a material increase or a material change in the character of traffic in the vicinity of the site, the LPA must, on receipt of the application, consult the Secretary of State for Transport where the increase or change relates to traffic entering or leaving a trunk road, the local highway authority where the increase or change relates to traffic entering or leaving a classified road or proposed highway (except where the local planning authority is the local highway authority), and the operator of the network which includes or consists of the railway in question and also the Secretary of State for Transport, where the increase or change relates to traffic using a level crossing over a railway (paragraph W(5)).

Where the application relates to prior approval as to the flooding risks on the site, the local planning authority must, on receipt of the application, consult the Environment Agency where the development is in an area within Flood Zone 2 or Flood Zone 3 (and also in an area within Flood Zone 1 which has critical drainage problems and which has been notified to the local planning authority by the Environment Agency) (paragraph W(6)).

In relation to both of the above cases (involving the assessment of transport and highways impacts of the development, or flooding risks, in relation to the building), the LPA must notify the consultees referred to in paragraphs W(5) and W(6), giving them not less than 21 days in which to respond (paragraph W(7)).

In all cases, the LPA is required either to give notice of the proposed development by displaying a site notice in at least one place on or near the land to which the application relates for not less than 21 days, describing the proposed development, giving the address of the proposed development, and specifying the date by which representations are to be received by the local planning authority or, alternatively, to serve a notice in that form on any adjoining owner or occupier (paragraph W(8)). Article 2(1) defines an "adjoining owner or occupier" as any owner or occupier of any premises or land adjoining the site. Note that the responsibility for giving notice of the development (or displaying a site notice) lies with the LPA, not with the applicant. Applicants should not remove or deface a site notice or tamper with it in any way, but are not themselves responsible for ensuring that it continues to be displayed for the requisite period.

14.4   Determining the prior approval application

The considerations that must be taken into account in determining a prior approval application vary as between the different Classes of development listed in Part 3. These have been noted in *Chapters 3* and *5 to 12* respectively, and the treatment of these criteria is discussed below, followed by the general considerations set out in paragraph W(10).

Both LPAs and applicants (and also objectors) should clearly understand that only those specific matters requiring approval in respect of the relevant Class of permitted development can be taken into account in connection with an application for prior approval of those matters. The following paragraphs are therefore applicable only to the Classes of development to which they specifically relate. The extent (if at all) to which other considerations can legitimately be taken into account is discussed in *paragraphs 14.4.13* to *14.4.17*.

14.4.1   Transport and highways

Transport and highway impacts are a consideration that must be addressed in *all* prior approval applications.

A number of prior approval applications have been refused by reason of transport and highways impacts, and this is potentially a significant factor where traffic or road conditions may affect the site or the development. It is appropriate in such cases to consider the current traffic movements associated with the existing use of the site by comparison with the traffic movements that can be expected following the residential or educational occupation of the site. However, notwithstanding an expected reduction, or no change, in the traffic movements associated with the site, road or traffic conditions locally could arguably make the site unsuitable or unsafe for residential or educational use in any event. The views of the highway authority may carry weight in this regard.

As mentioned in *paragraph 13.5* of *Chapter 13* and in *paragraph 14.1* above, the highways impacts of the development may in some cases involve consideration of the access to the highway, including the available sight lines and the possible need for an improved visibility splay, even if (for the reason explained in *paragraph 13.5*) the access itself does not form part of the prior approval application. Any works that may be required in this connection will either be the subject of permitted development under Part 2, Class B or, if that is not possible, they may require a separate planning application.

An example of how highway or traffic issues might be approached in practice is provided by an appeal decision in Somerset, where the LPA had refused a prior approval application in respect of a proposed residential conversion of an agricultural building under what was then Class MB (now Class Q in the 2015 Order) on highway and traffic grounds. The barn in question was one of a group where planning permissions had previously been granted for residential conversions, using the same access to the highway. It was argued by the LPA that there had been overriding reasons for granting planning permission in those cases, notwithstanding the traffic or highway objections at that time.

The determining factor in the present case seems to have been that when a previous planning permission had been granted, officers had taken the view that there would be a minimal effect on highway safety. There had been a dismissal on appeal of another proposed residential conversion in 2009, in which an objection from the highway authority had clearly been a factor, but there had been no objection from the highway authority in the present case. The Inspector was not satisfied on the evidence that the present proposal gave rise to any real risk to highway safety, and therefore allowed the appeal.

In an appeal in London SW6 in November 2014, the LPA objected to development under what was then Class J (now Class O in the 2015 Order). The site was within an area covered by a Controlled Parking Zone, and the Council feared that the proposal would result in additional over-night parking which could not be satisfactorily accommodated within the surrounding streets. The appellant submitted a Unilateral Undertaking which contained provisions to prevent future residents of the proposal having a residents' parking permit. Various survey data were produced relating to the incidence of parking in an area within a 200-metre distance of the appeal site (rather than being confined to the two immediately adjoining roads, as the Council had insisted).

The Inspector found that the prospect of an inability to have a residents' permit, combined with good access to shops, services and public transport would be a significant incentive against car ownership. Added to this, the high charge for on-street parking by pay-and-display and the likely relatively low car ownership levels (even assuming no other controls were in place), led the Inspector to conclude that it was highly unlikely that the resultant additional car parking generated by the proposal could not be satisfactorily accommodated within the surrounding area, and he therefore allowed the appeal.

By way of another example, in an appeal decision in the London Borough of Camden in May 2015, the Inspector concluded that the LPA's demand for a construction management plan and the provision of parking spaces for fourteen bicycles, could be met by the imposition of conditions on the prior approval. The LPA had also called for a financial contribution in respect of road improvements in the area, but the Inspector rejected this. On the other hand she agreed to a condition restricting applications for parking permits by future residents.

14.4.2   Contamination risks

Contamination risks in relation to the building are a consideration that must be addressed in all prior approval applications, except those under Classes C (café/restaurant conversions) and J (change of use to an assembly or leisure use). In the case of café/restaurant conversions under Class C, however, there are specific considerations as to odour impacts and the impacts of the storage and handling of waste that must be taken into account. (See *paragraphs 14.4.3* and *14.4.4* below.)

Contamination risks "in relation to the building" could potentially include both existing site contamination (if any) and any contamination risks that might arise from the new use, although the latter are clearly not going to arise where that use is a purely residential use.

Contamination risks are unlikely to arise at all in the majority of cases, but applicants should be aware of such issues if the site may possibly be affected by them. Paragraph W(10)(c) specifically provides that, in relation to the contamination risks on the site, the LPA must determine whether, as a result of the proposed change of use, taking into account any proposed mitigation, the site will be contaminated land as described in Part 2A of the Environmental Protection Act 1990, and in doing so they must have regard to the Contaminated Land Statutory Guidance issued by the Secretary of State for the Environment, Food and Rural Affairs in April 2012, and if they determine that the site will be contaminated land, they must refuse the prior approval application.

An example of contamination risks disqualifying an agricultural building from residential conversion under Class Q is provided by an appeal decision in North Devon in July 2015. The building had been a cattle barn. The possibility of contamination was recognised by the applicant and this issue had been addressed in a short report submitted on the appellant's behalf. Manure, but not slurry, had been stored outside the building. In a nearby building there was storage of agricultural fertilisers and fuel oil. It was suggested on the appellant's behalf that the possibility of any contamination within the building itself could be investigated and dealt with upon opening up the floors in the course of the conversion works, and that this could be catered for by a suitably worded condition.

The Inspector rejected this approach. The GPDO clearly requires the contamination issue to be fully addressed as one of the subjects of the prior approval application. The possible health risks posed by contamination clearly disqualify a building from residential conversion, and so they must be fully addressed at the application stage.

14.4.3   Odour impacts

In relation to **Class C** only (which permits the change of use of retail premises or of a betting office, pay day loan shop or casino to use as a café or restaurant), the LPA must consider the odour impacts of the development. This is a well known and well understood issue with regard to such premises. It may give rise to objections from neighbouring occupiers, although in many cases the matter can be adequately addressed by the installation of appropriate ventilation and/or extractors.

Class C(b) permits building or other operations for the provision of facilities for ventilation and extraction (including the provision of an external flue) which are reasonably necessary for the use of the building as a café or restaurant, and the power given to the LPA by paragraph W(13) to impose appropriate conditions enables the LPA to ensure that such equipment is installed and satisfactorily maintained. (See *paragraph 14.5* below.)

It is worth noting that any more general issues of possible risks of contamination or pollution (such as the discharge of fat into drains, etc.) is not covered by Class C, and that considerations relating to contamination risks generally do not apply to Class C, whereas this is a consideration in respect of a number of other Classes of development.

14.4.4   Impacts of waste storage and handling

In relation, again, to **Class C** only, the LPA must also consider possible impacts of the storage and handling of waste in relation to the development. This is another well known and well understood issue with regard to café and restaurant premises.

Class C(b) permits building or other operations for the provision of facilities for the storage of rubbish which are reasonably necessary for the use of the building as a café or restaurant, and the power given to the LPA by paragraph W(13) to impose appropriate conditions enables the LPA to ensure that such facilities are provided and are satisfactorily maintained. (See *paragraph 14.5* below.)

14.4.5 Opening hours

In relation to both **Class C** (conversion of retail premises or of a betting office, pay day loan shop or casino to use as a café or restaurant) and **Class J** (change of use of retail premises or of a betting office or pay day loan shop to use for assembly or leisure), the LPA must consider any impacts arising from the hours of opening of the development. This is another well known and well understood issue in relation to such uses.

If early or late opening may be a potential source of disturbance to neighbouring occupiers, an appropriate condition as to opening hours is frequently imposed on planning permissions in relation to such premises, and the power given to the LPA by paragraph W(13) to impose appropriate conditions enables them to ensure that appropriate opening hours are observed, having regard to the character of the neighbourhood and the proximity of residential or other premises that could be affected by the new use. (See *paragraph 14.5* below.)

It should be noted that, whereas Class C includes the change of use of a casino to a café or restaurant, Class J does not cover the change of use of a casino to an assembly or leisure use. That change of use is permitted instead by Class K, which has been in the GPDO for some years, and is not subject to any limitations, restrictions or conditions whatsoever.

14.4.6 Air quality

In relation to **Class P** only (which permits the residential conversion of a building used for storage within Use Class B8), the LPA must consider the impacts of air quality on the intended occupiers of the development. The thinking behind this is presumably that the sort of premises covered by Class P are likely to be located in what may loosely be described as 'an industrial area', and so there may be some general industrial uses in the vicinity that could potentially cause an air quality problem for residents of the converted building. The storage building might alternatively be located in the countryside near farming activities that might give rise to air quality issues.

If air quality issues do arise, it might be possible to address them through appropriate conditions under paragraph W(13) to provide for sealed windows, air filtration, etc. (see *paragraph 14.5* below), although the practicability of tackling any air quality issues by such means may perhaps be open to question. In practice, however, this is a problem that is rarely likely to be encountered.

14.4.7 Noise

In relation to prior approval applications under **Classes C, J, P, Q, R, S** and **T**, [but *not* Classes M, N or O], the LPA must consider the noise impacts *"of the development"* [*sic*].

The residential conversion of an agricultural building is extremely unlikely to have any noise impacts in itself and, so far as development under Class Q is concerned, this must be taken to refer to the impacts on the dwelling, and on its occupants, of the noise (if any) from the adjoining agricultural activities, unless it might be argued, by reference to the words used, that this would not be a noise impact *"of the development"*, but the Warwickshire appeal decision referred to below clearly did not adopt that approach.

However, in the case of development under Classes C, S or T, the conversion to use as a café, school or nursery could well have noise impacts on neighbours, and may be an important material consideration in such cases. Noise issues may be similarly relevant in those cases in which a prior approval application is required in respect of certain developments under Class R (conversion of an agricultural building to various flexible uses). However, the issue of noise is not a material consideration in relation to the residential conversion of other premises (under Classes M, N or O), even if raised by a neighbour as a ground of objection - see *paragraph 14.4.13* below.

Paragraph 123 of the NPPF states that planning decisions should aim to avoid noise from giving rise to significant adverse impacts on health and quality of life as a result of new development, that they should mitigate and reduce to a minimum other adverse impacts on health and quality of life arising from noise from new development (including through the use of conditions), and that they should recognise that development will often create some noise and existing businesses wanting to develop in continuance of their business should not have unreasonable restrictions put on them because of changes in nearby land uses since they were established.

This accords with the government's revised online Planning Practice Guidance, which confirms that the NPPF may be relevant in relation to the specific issues that have to be determined, such as (in this case) noise.

The government's online Planning Practice Guidance enlarges on this with advice on the relevance of noise to planning, whether noise can override other planning concerns, how to determine noise impact, how to recognise when noise could be a concern (and the factors that influence this), and how the adverse effects of noise can be mitigated (in particular the considerations relating to mitigating the impact of noise on residential developments). It is noticeable that the means of determining noise impact recommended by this practice guidance are far more impressionistic than the detailed technical advice formerly set out in PPG24 (now withdrawn).

Reference is made in the national Planning Practice Guidance to various advice on noise published by DEFRA, including the Noise Policy Statement for England ('NPSE') published in March 2010. A more detailed explanation of this policy is set out in the Explanatory Note to the NPSE, although it does not really go into specifics.

An example of a prior approval application in respect of the proposed residential conversion of an agricultural building being refused on grounds of noise, under what was then Class MB (now Class Q in the 2015 Order), is provided by an appeal decision in February 2015 in Warwickshire. The proposal was for the residential conversion of part only of a steel-framed barn. The Inspector held that continued movement of agricultural machinery and vehicles in the vicinity of the converted barn, which would also affect the enjoyment of the garden of the proposed dwelling, plus possible vibration and noise from the part of the building remaining in agricultural use, made it impractical or undesirable for the building to change from agricultural use to residential use, in accordance with paragraph MB.2(1)(e), and so the appeal was dismissed.

As explained in *paragraph 14.4.15* below, some policies in the Development Plan are also capable of being material considerations for this purpose, and these could include any adopted policies on noise. Any supplementary planning guidance issued by the LPA might also be a material consideration in relation to this issue.

14.4.8   Light impacts

Light impacts of the development, and in particular the effect on any occupier of neighbouring land of any artificial lighting to be used is a specified consideration only in relation to a prior approval application under **Part 4, Class E**, relating to temporary use for film-making. (See *paragraph 18.3* of *Chapter 18*.) This issue does not arise in respect of any of the classes of development under Part 3.

14.4.9   Flooding risks

Flooding risks are a consideration that must be addressed in the case of all prior approval applications, *other than* those under Class C (conversion of retail premises or of a betting office, pay day loan shop or casino to use as a café or restaurant), Class J (change of use of retail premises or of a betting office or pay day loan shop to use for assembly or leisure) and Class T (change of use of business premises, hotels, etc. to use as a state-funded school or registered nursery).

Flooding risks are also an issue for consideration in a prior approval application under Part 4, Class E - temporary use for film-making. (See *paragraph 18.3* in *Chapter 18*. As noted there, it would appear that, contrary to the position under Part 3, which is explained below, a flood risk assessment is required, at least in theory, in all cases under Part 4, Class E.)

Those developments in Part 3 in respect of which flooding risk is a material consideration comprise the various Classes of residential conversion (Classes M, N, O, P and Q), and other changes of use that apply to agricultural buildings (Classes R and S). However, the requirement for a site-specific flood risk assessment in paragraph W(2) will only arise where one or other of the criteria in paragraph W(6) applies.

Thus it is only in those cases where the application relates to prior approval as to the flooding risks on the site, that the local planning authority is required to consult the Environment Agency in the event that the development is in an area within Flood Zone 2 or Flood Zone 3 (or where the site is in an area within Flood Zone 1 which has critical drainage problems and which has been notified to the local planning authority by the Environment Agency). It is in the light of this post-application consultation with the EA, and in light of the site-specific flood risk assessment which the applicant is required to produce in such cases, that a determination will be reached on the risk of flooding.

The consideration of flooding risk is not confined to those cases where paragraphs W(2)(e) and W(6) apply; it is clearly an issue that has to be considered in all cases where this is a specified issue for determination in the prior approval application (i.e. development in all classes within Part 3, *except* Classes C and J). However, flooding risk is much less likely to be a live issue in these other cases, and the LPA cannot demand the production of a flood risk assessment at the application stage in these other cases. Whilst a possible requirement for a flood risk assessment cannot be altogether ruled out (under paragraph W(9) - see *paragraph 13.6 in Chapter 13*), it would be difficult to justify such a request under paragraph W(9) in the absence of any of the circumstances in which paragraph W(6) would apply.

A practical example of the way this issue may be approached in practice is provided by an appeal decision in London SW6 in November 2014. It was agreed by the Council that the site was in Flood Risk Zone 1, but had not been notified by the EA as having critical drainage problems. The appellants had in any event included information relating to investigations into the risk of flooding from surface water, groundwater, artificial sources and sewers, which in all instances were shown to be low or negligible. However, the Council also referred to water use and efficiency and to Sustainable Drainage Systems, but the Inspector agreed with the appellant that an assessment of the "flood risks on the site" would not properly include the additional matters referred to by the Council and he did not therefore seek to address them. The Inspector was accordingly satisfied that there was negligible flood risk on this site.

14.4.10 Retail and similar impacts

In relation to prior approval applications under **Class C** (change of use of retail premises or of a betting office, pay day loan shop or casino to use as a café or restaurant), **Class J** (change of use of retail premises or of a betting office or pay day loan shop to an assembly or leisure use) and **Class M** (residential conversion of retail premises or of a betting office or pay day loan shop, or from a mixed use involving a dwellinghouse and one of those uses), the LPA must consider whether it is undesirable for the building to change to the use in question, because of the impact of the change of use on adequate provision of services of the sort that may be provided by a building falling within Use Class A1 (shops) or, as the case may be, Use Class A2 (financial and professional services) [i.e. depending on which of those two use classes applies to the current use of the building that is to be converted], but only where there is a reasonable prospect of the building being used to provide such services, or (where the building is located in a key shopping area) on the sustainability of that shopping area.

No reference is made here to the potential impact of the change of use on the adequate provision of services of the sort that may be provided by a betting office, a pay day loan shop or a casino. It may therefore be the intention of this provision that the 'retail impact' test should apply only to buildings that are currently in use within Use Class A1 or A2 (bearing in mind the newly restricted scope of the latter use class, which now excludes betting offices and pay day loan shops) and that this test is not intended to apply to these other *sui generis* uses, which merely happen to be subsumed within the same Classes of permitted development. There seems to be no necessary implication that the same test should be applied to these other premises.

The 'retail impact' of such a change of use may well be a reason for the refusal of a prior approval application relating to the proposed change of use of a shop or of premises providing financial or professional services. The issue as to whether the change of use will have an adverse impact on the adequate provision of such facilities is not confined to premises located in town centres, but may depend on the availability of such facilities in the area in which the building in question is located or within reasonable reach of that location. However, this should not be a reason for refusal where it can be shown that there is no reasonable prospect of the building being used to provide such services in the future.

Where the building is located in a key shopping area, the criterion is simply the impact of the change of use on the sustainability of that shopping area. "Key shopping area" is not defined in the GPDO, but is no doubt to be taken to embrace those areas of primary shopping frontage identified as such in the Development Plan, or a corresponding designation identifying a particular shopping frontage or shopping area as being at the highest level of the retail hierarchy. In this case, the question of adequate provision of such facilities in that area, or the prospects of the building being used to provide such services, does not arise; the determining factor will simply be the issue (well-known to retail planners) of the likely impact of the change of use on the vitality and viability of the key shopping area.

A slightly different impact test is applied in respect of **Class P** (which permits the residential conversion of a building used for storage within Use Class B8). In this case, where the building to which the development relates is located in an area which the LPA considers is important for providing storage or distribution services or industrial services or a mix of those services, the authority must consider whether the introduction of, or an increase in, a residential use of premises in the area would have an adverse impact on the sustainability of the provision of those services.

The term "storage and distribution services" is defined for this purpose in paragraph P.3 as services provided from premises with a storage or distribution centre use (i.e. a use within Use Class B8), and the term "industrial services" is defined as services provided from premises with a light industrial or general industrial use (i.e. within Use Class B1(c) or B2).

This provision addresses an issue which may well be of concern both to the LPA and to nearby industrial and commercial enterprises. The introduction of a residential use into such an area might give rise in future to complaints of nuisance which would not have arisen in the absence of residential development being permitted in that area. This could adversely affect the commercial operation of such businesses, and could have an adverse impact on their future viability and consequently on the economic health of the area.

14.4.11 Rural development policy

One of the criteria to be considered by the LPA when determining an application for prior approval in respect of proposed development under **Class Q** or **Class S** (relating to the conversion of an agricultural building respectively to residential use or to use as a school or nursery), but *not* under Class R (change of use of an agricultural building to a flexible use within Use Class A1, A2, A3, B1, B8, C1 or D2), is *whether the location or siting of the building makes it impractical or undesirable* for the building to change from agricultural use to a residential use (under Class Q) or to use as a school or nursery (under Class S).

This initially proved to be a major stumbling block for applicants in obtaining approval of these proposed conversions of agricultural buildings. The drafting of the former Class MA (now Class S in the 2015 Order) and the former Class MB (now Class Q) was originally interpreted as giving an LPA a considerable measure of freedom to refuse the application on policy grounds. At least half of all such applications for residential conversion under Class MB up to the early part of 2015 are thought to have been refused (and there was anecdotal evidence that there had been an even higher rate of refusal in some areas). Furthermore, by early 2015, 9 out of 10 of the appeals against such refusals had been dismissed by the Planning Inspectorate (a significantly higher proportion than in other types of planning appeal).

This prompted the government to amend their online Planning Practice Guidance on 5 March 2015 to explain their view as to how these permitted development rights are intended to operate, and to address in particular the issue as to whether the 'sustainability' of the proposed development is intended to be a material consideration in determining an application for prior approval in respect of the proposed change to residential use. The revised ministerial guidance makes it clear that the permitted development right does not apply a test in relation to *sustainability of location*. This is deliberate, as the permission granted by the former Classes MA and MB (now Classes S and Q respectively) recognises that many agricultural buildings will not be in village settlements and may not be able to rely on public transport for their daily needs. Instead, the LPA can consider whether the location and siting of the building would make it *impractical or undesirable* to change use to a house (or to a school or nursery).

The revised practice guidance then goes on to explain what is meant by "impractical or undesirable" for a change to be made to the new use. Impractical or undesirable are not defined in the Order, and the LPA should apply a reasonable ordinary dictionary meaning in making any judgment. The word "impractical" indicates that the location and siting would "not be sensible or realistic", and the word "undesirable" suggests that it would be "harmful or objectionable".

When considering whether it is appropriate for the change of use to take place in a particular location, an LPA should start from the premise that the permitted development right grants planning permission, subject to the prior approval requirements. That an agricultural building is in a location where the LPA would not normally grant planning permission for a new dwelling is not a sufficient reason for refusing prior approval.

There may, however, be circumstances where the impact cannot be mitigated. So when looking at location, LPAs may consider that because an agricultural building is (for example) on the top of a hill with no road access, power source or other services, its conversion is impracticable. Additionally, the location of the building whose use would change may be undesirable if it is adjacent to other uses such as intensive poultry farming buildings, silage storage or buildings with dangerous machines or chemicals. These quoted examples clearly indicate ministers' intentions as to the restricted scope for refusing permission on grounds relating to the impracticability or undesirability of the proposed change of use by reference to the location and siting of the building.

When an LPA considers location and siting, it should not therefore be applying tests from the NPPF except to the extent that these are strictly relevant to the subject matter of the prior approval. So, for example, factors such as whether the property is for a rural worker, or whether the design is of exceptional quality or innovative, are unlikely to be relevant.

As discussed in *paragraph 14.4.15* below, adopted policies in the Development Plan are also capable of being a material consideration when determining a prior approval application, but it is clear from the revised ministerial practice guidance that adopted policies on development in the open countryside, development in the Green Belt (where applicable) and sustainable development, especially taking account of the availability or non-availability of easily accessible local services and any generation of car-borne movements that might arise from this, will not usually be relevant and are unlikely to be valid reasons for refusal of a prior approval application.

The practical application of the revised ministerial practice guidance on this issue is well illustrated by an appeal decision in Northamptonshire in April 2015, where applications in respect of a proposed barn conversion had been made in the alternative both for full planning permission and for prior approval in respect of permitted development under Class Q. The appeal against the refusal of planning permission was dismissed on the ground that the proposed development would be unsustainable, contrary to paragraph 55 of the NPPF, among various other reasons that militated against this type of development in the countryside, including the loss of the building's agricultural character, the incidence of car parking and the intrusion of domestic paraphernalia, all of which would have an adverse impact in policy terms.

However, the simultaneous appeal against the refusal of a prior approval application under Class Q for precisely the same development was allowed, because paragraph 55 of the NPPF does not apply to permitted development under Class Q, nor could the other reasons for the refusal of planning permission be applied to the same development as permitted development under Class Q.

A contrary example of the application of this principle was provided by an appeal decision in Surrey in September 2015. The proposal was for the residential conversion of a timber barn which was remotely located with no direct access to a highway. In light of ministerial practice advice, the Inspector accepted that it was inappropriate to approach the matter from the point of view of the sustainability of the location, but the appeal was nevertheless refused because the barn had no viable means of access and would require the construction of a new drive across the field in which it was situated. The Inspector observed that this would have an urbanising effect on the rural character of the area, and it was for this reason that the proposed residential conversion was held to be undesirable or impractical.

It is not clear from this appeal decision whether any consideration was given to the possibility that an access might be provided as permitted development under Part 2, Class B or that it might alternatively be the subject of a separate planning application (which would have to be decided on its own merits). It is perhaps open to question in these circumstances whether the issue of access should be taken into account in considering the desirability or practicability of the development in accordance with published ministerial practice advice. Considerations as to any "urbanising effect on the rural character of the area" arising from or in connection with the development would in any event appear to go beyond the issues that a decision-maker should take into consideration in determining a prior approval application under Class Q.

Another example of the location or siting of a building making it impractical or undesirable for the building to change from agricultural use to a residential use under Class Q is provided by an appeal decision in Yorkshire in August 2015. In this case, the Inspector concluded that a nearby building which would remain in agricultural use, although it was not intended to be used to house cattle or to store slurry, might nevertheless involve the movement of agricultural vehicles, which could be intrusive and harmful. This might also happen at unsocial hours, and could adversely affect the living conditions of residents in the converted building.

In addition to these points, there are various other 'rural' issues which may properly be taken into account when an LPA is considering whether the location or siting of the building makes it impractical or undesirable for the building to change from agricultural use to a residential use (under Class Q) or to use as a school or nursery (under Class S). Ecological issues are an obvious example.

This was confirmed by a planning appeal decision in Shropshire in July 2015. The LPA were of the opinion that bats (a protected species) might be found in the building. In the absence of any bat survey having been carried out, the Inspector dismissed the appeal against the refusal of the prior approval application.

14.4.12 Design issues

With regard to development under **Classes M(b)**, **N(b)** and **Q(b)** (certain residential conversions) the local planning authority has to determine whether their prior approval will be required as to the design or external appearance of the building, but only where the prior approval application includes building operations reasonably necessary to convert the building to residential use. This has already been considered in *paragraph 13.3* in *Chapter 13*. As discussed there, the LPA may reasonably require drawings and/or other details of the proposed design and external appearance of the building in order to reach such a determination.

In the case of development under Class C (change of use of various buildings to use as a café or restaurant), the LPA must determine whether their prior approval will be required as to the *siting*, design or external appearance of any facilities to be provided under **Class C(b)** (for ventilation and extraction, including the provision of an external flue, and for the storage of rubbish). As discussed in *paragraph 13.3* in *Chapter 13*, the LPA may reasonably require drawings and/or other details of the proposed design and external appearance of these works in order to reach such a determination.

In both cases, this will necessarily involve the exercise of aesthetic judgment, which may well be open to debate. The provisions of Part 7 of the NPPF (paragraphs 56 to 68), and the corresponding text in the government's online planning practice guidance, are unlikely to be of any practical assistance in this regard, and the LPA may resort instead to any supplementary planning guidance that they have published themselves with regard to design issues. This should not be treated as being prescriptive, although it may be regarded as a material consideration which can legitimately be taken into account in this context.

14.4.13 Consideration of responses to consultations

Paragraph W(10) provides that the local planning authority must, when determining an application, also take into account any representations made to them as a result of any consultation under paragraphs W(5) or W(6) and any notice given under paragraph W(8).

The consultations under W(5) or W(6) are those which are addressed to the statutory consultees relating to highway and traffic impacts and flooding risks. Those under W(8) relate to neighbour notifications and/or a site notice. Representations received under the last category may (and quite probably will) range far outside the matters requiring approval in respect of the Class of development in question, but the requirement to take into account "any" such representations does not justify a widening of the issues that the LPA may take into account in determining the prior approval application. The considerations that the LPA can take into account are strictly limited to the matters requiring approval in each Class of development, and any representations that go outside the scope of those matters must be excluded when determining the prior approval application.

The handling of representations in response to planning applications is well understood and, subject to the proviso mentioned above, the LPA can be expected to deal with such representations under paragraph W in exactly the same way.

14.4.14 The National Planning Policy Framework

When determining a prior approval application, the LPA must also have regard to the National Planning Policy Framework (issued by the Department for Communities and Local Government in March 2012) *so far as relevant to the subject matter of the prior approval*, as if the application were a planning application.

The words in italics were added to the GPDO with effect from 6 April 2014. This amendment became necessary because, when determining prior approval applications under the former Class J (now Class O in the 2015 Order), LPAs had been interpreting the former paragraph N (now paragraph W), including the words "as if the application were a planning application", as giving them a wide discretion to take into account other policy considerations in addition to the short list of matters requiring approval in Class J. The amendment makes it clear that the only policies in the NPPF that can be taken into account in determining an application for prior approval are those that are relevant to the strictly limited criteria set out in respect of the specified Class of development. This has been confirmed and reinforced by appeal decisions, where inspectors have been robust in excluding considerations that go outside those parameters.

This was further reinforced by an amendment to the government's online Planning Practice Guidance on 5 March 2015, which points out that this procedure was amended in April 2014 to make it clear that the local planning authority must only consider the NPPF to the extent that it is relevant to those matters on which prior approval is sought, for example, transport, highways, noise etc.

In relation to Class Q (residential conversion of an agricultural building) and Class S (conversion of an agricultural building to use as a state-funded school or registered nursery) in particular, the revised ministerial practice guidance explains in some detail how an LPA should approach the question as to whether the location or siting of the building makes it otherwise impractical or undesirable for the building to change from agricultural use to the proposed use. (See *paragraph 14.4.11* above.) The practice guidance makes it clear that when an LPA considers location and siting, it should not be applying tests from the NPPF except to the extent these are relevant to the actual subject matter of the prior approval. So, for example, factors such as whether the property is for a rural worker, or whether the design is of exceptional quality or innovative, are unlikely to be relevant.

14.4.15 The Development Plan

There is no requirement in paragraph W that the LPA must have regard to the development plan in determining a prior approval application under Part 3, and so section 38(6) of the Planning and Compulsory Purchase Act 2004 (which provides that, *if* [but only if] *regard is to be had to the development plan* for the purpose of any determination to be made under the Planning Acts, the determination must be made in accordance with the plan unless material considerations indicate otherwise) does not apply in these cases.

Relevant parts of the development plan are nevertheless capable of being material considerations, even in the absence of the statutory duty under section 38(6) of the 2004 Act. This is best illustrated by reference to advertisement control. Here, too, there is no requirement to have regard to the development plan in determining an application for advertisement control consent under the Control of Advertisements Regulations, but the judgment of Sullivan J (as he then was) in *J C Decaux Ltd v FSS* [2003] EWHC 407 (Admin) established that whilst consideration of advertisement control matters is confined to issues of safety and amenity, this does not mean that planning policies, whether statutory or non-statutory, are irrelevant. Provided the policies in question are concerned with the two issues that have to be considered in relation to the control of advertisements (as distinct from other matters, such as housing or employment) they are as a matter of law capable of being material considerations in relation to the two specified issues for the purposes of determining an application for advertisement control consent.

The same principle undoubtedly applies to the determination of prior approval applications under Part 3 of the Second Schedule to the GPDO. However, the extent to which the provisions of the development plan may be relevant to the determination of the application is clearly limited to those that relate to highway and traffic impacts, contamination risks, flooding risks or to the other prescribed issues in respect of the Class of development in question that the LPA must consider when determining whether their prior approval in respect of those matters will be required, or should be given. To that extent, any relevant parts of the development plan can (and arguably should) be taken into account as a material consideration, but should not be regarded as being prescriptive.

It is clear, however, that other considerations that might be taken into account in the determination of a planning application cannot be brought into the equation in the case of a prior approval application under Part 3. Thus, to take just one example, in the case of an application under Class O, it would not be open to the LPA to refuse the application on the ground that the dwelling or dwellings would have inadequate amenity space.

14.4.16 Other considerations

Old habits die hard, and planning officers have been tempted in quite a few cases to refuse prior approval applications for reasons that rely on a variety of other considerations beyond the scope of those that are prescribed in respect of the relevant Class of permitted development in Part 3. However, it is clear both from the revised ministerial practice guidance issued in March 2015, and from decisions by the Planning Inspectorate in determining appeals against the refusal of prior approval applications, that a robust approach is being taken in strictly limiting the consideration of planning issues to those that are within the confines of the matters prescribed as the subject of the prior approval application in respect of the relevant Class of permitted development.

A particularly clear example was referred to in *paragraph 14.4.11*, where an appeal in Northamptonshire was allowed under Class Q, whilst a simultaneous appeal against the refusal of planning permission for the same development was dismissed on the basis of various material considerations that would normally be taken into account in the determination of a planning application.

Another example is provided by an appeal in one of the outer London boroughs, decided in April 2015, where the LPA had attempted to argue that the prior approval application should be rejected for lack of details as to the servicing of the proposed dwelling and as to the provision or availability of amenity space. This was a proposal for the residential conversion of an agricultural building originally made under Class MB (now Class Q). The Inspector pointed out that paragraph Q.2 does not require appellants to provide information on servicing or amenity space. The lack of such information did not make it impractical or undesirable to convert the building to residential use. This appeal also led to a full award of costs to the appellant, by reason of the LPA's misinterpretation of the terms of Class Q. They had made irrelevant observations with regard to possible future extension of the curtilage, and had failed to demonstrate why the proposed residential conversion would be undesirable or impractical.

Another appeal decision under Class Q, also in April 2015, in West Sussex, dealt with the LPA's concerns as to a nearby solar farm which, they alleged, would make the proposed residential development undesirable because of the outlook towards the solar panels and an impression that residents would be 'hemmed in' by the solar farm. The Inspector does seem to have accepted that the issue of the outlook for residents in this case did relate sufficiently to the desirability or practicability of the proposed residential conversion (which is one of the specific issues for determination under Class Q) as to be a relevant issue, but felt that any concern on this ground could be addressed by imposing an agreed condition requiring the developer to carry out a landscaping scheme that had been submitted.

14.4.17 Human rights

An even more graphic example of other considerations being rejected, and which was something of a *cause celèbre*, is provided by the *'Utopia Village'* appeal in the London Borough of Camden, which was decided by the Secretary of State in March 2015. This was an appeal under what was then Class J (now Class O), which proposed the residential conversion of offices that had been used within Use Class B1(a), to form up to 53 dwellings. The Council refused the prior approval application, giving 15 reasons for refusal which ranged far beyond the scope of the three matters requiring approval in Class J (transport and highways impacts, contamination risks and flooding risks).

The Council (no doubt on legal advice) did not seek to defend its refusal on these 'extraneous' grounds but, in concert with third party objectors, they did attempt to resist the proposed development because of its alleged effect on neighbours by reason of overlooking and loss of privacy. The Council accepted that Class J did not offer an LPA the opportunity to assess the impact that the proposal would have on the residential amenity of the existing occupiers of surrounding buildings. Nevertheless, having accepted the limited scope of Class J, the Council argued that the harm would be so severe that the development would be in breach of Article 8 of the European Convention on Human Rights (the right to respect for a person's private and family life, his home and his correspondence).

The Inspector and the Secretary of State gave careful consideration to this argument, but both of them rejected it, because the legislative intent behind Class J and what was then Paragraph N [now paragraph W] of the GPDO was absolutely clear, even on the basis of the wording of paragraph N as it stood prior to 6 April 2014. This was reinforced by the amendment to paragraph N(8)(b) made in April 2014 [now paragraph W(10)(b) in the 2015 Order], which added the words *"so far as relevant to the subject matter of the prior approval"*. The effect of these words was to make it clear that when an application for prior approval is made under any Class in Part 3, considerations raised by the NPPF (or by the development plan or other policy documents) can only be considered insofar as they address the subject matter specifically requiring prior approval within that Class (in the case of Class O [formerly J], only transport and highways impacts, contamination risks and flooding risks).

The addition of the words *"so far as relevant to the subject matter of prior approval"* therefore makes it clear that other considerations cannot be taken into account. It follows that for a planning authority to take into account a matter such as loss of privacy, or overlooking, or some other matter which relates to residential amenity, where this is not the subject matter of the application for prior approval, would run contrary to "a fundamental feature of the legislation" (per Lord Nicholls in *Ghaidan v Godin-Mendoza* [2004] 2 A.C. 557, at 33) and would be incompatible with its underlying thrust. Class J [now Class O] represented a deliberate policy choice that matters such as residential amenity should not provide a basis to refuse prior approval under that class, because this would defeat the policy aims behind the creation of Class J [Class O]. Accordingly, even if there was a case where a grant of prior approval would lead to a breach of Article 8 of the ECHR, section 3 of the Human Rights Act 1998 does not permit an interpretation of the GPDO whereby the matters relevant to Article 8, but outside of the subject matter of the prior approval, can be treated as a basis to refuse prior approval.

Nonetheless, the Secretary of State did go on to consider, as a separate issue, whether there would in any event be a breach of Article 8, but concluded that the grant of prior approval in this case would not lead to any breach of Article 8. The Secretary of State agreed with his inspector that, for a breach of Article 8 to occur, the impact upon the interests protected by Article 8 "must be far greater than may be considered to be unreasonable in the normal 'planning balance'".

The Secretary of State pointed out that the Strasbourg court (the ECHR) has held that there is a breach of Article 8 in only a very small number of cases arising from a decision by a State party to the Convention to permit, or not to restrict, development. As a whole, the judicial authorities show that the threshold for interference with Article 8(1) by reason of a grant of development consent is high.

This is confirmed by *Lough v FSS* [2004] 1 W.L.R. 2557, where the Court of Appeal stated that it was not in every case in which a person affected by a development suffered a loss of amenity that there would be a lack of respect for a person's private and family life and their home which required justification under Article 8(1). Rather, the degree of seriousness required to trigger lack of respect for Article 8 rights will depend on the circumstances, but it must be substantial. In considering whether a lack of respect of those rights has occurred, it is relevant to consider not only the impact on individuals but also the reasonableness and appropriateness of the measure.

In this regard, the Secretary of State stated, it was relevant to consider not only the policy aims behind the introduction of Class J [now Class O] but also the wider interests of the community including property developers such as the applicant for prior approval in this case, whose property rights under Article 1 of the First Protocol to the Convention are also engaged.

The Secretary of State made it clear that he did not underestimate the impacts of the development of overlooking, nor doubt that that impact will be disturbing for those properties most affected by the development. Nevertheless, having regard to the need for a "substantial" interference with amenity before any question of a lack of respect for Article 8 rights will occur, he did not accept that this threshold had been crossed in this case. He noted that this is a densely occupied urban area, close to the centre of London, in which some degree of overlooking will often occur, whether in accordance with current planning policies or not. In those circumstances a development which (bearing in mind the existing commercial use of the building) will simply increase the hours during which a small number of properties will be overlooked did not, in the Secretary of State's view, give rise to a sufficient impact on amenity so as to amount to a lack of respect for privacy under Article 8(1) of the ECHR.

Furthermore, the balance required by Article 8 has been struck in the legislation itself, so that it is not necessary to consider, in an individual case, whether any interference under Article 8(1) has arisen, or whether, if so, that interference is justified under Article 8(2). The Secretary of State took the view that the former Class J itself [now Class O] is intended to strike a balance between the competing interests protected by Article 8, and the wider interests of the community (as well as the property rights of developers and neighbours) including the advancement of the policy aims underlying Class J, as it then was.

The Secretary of State therefore concluded that this was a case where it could properly be said that any balance required by Article 8 is carried out in the legislation itself. In considering the *Utopia Village* case, the Secretary of State continued to believe that Class J [now Class O] is justified by the benefits which it brings about. In future, the Secretary of State therefore expects local planning authorities, and inspectors hearing appeals against their decisions, to proceed on the basis that Class O is compatible with Article 8, so that the grant of prior approval in a particular case will be justified under Article 8(2) by the general benefits of the legislation, even in a case where there is a sufficiently substantial impact to raise an issue under Article 8(1).

In another appeal in the same London Borough in May 2015, the same argument by the LPA complaining of the extent of overlooking and loss of privacy, and also calling in aid Article 8 of the Human Rights Convention was again rejected by an inspector in that appeal.

14.5   Conditions

When the prior approval procedure was introduced in May 2013, it was unclear whether the local planning authority had any power to impose conditions when granting their approval. This uncertainty was removed by the addition of paragraph N(11) to the 1995 Order with effect from 6 April 2014 (now paragraph W(13) in the 2015 Order), which provides that the LPA may grant prior approval unconditionally or subject to conditions reasonably related to the subject matter of the prior approval.

This does not give the LPA *carte blanche* to impose any conditions they please; the conditions must be *reasonably related to the subject matter of the prior approval*. The approval does not relate to the entirety of the proposed development, but only to those matters which are specified for approval under each Class of development (highway and traffic impacts, contamination risks, flooding risks or the other considerations specified in the respective Classes of development). This does not seem to have been properly understood by some LPAs, who have purported to impose somewhat more wide-ranging conditions in some cases.

It follows from the foregoing that it is not within the power of an LPA to impose conditions on a prior approval which seek the provision of, or any contribution to, affordable housing or any other form of financial contribution. Equally, an LPA cannot impose any conditions as to the provision of public open space, play areas and the like. It would appear that a condition as to the time within which development must be commenced (in those cases where such a condition is not imposed by the relevant Class in Part 3 itself) would also be outside the scope of the conditions which could properly be imposed by the LPA when approving those matters in respect of which the prior approval application is made.

On the other hand, because highway and traffic impacts are a proper subject of the prior approval, conditions can be imposed that seek to secure the safety and convenience of road users, and also where necessary appropriate provision for car parking, cycle parking and other measures for the management of traffic associated with the development, possibly including conditions requiring works to the highway access. (See *paragraph 14.4.1* above.)

The inclusion, among the issues that may require prior approval by the LPA, in respect of developments under Class Q or Class S only, of an issue as to whether the location or siting of the building makes it otherwise impractical or undesirable for the building to change from agricultural use to the proposed new use, did appear at first (as explained in *paragraph 14.4.11* above) to widen significantly the scope of the LPA's discretion on planning issues in such cases, and this might also have been thought to extend to the conditions that could properly be imposed on a prior approval under the former Class MB (now Class Q in the 2015 Order). However, in light of the amended online Planning Practice Guidance issued on 5 March 2015, which emphasises the restricted scope of the LPA's discretion with regard to the impracticability or undesirability of the proposed residential conversion in the context of the location or siting of the building, it would seem that the scope for the imposition of conditions aimed at addressing such issues is similarly constrained.

Nevertheless, it has been suggested that such conditions may extend to ecological issues (which would certainly appear to relate to the building's location) so as to justify a pre-commencement condition requiring, for instance, a bat survey before development may commence, and the planning appeal decision in July 2015 mentioned in *paragraph 14.4.11* would seem to confirm this. It would therefore appear that such a condition could properly be imposed in the case of Class Q, if there is a demonstrable ecological justification for it.

In addition to the limitation of the range of conditions that may be imposed within the scope of the prior approval for each class of development under Part 3, it is clear from paragraph 206 of the NPPF that planning conditions should only be imposed where they are necessary, relevant to planning and to the development to be permitted, enforceable, precise and reasonable in all other respects. The advice set out in the government's online Planning Practice Guidance on the use of conditions may also be relevant (and, although it no longer has the ministerial *imprimatur*, the advice set out in former Circular 11/95 may also be helpful in determining what conditions would be acceptable in the circumstances).

Where conditions are imposed that are arguably unlawful, by reason of their falling outside the scope of the specified issues to which the prior approval relates, it may be tempting simply to ignore them, but a safer course would be to apply to the LPA under section 73 to remove those conditions and, if they refuse to do so, to appeal against that refusal. This would be preferable to making an immediate appeal against the offending conditions under section 78(1)(c), because in taking the latter course the appellant may potentially put the prior approval itself in jeopardy in that appeal (see section 79(1)(b)).

In an appeal in London SW6 in November 2014, the LPA had proposed that a number of conditions should be included if the appeal was successful. The suggested conditions related to compliance with all other conditions, postal address application, refuse storage and water efficient appliances. But Paragraph N(11) (now paragraph W(13) in the 2015 Order) required that conditions must be reasonably related to the subject matter of the prior approval. The conditions requested by the Council did not relate to the matters under consideration in this application and so the Inspector declined to impose these conditions on the prior approval.

14.6 Planning obligations

A question may arise as to whether the LPA can properly seek the execution of a deed under section 106 of the 1990 Act in connection with a prior approval application under Part 3. Clearly the very limited time that the LPA has in which to determine a prior approval application would make it impracticable to secure the execution of a section 106 agreement before the issue of the prior approval. Whether a refusal to grant prior approval without a planning obligation having been offered would be upheld on appeal is open to question. This cannot be entirely ruled out, but it would have to be justified on the basis set out below.

The alternative of imposing a condition requiring that the applicant should enter into a planning obligation may also be impracticable, as it has proved difficult to devise a legally effective condition that seeks to impose such a requirement, and it is doubtful whether such a condition would be within the restricted range of conditions permitted by paragraph W(13) (see *paragraph 14.5* above).

This does not, however, prevent a planning obligation under section 106 being proffered by an applicant, and there are some examples of this having been done. A planning obligation under section 106 need not be in any way tied to an application under the planning legislation, but can be entered into at any time, either as an *inter partes* agreement or as a unilateral deed. Crucially, it can be made conditional on the grant of consent or approval in respect of a particular development.

Where a planning obligation is associated with an application for consent or approval under the planning legislation, it is ministerial policy (as set out in paragraph 203 of the NPPF) that planning obligations should only be used where it is not possible to address unacceptable impacts through a planning condition. This is reinforced by paragraph 204, which advises that planning obligations should only be sought where they meet all of the following tests:

– necessary to make the development acceptable in planning terms;

– directly related to the development; and

– fairly and reasonably related in scale and kind to the development.

This reflects the provisions of Regulation 122 of the Community Infrastructure Regulations 2010, which put these principles into statutory form. Judgments in the High Court and the Court of Appeal have confirmed the need for a direct connection between the development and the benefits offered by the planning obligation, but have not been unduly demanding as to their precise nature. The range of potential material considerations is broad, subject to their being relevant to planning and related to the development in question.

It is, nevertheless, entirely open to an inspector on appeal to conclude that the development is acceptable without the planning obligation being entered into and that the requisite approval can therefore be granted without it. If a planning obligation is to be proffered in such circumstances, it would be advisable that its terms should make it conditional upon the Inspector's certifying that it is a necessary prerequisite to the grant of prior approval. If this is not done, the planning obligation will be binding on the landowner in any event (see *R (Millgate Developments Ltd) v Wokingham BC* [2011] EWHC 6 (Admin), which was subsequently upheld by the Court of Appeal).

Arguably, and particularly bearing in mind the limited scope for imposing conditions on the prior approval in respect of development under Part 3 (as discussed in *paragraph 14.5* above), a planning obligation should similarly be confined to subject matter that is relevant to those same issues (highways and traffic impacts, contamination risks, flooding risks, etc.). Reg 122 of the CIL Regulations and paragraph 203 of the NPPF would appear to confirm this.

Thus a planning obligation might well be used as a means of dealing with the provision or funding of various highway infrastructure, or making other provision for the management of traffic, car parking or cycle parking, etc. if the need for it clearly arises from the development. An agreement under section 278 of the Highways Act 1980 could alternatively be used for the same purpose.

On the other hand, there would appear to be no justification, in the context of an application for prior approval under Part 3, for a planning obligation to secure the provision of, or any contribution to, affordable housing, or as to the provision or funding of educational facilities, public open space, play areas and the like, no matter what planning policies may have been adopted by the LPA with regard to such matters.

14.7 Community Infrastructure Levy

While considering the issue of financial contributions, applicants should be aware that Community Infrastructure Levy may be payable on permitted development (see Regulation 64 of the Community Infrastructure Levy Regulations 2010). Primarily, this depends on whether a charging schedule has yet been adopted by the LPA.

The detailed rules relating to CIL lie outside the scope of the present work, but it is possible that liability may be avoided or minimised when existing floorspace is netted off in calculating the chargeable amount under Regulation 40. However, attention must be paid in this regard to the judgment of the High Court in *R (Hourhope Ltd) v Shropshire Council* [2015] EWHC 518 (Admin), relating to the actual use of the building prior to re-development.

One point that should be borne in mind in this connection is that, whilst CIL may be payable in some cases, potential liability to CIL is wholly irrelevant to the submission, processing and determination of a prior approval application. (See *paragraph 13.6* in *Chapter 13*.)

14.8 Appeals

An appeal against the refusal of prior approval under Part 3 may be made to the Planning Inspectorate under section 78(1)(c) of the 1990 Act. An appeal can also be made under this section against the imposition of particular conditions imposed by the LPA, but section 79(1)(b) could put the prior approval itself in jeopardy in these circumstances, and so (as suggested in *paragraph 14.5* above) an application under section 73 would be a preferable way of dealing with any offending conditions. If the section 73 application is refused by the LPA, this can then be appealed under section 78 without jeopardising the prior approval decision itself.

Prior approval appeals generally follow the same procedures and timetables as appeals relating to the refusal of planning permission. No appeal fee is payable. Even where such an appeal relates to the domestic conversion of a building, this does not make it a 'householder appeal' (nor does any prior approval application constitute a planning application for 'minor commercial development'), and so the time limit for appealing is the usual six months, not the abbreviated period of 12 weeks that applies to those other types of appeal.

Although it is not currently possible to make a prior approval application online, an appeal under section 78 can be made online through the Planning Portal, or an appeal form can be downloaded from that website and submitted to the Planning Inspectorate by post, if preferred.

An appellant must set out their full statement of case when making the appeal. The statement of case must contain full details of relevant facts and planning/legal arguments; it must contain all available evidence and must be accompanied by all documents (including analysis of the facts or copies of legal cases), maps and plans and any relevant extracts to which the statement refers.

The statement should respond to the reasons for refusal set out in the LPA's notification of their decision; it should cite the statutory provisions relied upon and any relevant case law (including the full report reference), and it should refer to any policy or practice guidance (such as the ministerial guidance discussed in this and the preceding chapters) that supports the appellant's case.

These appeals will usually be dealt with by the written representations procedure, but a Hearing is not ruled out if the circumstances of the case require it. (A full public inquiry was held into the '*Utopia Village*' appeal mentioned in *paragraph 14.4.17* above, but public inquiries are likely to be rare exceptions in prior approval appeals.) The appellant must state which procedure they would prefer, and give their reasons for this. However, it is for the Planning Inspectorate to decide upon the appropriate procedure, having considered any representations that may have been made by the parties in this regard.

The detailed procedural rules are beyond the scope of this book, and will depend on the appeal procedure adopted. Subject to this, the appeal will be dealt with in exactly the same way as any other planning appeal under section 78.

The issues to be considered by the Inspector will depend on the reasons given by the LPA for refusing their prior approval in respect of the proposed development, and may include a dispute as to whether the building in question qualifies for conversion under the terms of the relevant Class of Part 3. Issues such as the adequacy of the information supplied by the applicant may also be relevant in some cases.

Other issues for consideration may include the extent (if at all) that the LPA was entitled to take into account the considerations that led to their refusal of prior approval for the reasons stated by them, having regard to the criteria set out in the relevant Class of Part 3. The provisions of paragraph W(10) and its limitations, and the revised ministerial practice guidance issued in March 2015 will be very relevant in this context.

Where there is no dispute on any of the points mentioned above, issue may still be joined on the justification for the reasons stated by the LPA as supporting the refusal, in much the same way as in other planning appeals, but always bearing in mind the much narrower ambit of the considerations that are relevant to such cases, and in particular the very limited applicability of adopted planning policies and other planning considerations, as explained in the earlier parts of this chapter.

Where the LPA has refused its prior approval, but there is an issue as to whether they notified the applicant of this decision within the 56-day period, this may also be raised in such an appeal. (The 56-day rule is examined in detail in *Chapter 15*.) Where, however, the failure of the LPA to determine the application or to notify the applicant of that determination within the 56-day period is the sole determining factor in an appeal, the Planning Inspectorate seems to have taken the view that no appeal is required (or can be made) in such a case.

The author has been shown a letter from the Planning Inspectorate, written in May 2015 in response to an appeal which had been made against non-determination of a prior approval application in Gloucestershire, in which they stated that, because it would appear that the LPA did not determine the application within the required 56-day period, the applicant can proceed with the development in these circumstances, and no right of appeal applies. The LPA had the power to refuse the application on the basis that the development was not appropriate for the prior approval process but there was no indication in this case that they did so. In the circumstances, the Inspectorate stated that the appeal appeared to be invalid and no further action would be taken on it.

After further representations from the LPA, on the basis that the proposed development did not fulfil the conditions for permitted development under the relevant part of the GPDO, the Planning Inspectorate subsequently changed their minds in this case and accepted the appeal, but made it clear that the Inspector would address the LPA's position as a preliminary matter, and that the Inspector would only proceed to determine the appeal if satisfied that the prior approval procedure was applicable.

In the absence of any such other issues, though, it would appear that it is unnecessary (and in fact impossible) to appeal against the non-determination of a prior approval application. However, if there is any doubt in such a case as to the qualification of the pre-existing use under the terms of the relevant Class of permitted development in Part 3, or as to the nature and scope of the proposed development itself, and which has not been an issue that has been dealt with on appeal under section 78, it may in such circumstances be advisable to make an application for a Lawful Development Certificate under section 192 of the 1990 Act, as discussed at the end of *paragraph 14.9* below.

It should also be borne in mind that no appeal can be made against the refusal of an LPA to entertain a prior approval application in accordance with the provisions of section 70A(5)(b) (as mentioned at the end of *paragraph 14.2* above), provided that one or other of the conditions in subsections (3) or (4) have been met, and provided also that the LPA notifies the applicant of its refusal to entertain the application in accordance with section 70A(5)(b) within the 56-day time limit. In the absence of the applicant having been informed by the LPA within that time limit that they decline to entertain the application in accordance with section 70A(5)(b), the 56-day rule will operate, so that no appeal can then be made against the non-determination in any event, but the development may in those circumstances proceed, subject to the observations made above in this paragraph as to all other factors being in order.

Where an appeal is made and determined under section 78, an application for a full or partial award of costs may be made where the LPA is alleged to have acted unreasonably in refusing their prior approval, for example in relying on reasons for refusal that go outside the scope of the criteria applicable to that particular Class of development, the provisions of paragraph W(10) and/or the government's online practice guidance (as revised in March 2015). An award of costs may be made if the Inspector is satisfied that the appellant has thereby been put to unnecessary expense in having to appeal against the LPA's decision, and quite a few orders for costs have been issued on this basis against local planning authorities in prior approval appeals.

14.9 Lawful Development Certificate

It is the practice of some authorities upon notifying an applicant of their determination of a prior approval application to advise the applicant that if they want formal confirmation that the proposed development would be lawful (e.g. on the basis that it would comply with all of the limitations of the relevant Class of development in Part 3), they should submit an application to the authority for a Lawful Development Certificate.

In practice, this should be entirely unnecessary, as the LPA should refuse a prior approval application in circumstances where the development does not comply with all of the limitations of the relevant Class of development. If there is any doubt on this score, either as regards compliance with the qualifying criteria or as to the lawfulness of the existing use upon which the proposed permitted development depends, this should be resolved by the applicant, with the assistance if necessary of professional advice, before a prior approval application is made.

Where the applicant or their professional advisers are clear as to the position in this regard, an application for an LDC should not be necessary. The lawfulness of a use or development is not dependent on an LDC being issued. This has been confirmed in relation to the lawfulness of an existing use or development by the judgment of the High Court in *Hillingdon LBC v SSCLG* [2008] EWHC 198 (Admin). In the course of this judgment, attention was drawn to paragraph 16 of Annex 1 to Circular 17/92 which stated that sub-section (2) of section 191 (which provides that, for the purposes of the Act, uses of land and operations are lawful at any time if no enforcement action may then be taken in respect of them) applies *"whether or not an LDC has been issued under sections 191 or 192 of the 1990 Act."*

It may, on the other hand, be advisable to apply for a Lawful Development Certificate where the LPA has failed to determine a prior approval application within the 56-day period, or has failed to notify the applicant of its decision, in circumstances where the LPA is in fact disputing the qualification of the site for change of use under the relevant Class in Part 3, or is otherwise challenging the right to carry out the proposed development. If the applicant is correct in their assertion that they have the right to carry out the permitted development, then the expiry of the 56-day period would in principle enable the development to proceed, but caution may suggest that the correctness of the applicant's assertion as to the lawfulness of the proposed development should be tested by means of an application under section 192, before going ahead with the development.

The details of an LDC application are outside the scope of this book, but it may be helpful to readers to be reminded of the judgment in *F W Gabbitas v SSE and Newham LBC* [1985] J.P.L. 630, where it was held that the applicant's own evidence does not need to be corroborated by "independent" evidence in order to be accepted. If the local planning authority has no evidence of its own, or from others, to contradict or otherwise make the applicant's version of events less than probable, there is no good reason to refuse the application, provided the applicant's evidence alone is sufficiently precise and unambiguous to justify the grant of a certificate "on the balance of probability". This was helpfully summarised in paragraph 8.15 of Annex 8 to Circular 10/97. The Circular was cancelled in March 2014, but *Gabbitas* is now referred to in the government's online planning practice guidance on this topic.

14.10 Carrying out the development

Development that requires an application for prior approval cannot be begun before the receipt by the applicant from the local planning authority of a written notice of their determination that such prior approval is not required or giving their prior approval or, alternatively, before the expiry of 56 days following the date on which the application was received by the LPA without the authority notifying the applicant as to whether prior approval is given or refused. (As to this last point, see *paragraph 15.6 in Chapter 15*.)

Upon one of these three events occurring, development can then begin and, if it comprises only a change of use, and does not involve building operations under one or other of Classes C(b), M(b), N(b) or Q(b), it will not be *"begun"* until the change of use is actually made, that is to say until the residential occupation of the new dwelling actually commences or, at the earliest, when it is ready for immediate occupation for its new use. Any works for the adaptation of the building to residential use that affect only the interior of the building, or which do not materially affect the external appearance of the building, do not amount to development, under section 55(2)(a), but their completion so that the building is ready for imminent occupation for its new use may amount to a change of use so as to constitute the commencement of development for that purpose (see *paragraph 1.3.2 in Chapter 1*).

Thus the commencement of such internal works before the receipt by the applicant of a written notice of the LPA's determination that prior approval is not required or a written notice giving their prior approval, or (in the absence of any such notice) before the expiry of 56 days following the date on which the application was received by the LPA, is not prevented and does not affect the validity of the change of use as permitted development under Part 3, provided the change of use (which may include the completion of the adaptation itself to the point at which the property is actually ready for imminent occupation) is not made before the appropriate date. However, any building or other operations under Classes C(b), M(b), N(b) or Q(b) must not begin before one of the three prerequisite events mentioned above has occurred.

The development must be carried out in accordance with the details approved by the local planning authority, where their prior approval was required and given. Where prior approval is not required (because the LPA has so determined), or where the 56-day period expires without the LPA notifying the applicant as to whether prior approval is given or refused, the development must be carried out in accordance with the details provided in the prior approval application. In both cases, however, the LPA and the developer may agree otherwise in writing (see paragraph W(12)).

The applicant must, of course, also carry out the development in accordance with the conditions set out in the relevant Class in Part 3. So, for example, in the case of developments under Classes C, J, R, S or T, the development must begin within a period of three years beginning with the date on which any prior approval is granted for that development, or beginning with the date when the 56-day period expires without the LPA notifying the applicant as to whether prior approval is given or refused, and in the case of developments under Classes M, N and Q, it must be completed within three years of that date.

The development must also comply with any conditions imposed by the LPA on the prior approval, subject to the observations set out in *paragraphs 14.5* and *14.8* above.

It should also be borne in mind that the change of use of the building (as well as any permitted building operations) must also comply with the Building Regulations, although this will not affect the lawfulness of the permitted development under the planning legislation.

CHAPTER 15

THE 56-DAY RULE

15.0 Preliminary note

In the normal course of events, permitted development requiring prior approval can be begun upon the receipt by the applicant from the local planning authority of a written notice of their determination that prior approval is not required, or the receipt of a written notice giving their prior approval. However the provisions of paragraph W(11) include a 56-day rule, whereby the development can be begun upon the expiry of 56 days following the date on which the application was received by the LPA without the authority notifying the applicant as to whether prior approval is given or refused.

There is, however, one point that must be emphasised as strongly as possible. The 56-day rule has no application where the qualifying criteria in a particular case are not met. If the proposed development does not qualify as permitted development for any reason (and this would include any failure to comply with the conditions subject to which Part 3 grants deemed planning permission for this type of development), then it is simply not permitted development in any event. In those circumstances, any failure on the part of the LPA to notify the applicant as to whether prior approval is given or refused, either within the 56-day period or at all, cannot give rise to any right to carry out the development.

In the same way, if the prior approval application is not a valid application, because it does not comply with the terms of paragraph W(2), including the payment of the correct application fee, the 56-day period will not commence, and the 56-day rule will have no application in those circumstances.

15.1 General approach

The general approach to the 56-day rule is illustrated by the decision of the Court of Appeal in *Murrell v SSCLG* [2010] EWCA Civ 1367 (a case which actually involved the 28-day period for determination in respect of a prior notification of agricultural development under Part 6). This established that the GPDO does not make the running of time dependent on a decision by the local planning authority to accept an application as valid. Whether there was a valid application or not is an objective question of law. The application for determination as to whether prior approval is required does not need to be in any particular form and does not need to be accompanied by anything more than what is prescribed by the GPDO (see *Chapter 13*). It is not mandatory to use a standard form or to provide any information beyond that specified in the GPDO.

The appellant's application in *Murrell* complied with the requirements of the GPDO and was a valid application, contrary to the LPA's assertion. The GPDO does not require an application to be accompanied by proposed elevations or a block plan (and Part 6 does not require a location plan, although in *Murrell* a location plan was in fact provided with the application). It does not require multiple copies of any documents. Since use of a standard application form is not mandatory, the council was mistaken in stating that these were the only forms they could accept and in requesting the applicant to complete and return, in quadruplicate, a new standard form. Accordingly, the council's assertion that the application was invalid was wrong in law.

The Court of Appeal agreed that the council was entitled to ask for further information. It was not, however, entitled to refuse to treat the application as a valid application until that further information was received. The clock carried on ticking from the date of receipt of the application until the expiry of (in that case) the 28-day period.

15.2 Commencement of the 56-day period

There appears to be some confusion, not least on the part of some planning officers, as to the start date of the 56-day period. However, the wording of paragraph W(11) is perfectly clear on this point. The development cannot be begun before "the expiry of 56 days *following the date on which the application was received* by the local planning authority". Thus Day 1 of the 56-day period is the day immediately following the date on which the application is received by the LPA.

The incidence of weekends and public holidays has no effect on the 56-day period, except in those cases in which the application is submitted to the LPA by email, where section 336(4A) of the 1990 Act, and also Article 2(9) of the GPDO, will apply. Section 336(4A) provides that where an electronic communication is used for the purpose of serving or giving a notice or other document on or to any person for the purposes of this Act, and the communication is received by that person *outside that person's business hours*, it is to be taken to have been received on the next working day.

In this subsection, "working day" means a day which is not a Saturday, Sunday, Bank Holiday or other public holiday. It should be noted that this does not refer to 'normal' working hours, but to "that person's" (i.e. the recipient's) actual working hours, whatever they may be. Some local authorities, for example, close for business at 4.30 p.m. on a Friday afternoon, and there may be other variations in the working hours of certain authorities. This provision is further refined by Article 2(9) of the GPDO by defining "working day" as a day which is not a Saturday, Sunday, Christmas Day, Good Friday or a day which is a bank holiday in England under the Banking and Financial Dealings Act 1971. Article 2(9) also refers to "*the recipient's business hours*", but its effect is otherwise the same as section 336(4A).

The further complication of determining the precise date and time of receipt by the LPA of an application which is submitted electronically via the Planning Portal does not arise in these cases, because prior approval applications under Part 3 cannot, at the time of writing, be submitted via the Planning Portal, but must be submitted direct to the authority, either by hand, by post or by email. As to the last of these, section 329(1)(cc) of the 1990 Act permits the service of a notice using electronic communications where an address for service has been given, as it is on most local planning authorities' websites, and so there can be no doubt as to the validity of an application transmitted by email, so long as it complies (in the case of Part 3) with the requirements of paragraph W.

Lest there be any doubt on the point, the rules relating to the application being treated as having been received on the next working day apply only where the application is received electronically outside the authority's business hours. If it is received electronically within the authority's actual business hours, then Day 1 of the 56-day period will be the very next day, irrespective of whether the council's offices are open on that next day or not. Weekends and public holidays cannot delay the start of the 56-day period, provided the council's offices were open at the time when the application was received. (If received before office hours, the next working day will, of course, be the same day, and Day 1 of the 56-day period will be the next day after that.)

Some LPAs seem to be under the impression that time does not begin to run until they have 'validated' or registered the application, but this is not so (as the Court of Appeal's decision in *Murrell* confirms - see *paragraph 15.1* above). Provided the application complies with the requirements of paragraph W and is accompanied by the correct fee (see *paragraph 13.7* in *Chapter 13*), the 56-day period will begin to run on the day after it is deliv-ered to the LPA. If payment of the fee follows after the application itself, then the application may be considered to be complete upon subsequent receipt of the fee, and the 56-day period will then commence on the day after that date. (See *Infocus Public Networks Ltd v SSCLG* [2010] EWHC 3309 (Admin).)

Bearing in mind the practical importance of the 56-day rule, applicants should ensure that the date and time of receipt of the application by the LPA is reliably recorded. In the case of electronic delivery, it should usually be possible to confirm this by reference to email records, but receipt of an email cannot automatically be assumed, and the applicant should obtain confirmation of receipt, at the very least by requesting a delivery receipt on the outgoing email. A 'read receipt' can also be requested, but in the author's experience will only rarely receive a response. It would probably be best to address the email to the council's general email address, rather than to any particular department or named officer.

If a prior approval application is delivered to the authority electronically, payment of the fee will, of course, have to be separately arranged (see *paragraph 13.7* in *Chapter 13*). As mentioned above, the application cannot be treated as having been received by the authority until this fee is also received.

Delivery by post can most reliably be arranged by using the Royal Mail's Signed For® First Class service. This service aims to deliver a letter or parcel the next working day, and provides proof of delivery, including a signature from the receiver. You can check online (or by phone) quoting the reference number on the receipt and proof of posting to see when the item has been delivered, and this information can be printed off for future reference. If delivering an application in this way, it would be best not to send it to a PO Box number, but to address it to the actual address of the council's main offices (even if this is not the address of the Planning Department). It is the author's practice simply to address the envelope to "[XYZ] Council" at that address. The fee cheque should be enclosed, unless you have arranged to make the payment electronically.

Delivery by hand is also an option, but it would probably be best simply to address the envelope to "[XYZ] Council" and to deliver it to the council's main office (again with the fee cheque enclosed), rather than to the Planning Department. This makes it more likely that delivery can be effected without queries or difficulties arising.

15.3   Extending the 56-day period

There was no provision in the 1995 Order for any extension of time in respect of the determination of a prior approval application. However, Article 7 of the 2015 Order (after restating the basic rule that prior approval applications must be determined within 56 days) now allows the LPA to make a decision in relation to the application within such longer period as may be agreed by the applicant and the authority in writing (which can include an exchange of emails).

There is, of course, no obligation on the applicant to agree to such an extension of time, but if they do not do so a prudent authority might then refuse the application fairly promptly in order to avoid the 56-day rule coming into operation (which would result in the development being able to go ahead in any event). It is clear that any agreement to an extension of time would have to be explicit and unequivocal; it cannot be assumed or implied, nor can it be construed from only one side of a purported exchange of correspondence. There would need to be some written evidence that both parties had agreed to extend time. A nil response from the applicant to the LPA's request for more time would not prevent time from continuing to run for the purposes of the 56-day rule.

15.4   Has the application actually been determined?

A query may possibly arise as to the validity of the LPA's determination of the prior approval application (or whether it has in fact been determined at all). The addition of paragraph N(2A) to Part 3 in 2014 (now paragraph W(3) in the 2015 Order) largely removed the ambiguity in this regard that was inherent in the original drafting of former paragraph N, and this has been reinforced by the addition of further words at the end of what is now paragraph W(4) in the 2015 Order.

Paragraph W(4) now provides that for the purposes of section 78 of the 1990 Act the rejection of the prior approval application based on paragraph W(3) is to be treated as a refusal of that prior approval application. It does therefore amount to a determination of that application, even if the LPA is objectively wrong as to the non-compliance of the development with the qualifying criteria under the relevant Class of Part 3. Consequently, the correctness or otherwise of the LPA's opinion can only be tested by way of an appeal against this decision under section 78 of the 1990 Act.

However, as noted in *paragraph 14.2*, the adequacy of the information provided relates only to the issue as to whether it is reasonably sufficient to enable the authority to establish that the proposed development complies with the relevant conditions, limitations or restrictions, so as to qualify as permitted development under the Class in question. If the LPA purports to reject the application in relation to the adequacy of the information for other purposes, going outside the question of compliance with the qualifying criteria, this may perhaps call in question the validity of the decision. If the LPA's opinion on this point strays outside these stated parameters, it might possibly be argued that the authority has not actually determined the application, which could raise the possibility that the 56-day period might continue running.

In such cases, a notice or other written communication informing the applicant of the LPA's rejection of the prior approval application under paragraph W(3) is likely (in view of the provision now contained in paragraph W(4)) to be regarded as a valid determination of the application, leaving an appeal under section 78 as the only course that would then be open to the applicant (unless the applicant chooses instead to make a planning application). Thus it is unlikely that a wrongful or mistaken rejection of a prior approval application would result in the 56-day period continuing to run in these circumstances.

If the LPA has declined to entertain the prior approval application in reliance upon the power granted to it by section 70A(5)(b) of the 1990 Act (which is referred to at the end of *paragraph 14.2* in *Chapter 14*), the 56-day rule will not apply, provided that one of other of the conditions in subsections (3) or (4) have been met, and provided also that the LPA notifies the applicant of its refusal to entertain the application in accordance with section 70A(5)(b) within the 56-day period. If the provisions of section 70A(5) of the 1990 Act are observed by the LPA, the council's obligation to determine the application, whether within the 56-day period or at all, is at an end and the 56-day rule will not apply in these circumstances.

15.5 Notifying the applicant of the authority's decision

The critical event for the purposes of the 56-day rule is the authority's "notifying the applicant as to whether prior approval is given or refused". This would not seem to require a formal decision notice as such; any simple communication informing the applicant either that prior approval is given or that it is refused might suffice to meet this requirement. Nor does there seem to be any statutory obligation on the LPA to state their reasons for refusing prior approval, although it would no doubt be good practice to do so, and this does indeed appear to be the standard practice of most authorities.

Bearing in mind that sub-paragraphs (a) and (b) in paragraph W(11) refer to a *written notice* of the LPA's determination that their prior approval is not required, or giving their prior approval, it is clear that the notification of their determination must be in that form, but this does not preclude its being sent in electronic form, such as an email, bearing in mind that section 329(1)(cc) of the 1990 Act permits the service of a notice using electronic communications where an address for service has been given. Article 2(6) to (11) of the GPDO makes further provision as to the electronic service of notices.

Whilst it is clear that written notification of the LPA's determination must be given (i.e. dispatched) within the 56-day period, some doubt has been expressed as to whether that notification must also be received by the applicant within that time limit. The wording of paragraph W(11)(c) is not as clear as one might wish.

In paragraph W(11) of Part 3, sub-paragraph (a) refers to "*the receipt by the applicant* from the local planning authority of a written notice of their determination that such prior approval is not required" and sub-paragraph (b) refers to "*the receipt by the applicant* from the local planning authority of a written notice giving their prior approval". However, sub-paragraph (c) refers to "the expiry of 56 days following the date on which the application was received by the local planning authority without the authority *notifying the applicant* as to whether prior approval is given or refused".

Sub-paragraph (c) relates to both of these two alternative notifications, and (by implication) to the third possibility that the notice served by the authority may be to inform the applicant that prior approval is refused. It therefore seems clear from the context that sub-paragraph (c) must also be taken to refer to the *receipt by the applicant* of such a notice, so sub-paragraph (c) should in practice be read as - "the expiry of 56 days following the date on which the application was received by the local planning authority without *the receipt by the applicant* from the local planning authority of a written notice as to whether prior approval is given or refused".

The author is currently aware of three practical examples where this point has been in issue. The first of these was a case in North Somerset in 2009 (apparently not the subject of any appeal or other proceedings), where notification of the refusal of prior approval of a mobile phone mast (under what was then Part 24 in the 1995 Order, now Part 16 in the 2015 Order) was sent to the applicant by Second Class post on Day 52 or Day 53, but was not received by them until Day 57. The applicant relied on this as allowing them to proceed with the development. The resulting dispute appears to have been settled by negotiation, although the company continued to insist that they had been correct to treat the late receipt of the notification of the council's decision as being out of time.

The second example, was an appeal decision in Tower Hamlets, issued on 24 June 2013. This was an application for prior approval in respect of a telephone kiosk under what was then Part 24 (now Part 16 in the 2015 Order). The Inspector stated at the beginning of his decision letter that the authority had 56 days in which to give notice whether prior approval was required, *and for the applicant to receive such notice*. The Inspector clearly took the view that a written notification sent within the 56 days but not received by the applicant within that time would not comply with the 56-day rule, so that the right to carry out the development then became automatic, notwithstanding the LPA's decision and the purported notice of their refusal of the prior approval application.

On this basis, both parties agreed that the time within which the applicant should have *received* such notice expired on 26 December 2011. The authority sent out an undated letter on 23 December refusing prior approval. That letter was received by the appellant in the post on 29 December 2011, outside the 56-day period. However, a copy of this letter was also sent out by two emails at 4.32 p.m. on 23 December, one of which went to the email address given on the applicant's headed notepaper, and was received by them on that day.

As indicated above, there can be no doubt that, in accordance with section 329(1)(cc) of the 1990 Act, transmission of the letter by email to the applicant's stated email address was an effective communication of the written notice of the LPA's determination of the prior approval application, because an address for service had been given by virtue of its being shown on the applicant's headed notepaper (notwithstanding that the applicant had not confirmed on the application form that they would agree to receive communications by email).

The question, however, still arose as to whether the receipt of the email at or shortly after 4.32 p.m. on 23 December was actually in time. In this regard, the applicant relied on Section 336(4A) of the 1990 Act, which provides that where an electronic communication is used for the purpose of serving or giving a notice or other document on or to any person for the purposes of this Act, and the communication is received by that person *outside that person's business hours*, it is to be taken to have been received on the next working day, and in this subsection, "working day" means a day which is not a Saturday, Sunday, Bank Holiday or other public holiday. [They could equally have relied on Article 1(10) of the GPDO 1995 at that time - now replaced by Article 2(9) of the GPDO 2015.]

The Inspector drew attention to the words "that person's business hours". This does not mean 'normal' business hours, but the business hours which that person chooses to keep. Whilst it may be usual for offices to remain open until 5.00 p.m. or 5.30 p.m., some businesses do close down earlier on Friday afternoons and in the cited appeal case this was the last working day before the Christmas holiday, and it was therefore unsurprising that the applicant's office closed down for Christmas before 4.30 p.m. on that day. In any event, if a person keeps business hours that are different from the norm, it is their own business hours which apply for this purpose.

In this case, therefore, the email of 23 December had been received outside the applicant's working hours, and so (in accordance with section 336(4A)) it had to be taken to have been received on the next working day, which was Wednesday 28 December in this case, because Christmas Day fell on a Sunday and so there was an extra Bank Holiday on Tuesday 27 December. The Inspector accordingly held that the notification of the council's refusal of prior approval was received outside the 56-day period, and the applicant had been entitled (as they did) to go ahead with the erection of the telephone kiosk.

The third example is another appeal decision, issued in February 2015. This appeal related to a prior approval application under Part 3, Class MB [now Class Q], involving the residential conversion of a detached barn to produce two dwellings. The appellant claimed that he did not receive notification of the council's decision within the 56-day period. It was agreed by both parties that the 56-day period would have expired on 4 June 2014. The council's decision was dated 3 June, but the decision was not authorised under the council's scheme of delegation until 4 June. Thus the decision could not have been sent out until Day 56 at the earliest.

The applicant stated that he had received the decision by post on 9 June, and that the council's website was also updated with details of the decision on that day. He stated that the decision was not emailed to him. The council did not comment on or contradict any of this evidence. The Inspector therefore held that, if the decision was posted on 4 June it would have been received by the appellant after the 56-day period and therefore that the postal notification did not take place within the statutory period.

As in the Tower Hamlets appeal (under what was then Part 24, now Part 16 in the 2015 Order), the Inspector in this case clearly took the view that notification of the council's decision must not only be dispatched (whether by post or electronically) within the 56-day period, but that it must actually be received by the applicant within that period.

One other point that can be quickly disposed of is the implied suggestion (which has also been raised elsewhere) that publication of the council's decision on its website could be taken as 'notifying the applicant' of the council's decision. In the author's view, this could not amount to notification for the purposes of paragraph W(11)(c). Notification requires a written communication addressed to the applicant (or their agent), whether by post or by email, and merely posting information on the council's website would not suffice for this purpose.

On the basis of the three practical examples quoted above, there would appear to be an established consensus that notification of the LPA's determination of the prior approval application must not only be given by the authority within the 56-day period, but must also be received by the applicant within that period, and a proper construction of paragraph W(11), read as a whole, would seem to support this.

15.6 *Commencement of development in default of notification of a decision*

If there has been no determination of the prior approval application or if the applicant has not been notified of the authority's decision, the 56-day period must actually have expired before the development is begun; thus it cannot lawfully be begun until the day following the last day of the 56-day period. However, if the development does not involve building or other operations under Classes C(b), M(b), N(b) or Q(b), it will not be "*begun*" until the change of use is actually made, that is to say until the residential occupation of the new dwelling (or the use of the café or restaurant in the case of Class C) actually commences or, at the very least, until the new dwelling (or the café or restaurant) is ready for immediate occupation. Any works for the adaptation of the building to its new use that affect only the interior of the building, or which do not materially affect the external appearance of the building, do *not* amount to development (by virtue of section 55(2)(a) of the 1990 Act) and so the commencement of any such works does not amount to the beginning of development, but their completion may bring about a change of use, so as to constitute the commencement of the development. (This is discussed in more detail in *paragraph 1.3.2* of *Chapter 1*.)

Thus the commencement of purely internal works before the receipt by the applicant of a written notice of the LPA's determination that prior approval is not required or a written notice giving their prior approval, or (in the absence of any such notice) before the expiry of 56 days following the date on which the application was received by the LPA, is not prevented and does not affect the validity of the change of use as permitted development under Part 3, provided the change of use itself is not made before the appropriate date. However, where the works involve building operations under Classes

C(b), M(b), N(b) or Q(b), the development under that class will be begun when those building operations are commenced, and so (in the absence of prior approval or notification that it will not be required) this work must not begin until the 56-day period has expired.

One point which has already been noted, however, is that if the LPA has declined to entertain the prior approval application in reliance upon the power granted to it by section 70A(5)(b) of the 1990 Act (referred to at the end of *paragraph 14.2* in *Chapter 14*), the 56-day rule will not apply, provided that one or other of the conditions in subsections (3) or (4) have been met, and provided also that the LPA notifies the applicant of its refusal to entertain the application in accordance with section 70A(5)(b) within the 56-day period.

A final point to be borne in mind is that it will be lawful to begin the permitted development under Part 3 only if this development does indeed meet all the qualifications for that class of development, and only if it is in compliance with all the restrictions, limitations and conditions set out in Part 3. Non-determination of a prior approval application, or a failure by the LPA to notify the applicant of its decision, does not entitle a developer to proceed with a development which does not in fact qualify as permitted development under the terms of the GPDO. If there is any doubt about this, an applicant would be well advised to apply for a Lawful Development Certificate before proceeding with the development, as explained in *paragraph 14.9* of *Chapter 14*.

CHAPTER 16

TEMPORARY USE OF OPEN LAND

[NOTE: Because this book is concerned only with permitted changes of use, and does not deal with building, engineering or other operations (other than certain operations associated with permitted changes of use, which have been dealt with in earlier chapters), Part 4, Class A in the Second Schedule to the GPDO, which concerns the provision on land of temporary buildings and structures in connection with other operational development, is not covered here (although the development permitted by that Class in Part 4 may be relevant in the circumstances discussed in *paragraph 19.9* in *Chapter 19*, and is referred to there).]

16.1   The scope of the temporary use permitted

Part 4, Class B permits the temporary use of any land (other than a building, or land which is within the curtilage of a building) for any purpose, and the provision on the land of any moveable structure for the purposes of the permitted use. The reference to "any land" may be taken to embrace the whole of the relevant planning unit, subject to the exclusion of any building which is located within that planning unit and also the exclusion of its curtilage. (For the definition of the 'planning unit' and the 'curtilage' of a building, see *Appendix B*.)

The land can be used for *any* purpose, *except* as a caravan site or for the display of an advertisement. A "caravan site" is defined by Article 2(1) of the GPDO as land on which a caravan is stationed for the purpose of human habitation and land which is used in conjunction with land on which a caravan is so stationed. "Caravan" has the same meaning as for the purposes of Part I of the Caravan Sites and Control of Development Act 1960. (For a more detailed discussion of these definitions, see *paragraph 19.2* in *Chapter 19*.)

Although the use of land as a caravan site is excluded from the development permitted by Part 4 (and is catered for instead by Part 5 - see *Chapter 19*), other forms of camping are permitted by this provision for up to 28 days in any one calendar year, and certain organisations are permitted by Part 5, Class C to camp for an unlimited time - see *part 20.1* of *Chapter 20*.

The display of advertisements is governed by the Town and Country Planning (Control of Advertisements) (England) Regulations 2007 (as amended). Whilst the display of advertisements is a material change of use of the building or land on which they are displayed, planning permission for this change of use is deemed to be granted by virtue of section 222 of the 1990 Act, if the advertisements are displayed in compliance with the Control of Advertisements Regulations, and no further permission is necessary in that case.

A further prohibition applies to land which is, or is within, a site of special scientific interest (SSSI). Such land may not be used for motor car and motor-cycle racing, including trials of speed, and practising for these activities, or for any other motor sports; nor may it be used for clay pigeon shooting, or for any war game. "War game" is defined for this purpose as an enacted, mock or imaginary battle conducted with weapons which are designed not to injure (including smoke bombs, or guns or grenades which fire or spray paint or are otherwise used to mark other participants), but excludes military activities or training exercises organised by or with the authority of the Secretary of State for Defence.

Temporary use of the land under Part 4, Class B, is permitted for not more than 28 days in total in any calendar year, but the land may not be used for more than 14 days in total for the purposes of holding a market, or for motor car and motorcycle racing, including trials of speed, and practising for these activities.

It has been held that a "market" would include similar selling uses, such as a car boot sale, so that this type of use is governed by the 14-day limit (*Fitzpatrick v SSE* [1988] J.P.L. 564). The former limitation of clay pigeon shooting to no more than 14 days was removed in 1989, and so this is permitted for up to 28 days.

So far as concerns "motor car and motorcycle racing, including trials of speed, and practising for these activities", the judgment in *Hart DC v Benford* [2006] EWHC 240 (QB) demonstrates that whether motor-cycling activities do actually fall within this category is a matter of fact and degree in each case, and it cannot be assumed that any such activities automatically constitute "motor car and motorcycle racing, including trials of speed, and practising for these activities". If they do not, then the 28-day limit would apply.

Note that where land is used for one or other of the two restricted uses (a market or motor sport) for up to 14 days in any calendar year, the remainder of the annual 28-day limit can be utilised for any other purposes permitted by Class B.

The 14/28-day limit applies to the whole of any one planning unit; separate 14/28-day periods of use cannot be claimed in respect of different areas within a large planning unit, such as a farm, unless this genuinely comprises two or more planning units. (This is a question of fact - *Fuller v SSE* (1988) 56 P. & C. R. 84; [1988] 1 P.L.R. 1.) [For the definition of a planning unit, see *part B.1* of *Appendix B.*]

Use of a planning unit under the provisions of Part 4 does not give rise to any right to change the use permanently to that or any other use under section 55(2)(f) of the 1990 Act. So this provision cannot be exploited to engineer a change of use to any other use.

16.2   The temporary nature of the permitted change of use

It was established in *S Bucks DC v SSE* [1989] J.P.L. 491, [1988] 2 P.L.R. 1 that each change of use from the normal use of the land to a temporary use is a separate development, which is individually permitted by Class B of Part 4. It follows that if an Article 4 Direction were to be made preventing further permitted development under this class of Part 4, the fact that this permitted development has already been implemented during the calendar year in question does not bestow any accrued right to use the land for the remainder of the 14 or 28 days in that calendar year; the Article 4 Direction would prevent any further changes of use to a temporary use which would otherwise be authorised by Class B for the remainder of that calendar year and in future years.

The development permitted by Class B is restricted to purely temporary changes of use. It follows that if a change of use is permanent, or is intended to be permanent, then in the absence of planning permission it is unlawful from the outset, and it cannot in those circumstances be claimed that such a change of use has the benefit of the 14-day or 28-day use permitted by Class B of Part 4. There has in the past been considerable litigation on this point, but it is clear from the decided cases that enforcement action can be taken immediately if it appears to the LPA that a breach of planning control has occurred, in the form of a material change of use that is (or is intended to be) permanent, notwithstanding that at the relevant time the use would be within the 14-day or 28-day period permitted by Class B if it were a genuinely temporary use that was not intended to continue beyond the relevant time limit.

There has been at least one appeal decision in which it was held that the 28-day period under Part 4, Class B continued to run (and was therefore being used up) where a site was open for use by campers, even though there were no tents on the site at the time.

The provision on the land of any moveable structure for the purposes of the permitted use is considered in *paragraph 16.4* below, but the decision of the Court of Appeal in *Ramsay v SSETR* [2001] EWHC 277 (Admin) demonstrates that (to quote Keene LJ) the carrying out of operations on the land, either in anticipation of the proposed use or accompanying it, *may* in some cases be relevant to the issue of whether the proposed use is a temporary one within the GPDO or is instead a permanent change of use of the land. This would arise if the operations make it difficult or impossible for the site realistically to revert to its previous normal use (such as agriculture) in between the occasions when the land is used for the new use. If the physical changes have that effect, then one would be dealing with a material change of use from the previous use (which had to all intents and purposes ceased) to the new use, even though the latter only in practice involves activity on 28 days or less a year. It is duration *and reversion to normal use* which is of importance.

But Keene LJ observed that this is the only relevance which such physical changes to the land are likely to have to this issue. If physical changes to the land are allowed to take place *and they do not prevent the normal permanent use from continuing for most of the year*, there is no reason in principle why the rights under Part 4 Class B of the GPDO should not be available for another use which does not take place for more than 28 days in the year. Nothing in the wording of the GPDO would prevent the deemed permission from being available in such a situation. There is no reference in Class B of Part 4 to the character or appearance of the land as a criterion or to its planning merits generally, but only to the maximum duration of the use during each year.

In *Ramsay*, the Court of Appeal held that the Inspector and the judge at first instance had both been wrong in attaching the significance which they did to the physical changes to the site. It is the duration of the proposed use *and the reversion in between times to the normal use of the land* which are the critical factors. If the site is used for a temporary use on no more than 28 days (or 14 days where applicable) in any one year and it reverts after each occasion to its normal use for the rest of the year, then the deemed permission in Part 4, Class B covers the proposed use. Those conditions were met in *Ramsay*.

As explained in *paragraph 16.4* below, structures that are left in place (and may therefore be regarded as permanent) are not authorised by Class B, so that these will be building or engineering operations requiring planning permission, but (in accordance with *Ramsay*) their continuing presence on the land does not make the change of use itself permanent, if the use of the land can, and does in practice, revert to its normal use notwithstanding the presence of those structures. (Although this issue was not directly in point in *Hart DC v Benford* [cited in *paragraph 16.1* above], that case illustrates a situation where the presence of structures did not amount to evidence of a permanent change of use.)

16.3   Reversion to normal use of the land

By section 57(3) of the 1990 Act, where by a development order, a local development order or a neighbourhood development order planning permission to develop land has been granted subject to limitations, planning permission is not required for the use of that land which (apart from its use in accordance with that permission) is its normal use; but by sub-section (5), in determining for this purpose what is or was the normal use of land, no account is to be taken of any use begun in contravention of planning control.

The limitation in this case is the 14/28-day time limit, and permission is not therefore required to revert to the normal use of the land. If that normal use is for agriculture or forestry, no planning permission would be required in any event, because by virtue of section 55(2)(e) of the 1990 Act, the use of any land for the purposes of agriculture or forestry is not to be taken for the purposes of the Act to involve development of the land.

As noted above, the reference to the purpose for which the planning unit was normally used previously means the last lawful use - Section 57(5). A difficulty could arise if temporary use of the land under Part 4, Class B follows an extended period of disuse after the cessation of a previous authorised use. The right to resume the previous use does not last indefinitely, and so in those circumstances any right to resume the previous use may have been lost. (See *Bramall v SSCLG* [2011] EWHC 1531 (Admin).)

The combined effect of sub-sections (3) and (5) is to allow the reversion under section 57(3) to the normal use of the land, even if there were several temporary or even unlawful uses after the last lawful use prior to the time-limited permitted development to which sub-section (3) applies. This does not, however, apply where the use immediately preceding an unlawful use *in respect of which an enforcement notice has been served* was also unlawful. In that case, it is not possible, having regard to the terms of section 57(4), to go back to an earlier lawful use, and so planning permission will be required. (See *Young v SSE* [1983] 3 W.L.R. 382; [1983] 2 A.C. 662.)

16.4 *Moveable structures*

The development permitted by Class B includes the provision on the land of any moveable structure for the purposes of the permitted use. The term 'moveable structure' is really a contradiction in terms, because if the objects provided on the land for the purposes of the permitted use are truly moveable, and are immediately removed each time the permitted temporary use ceases, they are unlikely to be classed as structures within the terms of the 1990 Act. On the other hand, if these objects can truly be described as structures (for example earth banks or bunds) and they are left in place when the land reverts to its normal use, then their provision or erection on the land would in those circumstances amount to building or engineering operations under section 55 of the 1990 Act, and would not qualify as permitted development under Class B.

The wording of Class B does not require the removal of 'moveable structures' immediately following the cessation of a temporary use. The length of time they are left in place is relevant only to the question of whether they are in truth, and remain, 'moveable structures'. This is an issue that has troubled the courts on a number of occasions. It was established in *Cardiff Rating Authority v Guest Keen Baldwin* [1949] 1 KB 385 that there are three primary factors to be considered - size, permanence and physical attachment. If an object brought onto the land is purely temporary, then it will probably not be regarded as a structure, but how temporary is 'temporary'? Even the presence of an item on site for a few months has been held to be enough for the item in question to be regarded as permanent. In *Skerritts of Nottingham v SSETR (No.2)* [2000] 2 P.L.R 102; [2000] J.P.L. 1025, a marquee which was erected for eight months of the year was held to be sufficiently permanent to be regarded as a structure.

If the object is so large that it cannot be moved without being dismantled, then that too is an indication that it is probably a structure. On the other hand, if dismantling is a relatively quick and easy operation, this may indicate that the item does not constitute a structure (*James v Brecon CC* (1963) 15 P. & C. R. 20), but this did not prevent the items in question being regarded as structures in the more recent '*Woolley Chickens*' case [*R (Save Woolley Valley Action Group Ltd) v Bath and North East Somerset Council* [2012] EWHC 2161 (Admin)].

As to whether a 'temporary' object has in practice become permanent, so as to make it a building or structure, in *Skerritts* Schiemann LJ put the point in this way:

"in situ for how long, to which I would answer: for a sufficient length of time to be of significance in the planning context".

In *R (Hall Hunter Partnership) v FSS [2006] EWHC 3482 (Admin)*, the High Court upheld an inspector's finding that the installation of polytunnels, which remained in one particular location for three months, amounted to the erection of a building. This had been found by the Inspector to be sufficient to be of consequence in the planning context.

In the "*Woolley Chickens*" case, which involved 'mobile' poultry sheds, the units were permanently in their field, and there was no limit on the length of time they would remain there - they could be there for years. The ability to move them around the field did not remove the significance of their presence in planning terms. The visual and landscape impact of the units would not be affected to any material extent by any periodic changes to their position in the field.

It follows that structures that are left in place for a significant length of time (and which may therefore be regarded as permanent) are not authorised by Part 4, Class B, so that these will be building or engineering operations requiring planning permission, but (in accordance with *Ramsay*) their continuing presence on the land does not make the change of use itself permanent, if the land can, and does in practice, revert to its normal use notwithstanding the presence of those structures. (Although this issue was not directly in point in *Hart DC v Benford* [cited in *paragraph 16.1* above], that case illustrates a situation where the presence of structures did not amount to evidence of a permanent change of use.)

CHAPTER 17

TEMPORARY CHANGES OF USE OF VARIOUS BUILDINGS

17.1 Temporary use as a state-funded school

Classes S and T in Part 3 of the Second Schedule to the GPDO (originally Classes MA and K respectively in the 1995 Order) were introduced as a means of facilitating the provision of 'free' schools, because it was perceived that the planning system was too slow and inflexible to enable such schools to be established as rapidly as the government wished. As a further means of speeding up the establishment of these 'free' schools, Part 4 of the Second Schedule was also amended to enable various premises to be used as a school for a temporary period while a permanent site is being developed or converted for use by the school.

17.1.1 The development permitted

Part 4, Class C permits the use of a building and any land within its curtilage as a state-funded school for a single academic year. (Note that, unlike Classes S and T in Part 3, the temporary permission granted by Class C of Part 4 does not extend to use as a registered nursery.)

"State-funded school" means a school funded wholly or mainly from public funds, including an Academy school, an alternative provision Academy or a 16 to 19 Academy established under the Academies Act 2010, or a school maintained by a local authority, as defined in section 142(1) of the School Standards and Framework Act 1998. "Academic year" means any period beginning with 1 August and ending with the next 31 July.

The definition of the building's curtilage is not restricted in any way, and so the generally accepted definition of the word discussed in *paragraph B.2.1* in *Appendix B* applies.

Under paragraph C.2(a), the site must be one which is approved for use as a state-funded school by the Secretary of State who has policy responsibility for schools, and the relevant Minister must notify the LPA of the approval and of the proposed opening date of the school.

The site must be used as a state-funded school and for no other purpose. This precludes any other purpose falling within Use Class D1 (non-residential institutions), except to the extent that the other purpose is ancillary to the primary use of the site as a state-funded school.

The permission is granted for only one academic year and it may be used only once in relation to a particular site, which must then revert to its previous lawful use at the end of the academic year.

Where the pre-existing use of the building is or was as a public house or wine bar etc. (under Use Class A4), it is subject to the provisions referred to in *paragraph 17.1.2.* below.

17.1.2   Exclusions and other conditions

Only a building that falls wholly and exclusively within a single use class within the Use Classes Order can qualify for such temporary use. If a building has a *sui generis* use (including a mixed use, even if the various elements of that use would by themselves fall within one or other of the use classes) its use cannot be changed under this Class of permitted development.

Development is not permitted by Class C if the building is a listed building or is a scheduled monument (although the exclusion in respect of a listed building does not specifically extend to a building within its curtilage, where the curtilage building is not itself listed). Nor is it permitted where the site is or forms part of a military explosives storage area or a safety hazard area.

So far as a building which is within the curtilage of a listed building is concerned (which is not specifically disqualified from temporary change of use under Part 4, Class C), readers should refer to the discussion in *paragraph 5.2.3* in *Chapter 5* regarding the effect of section 1(5) of the Listed Buildings Act in this context, which may still have the effect of disqualifying the building from change of use under Part 4, Class C.

Development is also precluded where the building is within a safety hazard area or a military explosives storage area. The definitions of a "safety hazard area" and of a "military explosives storage area" are set out in Article 2(1), and are quoted at the end of *paragraph 3.2.3* in *Chapter 3.*

Finally, development under Class C is not permitted if the building in question is used within Use Class A4 (drinking establishments), where that building has been either nominated or designated as an "asset of community value" ('ACV'). (For a detailed explanation of the extent of this restriction, see *paragraph 3.1.3* of *Chapter 3.*) Even if the site has been approved for use as a state-funded school by the schools minister, this does not override this exclusion (except in the circumstances described below).

In the case of a building which is not an asset of community value but which is used for a purpose falling within Use Class A4, it is a condition that, before beginning the development, the developer must send a written request to the LPA as to whether the building has been nominated for designation as an ACV. This request must include the address of the building, the developer's contact address (and the developer's email address if the developer is content to receive communications electronically). The relevant procedure is discussed in detail in *paragraph 3.1.3* of *Chapter 3.*

However, there is a transitional provision in Article 8(2), preserving the saving effect of Article 6 in the March 2015 amendment order (which has been otherwise repealed by the consolidated 2015 Order). This provides that if a change of use is carried out in accordance with the requirements of Class C, *and the site was approved for use as a state-funded school by the relevant Minister prior to 6 April 2015*, Class 4, Part C of the 1995 Order continues to apply to that development, so that the restriction and/or condition mentioned above relating to Assets of Community Value does not apply to that development. This saving provision will cease to have effect after 14 April 2018.

There is no prohibition of this temporary change of use in National Parks, Areas of Outstanding Natural Beauty, World Heritage Sites, Conservation Areas or Sites of Special Scientific Interest.

Except for the approval of the schools minister mentioned in *paragraph 17.1.1*, no prior approval in respect of this temporary use is required.

17.1.3   *Operational development*

Perhaps rather surprisingly, bearing in mind the strictly limited time during which a building can be used as a school under Class C of Part 4, operational development under Part 7 is nevertheless permitted in such cases. Paragraph O in Part 7 confirms this. It specifically provides that, for the purposes of Part 7, "school" includes a building permitted by Class C of Part 4 to be used temporarily as a school, from the date the local planning authority is notified as provided in paragraph C.2(b) of Part 4.

Class M of Part 7 permits the erection, extension or alteration of a school building within the curtilage of an existing school, for use as part of, or for a purpose incidental to, the use of that school, and there is no exclusion of this permitted development right by paragraph M.3 (in contrast to buildings whose use has been changed under Class S of Part 3). Class M of Part 7 refers specifically to an "existing" school. It is clear, therefore, that the permitted development right under Class M cannot arise until after the temporary use as a school permitted by Part 4 has commenced.

Development under Class M of Part 7 is subject to various limitations and restrictions (set out in paragraph M.1), and this development is subject to a condition that it is only to be used as part of, or for a purpose incidental to, the use of that school. There is no requirement for the removal of any such built development when the site ceases to be used as a school, but this would appear to leave the use of any such extra buildings or structures in limbo when the temporary school use ceases.

Class N of Part 7 permits the provision of a hard surface within the curtilage of any school, to be used for the purposes of that school, and the replacement in whole or in part of such a surface. ('Curtilage' is not defined for the purposes of Part 7, and so the generally accepted definition of this term applies - see *paragraph B.2.1* in *Appendix B*.) Although Class N of Part 7 does not refer to an "existing" school, it is clear from its wording that the permitted development right under Class N cannot arise until after the temporary use as a school permitted by Part 4 has actually commenced. Before this occurs, the premises cannot properly be described as a 'school'. (The provisions of Part 7, Classes M and N are discussed in more detail in *paragraph 10.1.5* of *Chapter 10*.)

In the same way, various minor operations are permitted under Part 2. These are briefly summarised in *paragraph 5.2.9* of *Chapter 5*, and they include in Class A the erection, construction, maintenance, improvement or alteration of a gate, fence, wall or other means of enclosure up to 2 metres high at a school, even where this adjoins a highway used by vehicular traffic (provided that any part of it which is more than 1 metre above ground level does not create an obstruction to the view of highway users so as to cause danger to them). Paragraph A.2 in Part 2 confirms that, for the purposes of Class A, "school" includes a building permitted by Class C of Part 4 to be used temporarily as a school, from the date the local planning authority is notified as provided in paragraph C.2(b) of Part 4. Operations permitted by Part 2 also include the formation or laying out of an access to a highway, as discussed in *paragraph 5.2.9*.

17.2   Temporary use of various business premises

17.2.1   The development permitted

Part 4, Class D permits a change of use of a building and any land within its curtilage from a use falling within Use Class A1 (shops), A2 (financial and professional services), A3 (restaurants and cafés), A4 (drinking establishments), A5 (hot food take-aways), B1 (business), D1 (non-residential institutions) or D2 (assembly and leisure), or from use as a betting office or pay day loan shop, to a "flexible" use falling within Use Class A1 (shops), A2 (financial and professional services), A3 (restaurants and cafés) [but *not* Use Classes A4 or A5] or Use Class B1 (business) for a single continuous period of up to two years beginning on the date the building and any land within its curtilage begins to be used for one of the flexible uses, or on the date given in the notice to the LPA under paragraph D.2(a) (mentioned in *paragraph 17.2.2* below), whichever is the earlier.

17.2.2   Exclusions, restrictions and other conditions

Development is not permitted by Class D if it relates to more than 150 sq m in the building.

The definition of the building's curtilage is not restricted in any way, and so the generally accepted definition of the word discussed in *paragraph B.2.1* in *Appendix B* applies. The area of the curtilage is not taken into account in any way in relation to the floorspace limit mentioned above.

Development is not permitted by Class D if the building is a listed building or is a scheduled monument (although this exclusion does not specifically extend to a building within the curtilage of a listed building, where the curtilage building is not itself listed). Nor is it permitted where the site is or forms part of a military explosives storage area or a safety hazard area.

As noted in the preceding paragraph, the definitions of a "safety hazard area" and of a "military explosives storage area" are set out in Article 2(1), and are quoted at the end of *paragraph 3.2.3* in *Chapter 3*.

So far as a building which is within the curtilage of a listed building is concerned (which is not specifically disqualified from temporary change of use under Part 4, Class D), readers should refer to the discussion in *paragraph 5.2.3* in *Chapter 5* regarding the effect of section 1(5) of the Listed Buildings Act in this context, which may still have the effect of disqualifying the building from change of use under Class D.

Development is also precluded under Class D if the building in question is used within Use Class A4 (drinking establishments), where that building has been either nominated or designated as an "asset of community value" ('ACV'). (For a detailed explanation of the extent of this restriction, see *paragraph 3.1.3* of *Chapter 3*.) This restriction applies regardless of whether any notification of the change of use has been given to the LPA under paragraph D.2(a) (as to which see below).

In the case of a building which is not an asset of community value but which is used for a purpose falling within Use Class A4, the same conditions apply as they do to development under Class C. (See *paragraph 17.1.2* above and *paragraph 3.1.3* of *Chapter 3*.)

However, there is a transitional provision in Article 8(2), preserving the saving effect of Article 6 in the March 2015 amendment order (which has been otherwise repealed by the consolidated 2015 Order). This provides that if a change of use is carried out in accordance with the requirements of Class D, a*nd the developer has notified (or further notified) the local planning authority under paragraph D.2(a) of Part 4 of that Schedule of the change of use prior to 6 April 2015*, Class 4, Part D of the 1995 Order continues to apply to that development, so that the restriction and/or condition mentioned above relating to Assets of Community Value does not apply to that development. This saving provision will cease to have effect after 14 April 2018.

Although further changes of use within the specified use classes can take place within the two-year period, a change of use under Class D cannot be made again in the future.

Under paragraph D.2(a), the developer must notify the local planning authority of the date the site will begin to be used for one of the flexible uses, and what that use will be, before the use begins, and at any given time during the two-year period referred to in Class D the site can be used at any one time only for one of the use classes comprising the flexible use, but the site may at any time during the two-year period change use to a use falling within one of the other use classes comprising the flexible use, subject to further notification to the LPA. However, no prior approval is required.

For the purposes of the Use Classes Order and the GPDO, during the period of flexible use the site will retain the use class it had before changing to any of the flexible uses under Class D. So the temporary change of use permitted by Class D cannot be exploited to engineer a further change of use under the terms of Part 3. On the other hand, if minor operational development under Part 2 of the Second Schedule to the GPDO (summarised in *paragraph 5.2.9* of *Chapter 5*) is genuinely required in connection with the temporary change of use permitted by Part 4, Class D, then there would appear to be nothing in principle to prevent this.

CHAPTER 18

TEMPORARY USE OF BUILDINGS OR LAND FOR FILM-MAKING

18.1   The development permitted

Part 4, Class E is a new class of permitted development, first introduced on 15 April 2015.

Class E(a) permits the temporary use of any land or buildings for a period not exceeding 9 months in any 27-month period for the purpose of commercial film-making. The reference to *"any land or buildings"* may be taken to embrace the whole of the relevant planning unit (as to which, see *part B.1* of *Appendix B*).

"Commercial film-making" means filming for broadcast or transmission, but does not include the filming of persons paying to visit the site to participate in any leisure activity on that site, including motor car and motorcycle racing including trials of speed or other motor sports, and practising for those activities, or clay pigeon shooting or any war game. [The definition of a "war game" is the same as it is for the purposes of Class B in Part 4 (see *paragraph 16.1* in *Chapter 16*).]

The term "broadcast or transmission" used within the definition of commercial film-making means broadcast of the film or television programme by a television programme provider, or any other person for commercial gain, the transmission of it (including over the internet) by a television programme provider, or by any other person for commercial gain, or theatrical release of it at the commercial cinema. "Television programme provider" in this context has the meaning given in section 99(2) of the Broadcasting Act 1996.

Class E(b) permits the provision on such land, during the filming period under Class E (i.e. the period, not exceeding 9 months in total, during which the land or building is used for commercial film-making, including activities preparatory to, or otherwise related to, that film-making), of any temporary structures, works, plant or machinery required in connection with that use. However, the height of any temporary structure, works, plant or machinery provided under Class E(b) must not exceed 15 metres, or 5 metres where any part of the structure, works, plant or machinery is within 10 metres of the "curtilage" [*sic*] of the land.

The use of the word "curtilage" in this context is anomalous. It is presumably meant to refer to the boundary of the land in question. A further problem arising from the drafting of Class E is the definition of "site" in paragraph F, which, for the purposes of Part 4, means "the building and any land within its curtilage", but Class E can clearly apply to any land, even if there is no building on it. One can only make sense of these definitions by assuming that where the word "site" is used, it refers to a building and the curtilage of that building, but not to the whole of the planning unit of which that building and its curtilage form a part. On the other hand, the words "any land" in the first line of Class E(a) and "such land" in Class E(b) are clearly capable of applying to all the land within a particular planning unit. [See *Appendix B* with regard to the identification of the planning unit and the definition of "curtilage".]

18.2   *Exclusions and restrictions*

Development is not permitted by Class E if the land in question, or the land on which the building in question is situated, is more than 1.5 hectares in area.

The development permitted does not include the use of the land for over-night accommodation.

Development under Class E is precluded if the land or building is on 'article 2(3) land' (i.e. if it is in a conservation area, an area of outstanding natural beauty, the Broads, a National Park or a World Heritage Site).

Development under Class E is also precluded if the land or the site on which the building is located is or forms part of a site of special scientific interest, or of a safety hazard area or military explosives storage area, if the land or building is, or contains, a scheduled monument, or if the land or building is a listed building or is within the curtilage of a listed building.

As noted earlier, the definitions of "safety hazard area" and of "military explosives storage area" are set out in Article 2(1) of the GPDO, and are quoted at the end of *paragraph 3.2.3* in *Chapter 3*.

So far as a building within the curtilage of a listed building is concerned, the relevant curtilage in this context (consistent with the interpretation of other legislative provisions prohibiting or restricting development within the curtilage of a listed building) must be taken to refer to the curtilage of the building *at the time when it was first listed*. (See *paragraph B.2.2* in *Appendix B* and the judgment in *R (Egerton) v Taunton Deane BC* cited in that paragraph.) The inclusion in the listing of any building attached to the listed building is also discussed at *paragraph B.2.3*.

18.3   *Prior approval*

Before beginning the start of each new filming period (see the definition of "filming period" in *paragraph 18.1*), the developer must apply to the local planning authority for a determination as to whether the prior approval of the authority will be required as to:

(a)   the schedule of dates which make up the filming period in question and the hours of operation;

(b)   transport and highways impacts of the development;

(c)   noise impacts of the development;

(d)   light impacts of the development, in particular the effect on any occupier of neighbouring land of any artificial lighting to be used; and

(e)   flooding risks on the site.

The determination of the prior approval application in respect of these issues is governed by paragraph E.3 (see below).

The prior approval application must be accompanied by a written description of the proposed development, a plan indicating the site and showing the proposed development, the developer's contact address, the developer's email address (if the developer is content to receive communications electronically) and a site-specific flood risk assessment, together with the appropriate application fee.

In contrast to the provisions of Part 3, there is no specific provision as to the making of an application under Class E(b) at the same time as an application under Class E(a), but (bearing in mind paragraph E.3(3) - referred to below), where prior approval is required in respect of a proposed development under Class E(b), it would clearly be advisable, if not essential, that both should be dealt with together.

The extent to which drawings of proposed temporary structures are required is also debateable, bearing in mind that paragraph E.3(2)(b) refers only to "a plan", although this must not only indicate the site, but must also "show the proposed development". As in the case of prior approvals under Part 3, the power given to the LPA by paragraph E.3(3) to reject a prior approval application if, in their opinion, the developer has provided insufficient information to enable the authority to establish whether the proposed development complies with the applicable conditions, limitations or restrictions in Class E (for example, as to the height of any temporary structures, etc.) may in practice persuade film-makers that they need to provide sufficient drawings and other information to enable the various impacts of the proposed development to be properly assessed. The application can also be rejected under paragraph E.3(3) if, in the opinion of the LPA, the proposed development does not in any event comply with any of those conditions, limitations or restrictions.

Unfortunately (in contrast to paragraph W(2)(e) in Part 3), paragraph E.3(2)(e) of Part 4 does not make the provision of a flood risk assessment dependent upon the requirement in paragraph E.3(6) for the Environment Agency to be consulted. Thus, in theory, a site specific flood risk assessment must be provided in every case. In practice, it is to be hoped that LPAs will agree that the time and expense of doing so would not be justified where none of the conditions referred to in paragraph E.3(6) applies to the site.

The fee payable where the application relates only to the temporary change of use for film-making is £80. Where the application relates both to that change of use and to associated operational development to be carried out as permitted development in connection with the film-making use, the combined fee is £172 - see the Town and Country Planning (Fees for Applications, Deemed Applications, Requests and Site Visits) (England) Regulations 2012, Reg.14(1)(za) and (zb). The local planning authority is not entitled to demand any other fees in connection with the prior approval application.

The other provisions in paragraph E.3 largely mirror the provisions of paragraph W in Part 3, including consultations, the posting of a site notice and serving notice on neighbours (all of which are the LPA's responsibility), and readers are recommended to refer to *Chapters 13, 14* and *15* with regard to the processing and determination of the prior approval application although, so far as a request for further information by the LPA is concerned, paragraph E.3(9) does not allow for additional details of any proposed temporary structures, plant or machinery, etc. to be demanded (unlike paragraph W(9)(c) in Part 3).

The only consideration that has to be taken into account which is not to be found in any of the classes of development permitted by Part 3 is that relating to light impacts of the development, and in particular the effect on any occupier of neighbouring land of any artificial lighting to be used (and this is listed at *paragraph 14.4.8* in *Chapter 14*). This would fall to be considered in the same way as it would in the case of a planning application where such an issue arises. The relevance of the NPPF and the Development Plan, etc. in this context is also discussed in *Chapter 14*.

As indicated above, the 56-day rule applies (see *Chapter 15*), as does the power of the LPA to impose conditions on the prior approval, subject to the constraints mentioned in *paragraph 14.5* in *Chapter 14*.

There is no provision in Class E for the permitted development to be commenced within a specified time limit after prior approval is given but, bearing in mind that the matters on which the LPA's prior approval are required include the schedule of dates which make up the filming period in question and the hours of operation, this in itself will govern the dates when this development can take place. Furthermore, the LPA is entitled to impose a condition requiring compliance with the approved schedule and specified hours of operation. Where the circumstances justify it, the condition could be more restrictive than the hours of operation proposed in the application, although such a condition would have to be relevant to one or more of the specific matters that are the subject of the prior approval.

It is a condition of the development permitted by Class E that any structure, works, plant or machinery provided under this permission must, as soon as practicable after the end of each filming period, be removed from the land, and that the land on which any development permitted by Class E has been carried out must, as soon as reasonably practicable after the end of the filming period, be reinstated to its condition before that development was carried out. (The definition of a "filming period" is set out in *paragraph 18.1 above*.)

CHAPTER 19

TEMPORARY USE AS A CARAVAN SITE

19.1 The scope of the temporary use permitted

Part 5, Class A of the Second Schedule to the GPDO permits the temporary use of land, other than a building, as a caravan site in accordance with paragraphs 2 to 10 of Schedule 1 to the Caravan Sites and Control of Development Act 1960. These are all cases where a caravan site licence is not required. However, this permitted development right does not extend to use for winter quarters under paragraph 10 of that schedule (see *paragraph 19.10* below).

It should also be noted that removal of the exemption from the requirement for a site licence, by an order made under Paragraph 13 of Schedule 1 to the 1960 Act, has the effect of removing the corresponding permitted development right under Part 5, Class A. (This is explained in more detail in *paragraph 19.11* below.)

Thus, if the use of a site is not exempt from the requirement to obtain a caravan site licence, either because the use does not meet all the criteria of the relevant paragraph in Schedule 1 to the 1960 Act or because the exemption has been withdrawn by an order made under Paragraph 13 of that schedule, then the use of the site for the temporary stationing of a caravan or caravans for the purpose human habitation cannot be permitted development under Part 5, Class A, of the Second Schedule to the GPDO.

The exemptions under Schedule 1 of the 1960 Act fall into two distinct categories. First, certain leisure or holiday caravanning is exempted, and these uses are covered by paragraphs 2 to 6 of the schedule. Secondly, there are certain work-related uses covered by paragraphs 7 to 10 of the schedule.

However, the development permitted by Part 5, Class A, does not extend to the uses specified in paragraphs 11 and 11A of the schedule (the use as a caravan site of land occupied by the local authority in whose area the land is situated, and the use of land occupied by a county council as a caravan site providing accommodation for gypsies). Whilst these uses are exempt from site licensing under the 1960 Act, they are not permitted development and therefore require planning permission.

The reference in Class A to *"land, other than a building"* may be taken to refer to the whole of the planning unit in question, but excluding any building located within that planning unit. On the other hand, land within the curtilage of any such building is not precluded from use under Class A. (As to the identification of the planning unit, see *part B.1* of *Appendix B.*)

The temporary use of land as a caravan site for leisure or holiday purposes under Part 5 of the Second Schedule to the GPDO does not fall within Use Class

D2, and is therefore a *sui generis* use. These provisions cannot therefore be exploited to engineer a change of use to other types of leisure development.

19.2   The definition of "caravan site" and "caravan"

A "caravan site" is defined by Article 2(1) of the GPDO as land on which a caravan is stationed for the purpose of human habitation and land which is used in conjunction with land on which a caravan is so stationed. "Caravan" has the same meaning as for the purposes of Part I of the Caravan Sites and Control of Development Act 1960. The definition of a caravan contained in section 29(1) of this Act is:

"any structure designed or adapted for human habitation which is capable of being moved from one place to another (whether by being towed, or by being transported on a motor vehicle or trailer) and any motor vehicle so designed or adapted"

This definition of a 'caravan' for the purposes of the 1960 Act was extended by section 13 of the Caravan Sites Act 1968 to include significantly larger structures, referred to in the heading to that section as 'twin unit caravans', and often referred to as 'static' caravans or 'mobile homes'.

This provides that a structure designed or adapted for human habitation which is composed of not more than two sections separately constructed, and designed to be assembled on a site by means of bolts, clamps or other devices, and which is, when assembled, physically capable of being moved by road from one place to another (whether by being towed, or by being transported on a motor vehicle or trailer), is not to be treated as not being a caravan within the meaning of Part I of the Caravan Sites and Control of Development Act 1960 by reason only that it cannot lawfully be moved on a highway when assembled.

This is subject to dimensional limits – it must not be more than 65.616 feet (20 metres) in length (exclusive of any drawbar) and 22.309 feet (6.8 metres) in width, with the overall height of the living accommodation (measured internally from the floor at the lowest level to the ceiling at the highest level) not exceeding 10.006 feet (3.05 metres). The current dimensions were set by the Caravan Sites Act 1968 & Social Landlords (Permissible Additional Purposes) (England) Order 2006 (Definition of Caravan) (Amendment) (England) Order 2006 (S.I. 2006 No. 2374).

19.3   Cessation of the temporary use

The permitted development under Part 5 is subject to the condition that this use must be discontinued when the site ceases to qualify for exemption under these provisions, and that all caravans on the site must then be removed as soon as reasonably practicable. The well-known judgment in *R (Hall Hunter Partnership) v FSS* [2006] EWHC 3482 (Admin), in addition to dealing with the planning status of polytunnels, addressed the provisions of Part 5 in relation to the use of land as a caravan site to accommodate seasonal agricultural workers (referred to below in *paragraph 19.8*) and, in particular, the condition set out in paragraph A.1 that '*the use shall be discontinued........ and all caravans on the site shall be removed as soon as reasonably practical*' when the provisions of Schedule 1 to the 1960 Act cease to apply.

In *Hall Hunter* there was no dispute that in November or by early December 2004, all the caravans were removed from the site and stored elsewhere until they returned in February 2005. However, the infrastructure, comprising the pathways, the drainage, and the electrical and water supplies serving the caravans, all remained in place throughout the year.

The appellant relied on *Ramsay* (cited at *paragraph 16.2* in *Chapter 16*) to support their contention that in the winter period, the land remained available for other uses such as the parking of vehicles associated with the farm and the storage of agricultural equipment, although there was no clear evidence that such use had occurred to a material extent. In the appeal decision that was under challenge in the High Court, the Inspector held that whilst it would not be impossible for this area to be used for some agricultural purpose such as incidental parking or storage, it was clearly separated from the surrounding land by an earth bund and fencing, with access limited to a group of farm buildings, and care would be needed in such use to prevent damage to the infrastructure.

The Inspector concluded that, realistically, to all intents and purposes, the land remained designed and fitted out for use as a caravan site and it would not lose the characteristic of a caravan site merely because the caravans are removed for the time being. As a matter of fact and degree, the use as a caravan site would not be discontinued and the scheme would not be in compliance with the condition in paragraph A.1 of Part 5, Class A.

The court upheld the Inspector's decision. Sullivan J (as he then was) noted that there are two separate aspects to the condition in A.1 of Class A; not only must the use as a caravan site be discontinued, but all caravans on the land must also be removed. Since caravans cannot by definition be occupied on the site once they have been removed from it, the condition envisages that there may be circumstances where mere removal of the caravans may not be sufficient to bring the use of the land as a caravan site to an end.

Whether removal of the caravans will of itself be sufficient to bring a use as a caravan site to an end will be very much a matter of fact and degree in each case. When the caravans have departed, do they leave behind an agricultural field or do they leave behind an empty caravan site with all the necessary infrastructure, pathways, services et cetera waiting for them to return? The Inspector's conclusion in this regard was unassailable.

19.4   *Caravans within the curtilage of a dwellinghouse*

It will be noted that the development permitted by Part 5 does not include the use of land as a caravan site in accordance with paragraph 1 of the Schedule, which exempts such a use from the site licensing requirements of the Act if this use is incidental to the enjoyment as such of a dwellinghouse within the curtilage of which the land is situated. It would seem that the exclusion of this use from the development permitted by Part 5 was probably based on the assumption that such a use would be exempt from the definition of development by virtue of section 55(2)(d). It is in fact capable of being a primary use of the land within Use Class C3, although the exemption from site licensing under the 1960 Act would only apply to a caravan that is situated within the curtilage of the dwelling (see *part 2* of *Appendix B*) and provided also that its use remains *incidental* to the enjoyment of the dwellinghouse as such (as distinct from its being an ancillary use or part of the primary residential use).

If, however, the stationing of a caravan within the curtilage of a dwellinghouse may be seen as a building operation (on the basis of the judicial authorities referred to in *paragraph 16.4* of *Chapter 16*, which apply generally, and not just in the context of Part 4, Class B) then, although the exemption from the requirement for a caravan site licence would still apply, such operational development does not come within the exemption provided by section 55(2)(d).

In practice, the stationing of a caravan within the curtilage of a dwellinghouse may be permitted development within Part 1, Class E of the Second Schedule to the GPDO (subject to its precise positioning in relation to the house, and compliance with the other conditions in that part of the GPDO, and provided that is genuinely required for a purpose incidental to the enjoyment of the dwellinghouse as such, and is not used as part of the primary residential use of the dwelling or used as a separate dwelling), unless permitted development rights under Part 1 have been removed either by a condition attached to a planning permission or by an Article 4 Direction. However, as operational development, this lies outside the scope of the present work.

19.5   *Temporary caravan camping on a small site*

Paragraph 2 exempts the use of land as a caravan site by a person travelling with a caravan who brings the caravan onto the land for a period that includes not more than two nights, provided that during that period no other caravan is stationed for the purpose of human habitation on that land or on any adjoining land in the same occupation, and provided also that a caravan or caravans have not been stationed anywhere on that land or on any adjoining land in the same occupation for an aggregate of more than 28 days during the preceding 12 months.

Similar considerations apply to this 28-day use as apply under Part 4, Class

B. Thus if the use as a caravan site exceeds 28 days in any one 12-month period, or is intended from the outset to exceed that limit, then in the absence of planning permission it is unlawful, and it cannot in those circumstances be claimed that such a use has the benefit of being permitted development under Part 5, Class A.

From the decided cases under Part 4, Class B it is clear that enforcement action can be taken immediately if it appears to the LPA that a breach of planning control has occurred, in the form of a use that exceeds (or is intended to exceed) the 28-day limit, notwithstanding that at the relevant time the use would be within the 28-day limit permitted. The same would clearly apply to Part 5, Class A if it appears that the use as a caravan site is likely or is intended to exceed the 28-day limit. The same would also apply to exceeding the 2-night limit of stay and/or having more than one caravan on the site at a time (unless the site is not less than 5 acres in size, and reliance is placed instead on paragraph 3 - see *paragraph 19.6* below).

It also follows that the 28-day limit applies to the whole of any one planning unit (i.e. "that land or any adjoining land in the same occupation"). Separate 28-day periods of use cannot be claimed in respect of different areas within a larger planning unit, such as a farm, unless this genuinely comprises two or more planning units. (This is a question of fact - *Fuller v SSE* (1988) 56 P. & C. R. 84; [1988] 1 P.L.R. 1.) [For the definition of a planning unit, see *part B.1* of *Appendix B*.]

19.6   *Temporary caravan camping on larger sites*

In the case of larger sites, paragraph 3 exempts the use as a caravan site of land which, together with any adjoining land which is in the same occupation and has not been built on, provided it comprises not less than 5 acres. Here again, there is a proviso that the land must not have been used as a caravan site for an aggregate of more than 28 days during the preceding 12 months. In addition, in that period, not more than 3 caravans must have been stationed there at any one time. This exemption is not subject to the 2-night limit in paragraph 2, although every night that there is a caravan on the site will eat into the 28-day limit within any 12-month period. Nor, under paragraph 3, is the use limited to a single caravan at a time. The paragraph is awkwardly drafted, but its effect is clearly to limit the number of caravans at any one time to no more than three.

The observations as to the 28-day limit in *paragraph 19.5* above apply equally to a use that is claimed to be permitted in accordance with Paragraph 3, including the application of that time limit to the entire planning unit, so that 28-day uses for this purpose cannot be claimed in respect of separate parts of the same planning unit. Similarly, having more than three caravans on the land at any one time would render the use of the site for this purpose unlawful.

19.7 Temporary caravan camping by exempted organisations

Paragraph 4 exempts the use as a caravan site of land which is occupied by an organisation which holds for the time being a certificate of exemption granted under paragraph 12 of the First Schedule to the 1960 Act, if the use is for purposes of recreation and is under the supervision of that organisation. Certificates of exemption have been issued to the Caravan Club and to the Camping Club of Great Britain and Ireland. There is an informal procedure whereby those organisations have undertaken to obtain the agreement of the LPA to the opening of a site which is exempted under this paragraph.

There is a further exemption for the certificated organisations under paragraph 5, whereby the use of land as a caravan site is exempted where a certificate approving the site has been issued under this paragraph by one of those exempted organisations, provided that not more than 5 caravans are at any one time stationed for the purpose of human habitation on the land to which the certificate relates. The paragraph authorises an exempted organisation to issue a certificate, for not more than a year at a time, which may be renewed each year, stating that the land has been approved by the exempted organisation for use by its members for the purposes of recreation. The organisation must notify the DCLG of the details of any such certificates that it issues. Again, the exempted organisations have undertaken to inform LPAs as soon as possible when they issue an approval certificate for a site under this paragraph.

In addition, paragraph 6 exempts the use of land as a caravan site if the use is for a meeting lasting not more than 5 days for members of one of the exempted organisations mentioned above, and is under its supervision and in pursuance of arrangements made by that organisation.

19.7.1 Certification of exempted organisations

As mentioned in *paragraph 19.7* above, the only two organisations to which Certificates of exemption have been issued are the Caravan Club and the Camping Club of Great Britain and Ireland, but paragraph 12 of the First Schedule to the 1960 Act gives the Secretary of State power for the purposes of paragraphs 4, 5 and 6 of that Schedule to grant a certificate of exemption to any organisation as to which he is satisfied that its objects include the encouragement or promotion of recreational activities. However, a certificate granted under paragraph 12 may be withdrawn by the Secretary of State at any time.

These provisions in Part 5, Class A (and in the First Schedule to the 1960 Act) are entirely separate from the permitted development under Part 5, Class C (explained in *paragraph 20.1* of *Chapter 20*) allowing the use of land for the purposes of recreation or instruction by other organisations that hold certificates under section 269 of the Public Health Act 1936.

19.8 Temporary accommodation for agricultural or forestry workers

Paragraph 7 exempts the use as a caravan site of agricultural land for the accommodation during a particular season of a person or persons employed in farming operations on land in the same occupation. This does not permit the provision of a permanent caravan site, even if it is used only for the accommodation of seasonal workers (*North v Brown* (1974) 231 E.G. 737).

In *Vale of White Horse District Council v Mirmalek-Sani* (1993) 25 H.L.R. 387, caravans used for accommodating workers on a poultry farm were occupied all year round. It was held that this did not fall within the exemption under paragraph 7 and therefore required both a site licence and planning permission. Attention has also been drawn in *paragraph 19.3* above to the judgment in *R (Hall Hunter Partnership) v FSS*, so far as the seasonal nature of the use is concerned, and compliance with the requirement to remove the caravans when the seasonal use comes to an end.

Paragraph 8 exempts the use as a caravan site of land used for the purposes of forestry (including afforestation) for the accommodation during a particular season of a person or persons employed on land in the same occupation. As in the case of paragraph 7, this does not permit the provision of a permanent caravan site, even if it is used only for the accommodation of seasonal workers, nor must it be used other than on a seasonal basis.

This permitted change of use relates only to the stationing of a caravan for residential purposes. It has been held that the stationing of a caravan on agricultural land to provide a weatherproof place for the storage and mixing of food for cattle was ancillary to the agricultural use of the land and did not amount to a material change of use (*Wealden DC v SSE* [1988] J.P.L. 268). However, such a caravan might now be regarded as a building or structure, in light of the decision in *R (Save Woolley Valley Action Group Ltd) v Bath and North East Somerset Council* [2012] EWHC 2161 (Admin), applying and extending the rules established by *Cardiff Rating Authority v Guest Keen Baldwin* [1949] 1 KB 385 and *Skerritts of Nottingham v SSETR (No.2)* [2000] 2 P.L.R 102; [2000] J.P.L. 1025.

19.9 Temporary accommodation for workers on building and engineering sites

Paragraph 9 exempts the use as a caravan site of land which forms part of, or adjoins, land on which building or engineering operations are being carried out (being operations for the carrying out of which planning permission has, if required, been granted) if that use is for the accommodation of a person or persons employed in connection with those operations.

There are several points that are relevant in deciding whether this exemption applies (and therefore whether the use is permitted under Part 5). First, it is not necessary that the caravan should be located on the site (or planning unit) on which the building or engineering operations are being carried out. It has been established in other contexts that 'adjoining' need not mean immediately contiguous, but it must be nearby.

The next point is that the building or engineering operations must be lawful, i.e. if they need planning permission then it is a necessary qualification that planning permission has been granted (or is deemed to be granted by virtue of a development order). Furthermore, they must be in the course of being carried out. Occupation in anticipation of building or engineering operations, or after those operations have been completed or have been abandoned is not permitted by Class A of Part 5.

Finally, the person or persons occupying the caravan(s) must be "employed in connection with" those building or engineering operations. The term "employed" does not necessarily denote paid employment; it suffices that the persons in question are 'engaged' in a general sense in connection with those works. It is not necessary that they should be directly engaged in the building or engineering operations themselves, provided they are engaged in some way *in connection with* those operations. This would clearly include somebody doing a self-build, and might reasonably include their dependants. However, if they are employing contractors and are not directly involved in the work or, at the very least, in project-managing the work, it would appear that the exemption under Paragraph 9 (and the permitted development under Class A of Part 5) would not cover that person and their family living in a caravan on or adjoining the site pending the completion of their new home.

These points were considered by the Divisional Court in *Adams v Shadey* (25 April 1985, unreported - Q.B.D, Farquharson and Tudor Price JJ), summarised in [1987] J.P.L. 185 (*Caravans and self builders* - P.T. Adams). The court reached the following conclusions:

(a)   For the purposes of both paragraph 9 of the First Schedule and permitted development under Class XXII [now Part 5, Class A of the Second Schedule to the 2015 GPDO] "employed in connection with" includes "undertaking";

(b)   The exemption is satisfied if *some* work is being carried out over an extended period on the site;

(c)   More than one caravan may be acceptable as being for the accommodation of the undertaking builder;

(d)   The issue of whether the undertaker is entitled within the exemption to have his wife and family live with him in the caravan(s) is not formally settled by this decision.

As to the last point, residence by other family members would certainly not appear to be ruled out. Provided that, as a matter of fact and degree, the residential occupation of the caravan does qualify by reason of its being for the accommodation of a person or persons employed in connection with relevant building or engineering operations, the purposes for which they can sleep and live in the caravan would not appear to be circumscribed by the terms of paragraph 9. As the commentator pointed out in the J.P.L. article cited above, there are strong social and moral reasons why those purposes should be taken to include the pursuit of an ordinary family life, which would often release money, by the sale of the matrimonial home, and so speed the work.

Later judgments such as *Hammond v SSE* (1997) 74 P. &C. R. 134 and *R (Grange) v Harrogate BC* [2009] EWHC 1997 (Admin) were largely fact-dependent and are of no real assistance in elucidating the statutory rules.

While considering Part 5, Class A in relation to Paragraph 9 in the First Schedule to the 1960 Act, it may also be relevant to bear in mind Part 4, Class A, which permits the provision on land of buildings, *moveable struc-tures*, works, plant or machinery required temporarily in connection with and for the duration of operations being or to be carried out on, in, under or over that land or on land adjoining that land. As in the case of Part 5, the development is not permitted if planning permission is required for those operations but has not been granted, or is not deemed to be granted.

"Moveable structures" could arguably include caravans. The conditions apply-ing to this permitted development are not so restrictive as those applying to Part 5, Class A (in accordance with the qualifying criteria of Paragraph 9 in the First Schedule to the 1960 Act). The "moveable structure" need only be *required temporarily in connection with the operations.* "Required" means reasonably required - *R (Wilsdon) v FSS* [2006] EWHC 2980 (Admin). "Operations" in this context must be taken to refer to operational develop-ment - *R (Hall Hunter Partnership) v FSS* [2006] EWHC 3482 (Admin).

Apart from these points, and the need to establish as a matter of fact and degree that the structure is genuinely "required temporarily" in connec-tion with relevant operational development, there is no other limitation as to the scope of that requirement, so it would appear that the permitted development right under Part 4, Class A could possibly be relied upon to allow temporary sleeping accommodation, even for persons not directly involved in the actual building work, for as long as the operational develop-ment continues. However, unlike the development under Part 5, Class A, this would not come within Paragraph 9 of the First Schedule to the 1960 Act, and so a caravan site licence would be required in this case (if the 'moveable structure' takes the form of a caravan), notwithstanding that for planning purposes it is permitted development under Part 4.

19.10 Travelling showmen's sites

Paragraph 10 exempts the use of land as a caravan site by a travelling showman who is a member of an organisation of travelling showmen which holds for the time being a certificate granted under this paragraph and who is, at the time, travelling for the purposes of his business. However, the development permitted by Part 5, Class A does *not* extend to the use of the site by such a person as winter quarters (i.e. for some period falling between the beginning of October in any year and the end of March in the following year), notwithstanding that this aspect of the use of the site is also exempted by Paragraph 10 from the requirement for a site licence.

For the purposes of this paragraph, the Secretary of State may grant a certificate to any organisation recognised by him as confining its membership to bona fide travelling showmen; and a certificate so granted may be withdrawn by the Secretary of State at any time.

The decision of the Court of Appeal in *Holmes v Cooper* [1985] 3 All E.R. 114 established that the exemption under Paragraph 10 is not to be applied on a pitch-by-pitch basis, but must be judged in relation to the site as a whole. It follows that in order to qualify for exemption under Paragraph 10 (and therefore to qualify as permitted development under Part 5, Class A), *all* the caravans on the site must be occupied by persons meeting the criteria set out in that paragraph.

The evidence in that case showed that the majority of people on the site were travelling showmen and members of the Showmen's Guild, but that there were also people on the site who did not come within that description. In those circumstances, the Court of Appeal did not accept that the occupation of the site was exempt under Paragraph 10. They rejected the contention that the exemption should apply if a substantial, or even predominant, use of the site was for travelling showmen. In this case, the evidence did not in any event indicate that those show people who were on the site were there at a time when they were travelling for the purposes of their business, as paragraph 10 requires.

19.11 Power to withdraw certain exemptions

Under Paragraph 13 of the First Schedule to the 1960 Act, a local authority may apply to the Secretary of State for an order that some or all of paragraphs 2 to 10 will not apply in relation to specified land in their area. The effect of such an order is to make it necessary for a site licence to be obtained where there would otherwise have been an exemption from that requirement.

The relevance of Paragraph 13 in the context of Part 5, Class A, is that each of Paragraphs 2 to 10 in Schedule 1 to the 1960 Act begins with the words: "*Subject to the provisions of Paragraph 13 of this Schedule.....*".

Not only is the exemption from the requirement for a site licence subject to the proviso that no order removing that exemption has been made by the Secretary of State under Paragraph 13, but this is clearly one of the "circumstances" referred to in Paragraph A.2 of Part 5, Class A ("cases where a caravan site licence is not required"). Thus where an order has been made on the application of the local authority under Paragraph 13, this has the effect not only of removing the exemption from the requirement for a site licence but also of removing the permitted development right under Part 5, Class A.

CHAPTER 20

OTHER CAMPING AND RECREATIONAL USES

20.1   Use for camping and recreation by certain organisations

Part 5, Class C (formerly Part 27 in the 1995 Order) permits the use of land by members of a recreational organisation for the purposes of recreation or instruction, and the erection or placing of tents on the land for the purposes of the use.

For the purposes of this provision, a "recreational; organisation" means an organisation holding a certificate of exemption under section 269 of the Public Health Act 1936. (This section relates to the power of a local authority to control the use of 'moveable dwellings'.)

Development under this provision is not permitted if the land is a building (of any sort) or is within the curtilage of a dwellinghouse. This does not prevent such a use within the curtilage of a building which is not a dwellinghouse. Subject to these points, it may be taken that the word "land" in this context refers to the whole of the relevant planning unit (as to which, see *part B.1* of *Appendix B*).

The organisations holding a certificate of exemption under the 1936 Act are the Boys' Brigade, Scout Association, Girl Guides, Salvation Army, Church Lads and Church Girls Brigade, National Council for the Y.M.C.A., Army Cadet Force Association, Caravan Club, Camping and Caravanning Club, and the London Union of Youth Clubs. Subject to the user being one of these qualifying recreational organisations, the use is not subject to any conditions, and there is no time limit on the period in any one year during which camping, or recreation and instruction, can take place.

The change of use permitted by Part 5, Class C is not a temporary change of use; the use of the land under Class C may be permanent, and is not restricted as to period, physical extent or numbers. It is not confined to camping, but covers all types of recreation or instruction provided for members of any of those organisations.

20.2   Other camping uses

Use as a campsite may be permitted development only in the two limited cases described in *Chapter 16* and in *paragraph 20.1* above, that is either as a '28-day use' under Part 4, Class B or as a use by a recreational organisation holding a certificate of exemption under section 269 of the Public Health Act 1936, under Part 5, Class C. Any use for camping in tents, caravans, huts or other temporary or moveable (or permanent) structures outside the confines of these two classes of permitted development will require planning permission.

There has been at least one appeal decision in which it was held that the 28-day period under Part 4, Class B continued to run (and was therefore being used up) where a site was open for use by campers, even though there were no tents on the site at the time.

There is a separate licensing system under the Public Health Act 1936 for camping (other than in caravans, which is now covered by the Caravan Sites and Control of Development Act 1960). A licence under section 269 of the 1936 Act is required if camping is carried on for more than 42 days consecutively or for an aggregate of more than 60 days in any 12 consecutive months. The licensing provisions of section 269 do not apply only to camping in tents but to any "moveable dwelling".

It follows that if a camping use is one that requires a licence under the 1936 Act, it will also require planning permission, because (by definition) it will exceed the 28-day limit under Part 4, Class B, and will not be a use by a recreational organisation exempted from the licensing requirement under section 269.

Appendix A

Loss or removal of permitted development rights

Permitted development rights that would otherwise be exercisable under the GPDO may be excluded in several ways. These are discussed in the following paragraphs, but it should also be noted that a special development order, where made, may restrict or remove permitted development rights under the GPDO, but a local planning authority does not have the power to restrict or remove permitted development rights under the GPDO by means of a local development order. An LPA does, on the other hand, have the power to do this by means of a direction made under Article 4 of the GPDO (as explained in *paragraph A.8* below).

A.1   *The pre-existing use*

Before a change of use can be made as permitted development under Parts 3, 4 or 5 of the Second Schedule to the GPDO, the relevant building or land must be in use for the specified qualifying purpose at that time (or, if it is not in actual use, the right in planning terms to use it for that purpose must still subsist at that time, as discussed below in *paragraphs A.2* and *A.3*). As explained in *paragraph A.4*, that pre-existing use must also be a lawful use.

The pre-existing use must fall wholly within the definition of the qualifying use set out in the relevant Class of permitted development in the Second Schedule. This may be within a single Use Class (such as a use within Use Class B8 where a residential conversion is proposed under Part 3, Class P) or within a specified part of a Use Class (such as Use Class B1(a) - use as an office, where a residential conversion is proposed under Class O), or it may be a specified *sui generis* use (such as a Casino where a change of use is proposed under Class K to a use within Use Class D2 - assembly and leisure). In the case of a proposed change of use of an agricultural building, there is a detailed and precise definition of the qualifying use for the purposes of the relevant Classes in Part 3 which permit various changes of use of such a building. In all cases, if the pre-existing use of the building in question does not fall wholly within the definition of the qualifying use, then the proposed change of use cannot be permitted development, and will require planning permission instead.

It is particularly important in this context to understand that a pre-existing use that falls within the scope of more than one of the use classes in the Use Classes Order is a *sui generis* use, notwithstanding that each of the elements of that use would by itself come within the UCO. It is quite common for such a mixed use to be described for convenience as (for example) "a B1/B8 use", but the fact remains that such a mixed use is outside the scope of the Use Classes Order, and a proposed change of use from such a mixed use cannot therefore be permitted development, and so will require planning permission. The sole exception to this rule is a B1/B2 use, as provided by article 3(4) of the Use Classes Order – see *paragraph 4.1* in *Chapter 4*.

Similarly, a pre-existing use of a building or land which is ancillary to a different primary use of the planning unit which the building or land comprises, or of which it forms part, will not meet the qualifying criteria of the various classes of development permitted by Part 3, notwithstanding that this ancillary use, if it were a free-standing primary use of the planning unit, would by itself qualify for the purposes of the relevant permitted change of use under Part 3. Here again, a proposed change of use in such a case cannot be permitted development, and so will require planning permission.

There is, however, one proviso that should be borne in mind. A use in one planning unit cannot be ancillary to an activity carried on in a different planning unit (see *Westminster City Council v British Waterways Board* [1985] A.C. 676; [1984] 3 All E.R. 737). In order for one use to be ancillary to another use, the secondary or subsidiary use in question must be carried on in the same planning unit as the primary use.

It should also be borne in mind that a use which is included in and ordinarily incidental to any use in a specified use class is not excluded from the use class in which the primary use falls, merely because the same use is specified elsewhere in the UCO as a separate use (see Article 3(3)). Thus an incidental or ancillary use will not prevent the primary use from qualifying for change of use under Part 3, always provided that the incidental or ancillary use has not grown to such an extent as actually to become a mixed use together with what was originally the primary use (see, for example, *Wallington v SSW* [1990] J.P.L. 112).

A.2 Loss or abandonment of the pre-existing use

Where a building is not in actual use for the qualifying use immediately before the proposed change of use under Part 3, it will be necessary to ascertain whether the right, in planning terms, to use the building for that purpose still subsists, or whether it has been abandoned or lost, as discussed below. In relation to those classes of permitted development in Part 3 where the use must have existed on or before a qualifying date, it will be necessary to consider the position both before and after the qualifying date, as explained below in *paragraph A.3*.

The decision of the House of Lords in *Pioneer Aggregates (UK) Ltd v SSE* [1985] 1 A.C 132 confirmed the general principle that a valid permission capable of implementation cannot be abandoned by the conduct of an owner or occupier of the land. Notwithstanding this, the House of Lords accepted that there could nonetheless be abandonment of a use. The two principles are not easy to reconcile, but the House of Lords in *Pioneer Aggregates* expressly accepted the position regarding the abandonment of a use as stated in *Hartley v MHLG* [1970] QB 413.

In that earlier case, the Court of Appeal had held that where there had been an existing use on a site which had ceased, the Minister had been entitled to find as a fact that the previous use had been abandoned by the owner or occupier of the land. This was not a case of abandoning a planning permission. However, the issue was one of fact, as the Court of Appeal had emphasised in that case.

Abandonment of a use depends on the circumstances. If the land has remained unused for a considerable time in such circumstances that a reasonable man might conclude that the previous use had been abandoned, then a decision-maker may hold it to have been abandoned. In other words (*per* Widgery LJ), it is perfectly feasible in this context to describe a use as having been abandoned when one means that it has not merely been suspended for a short and determined period, but has ceased with no intention to resume the use at any particular time.

The test as to whether or not a use has been abandoned is an objective one. There are four factors to be taken into account – the intention of the owner, the physical condition of the building, the period of non-use and whether there have been any other uses following the cessation of the previous use. The subjective intention of the owner is to be ascertained and weighed in the balance, but it is not determinative. A mere assertion that the owner did not intend to abandon the use may not be sufficient in itself to negative the objective facts. (See *Hughes v SSETR* [2000] 1 P.L.R. 76.)

In addition to abandonment, existing use rights can be lost in other ways. This can arise where what has been described as "a new planning unit" has been created. A line of cases (reviewed in *Newbury DC v SSE* [1981] A.C. 578) had shown that existing use rights can be lost by reason of a new development sanctioned by a planning permission. The existing use right disappears because the character of the planning unit has been altered by the physical fact of the new development. Another way of putting this is that "the planning history of the site begins afresh......with the grant of this permission......*which was taken up and used.*" (see *Prossor v MHLG* (1968) 67 L.G.R. 109, 113). The point of the words in italics in this passage is that where the evidence fails to establish the creation of a new planning unit by development actually having been carried out on the land, the grant of planning permission for some other development on the land does not in itself preclude a landowner from relying on an existing use right.

The same point arose in *Petticoat Lane Rentals Ltd v SSE* [1971] 1 W.L.R. 1112. Physical alteration of the planning unit will normally be made only in implementation of planning permission for the erection of new buildings, but it might be made in implementation of planning permission for a change of use in some circumstances. This could alternatively be described as creating "a new chapter in the planning history" of the site, where incompatible acts have been carried out, such as physical development incompatible with continuance of the existing use. The House of Lords in *Newbury* did not think that the principle should be limited to cases of planning permission for rebuilding, although it will only seldom apply to planning permission for a change of use.

The right to use a building or land for a particular use can also be lost if it is supplanted by some further change of use (whether authorised by planning permission or not). It is not then possible to revert to the previous use without obtaining a fresh planning permission for change of use to that previous use (see again *Petticoat Lane Rentals Ltd v SSE*, cited above). This is subject to the exceptions set out in section 57 of the 1990 Act, but those are unlikely to apply in practice to cases where it is sought to make a change of use under Part 3 of the Second Schedule to the GPDO.

Finally, existing use rights can be lost where a building is demolished or is accidentally destroyed (for example by fire or storm). This point was established by the decision of the Court of Appeal in *Iddenden v SSE* [1972] 1 W.L.R. 1433; (1973) 26 P. & C. R. 553. This rule has been applied in a number of barn conversion cases, where planning permission for the residential conversion of the barn took the form of permission for change of use, but was held to be lost upon the complete demolition or destruction of the pre-existing building. (See *Hadfield v SSE* [1996] E.G.C.S 114.)

The same would clearly apply to permitted development under Part 3 of the Second Schedule to the GPDO for the residential or other conversion of an agricultural building. Where the building is wholly or substantially destroyed, there is no implied permission to rebuild if necessary. (See the judgment of the Court of Appeal in *North Norfolk DC v Long* (1983) 267 E.G. 251; [1984] J.P.L. 45, which confirmed that there is no permission for any reconstruction in the absence of express authorisation of any such works by the permission.)

In any event, Article 3(9) makes it clear that the development permitted by most parts of the Second Schedule to the Order (including Part 3) does not permit any development which requires or involves the demolition of a building, except for part only of the building; and the extent of such partial demolition is strictly limited by those classes in Part 3 that permit building or other operations.

A.3   Continuation of the pre-existing use

In Part 3, Class J (change of use of a shop, financial or professional services or similar premises to a use within Use Class D2 - assembly and leisure), Class M (residential conversion of shops, financial or professional services and similar premises), Class N (residential conversion of an amusement arcade or centre or of a casino), Class O (residential conversion of an office building), Class P (residential conversion of a storage building), Class Q (residential conversion of an agricultural building), Class R (change of use of an agricultural building to a flexible use within Use Class A1, A2, A3, B1, B8, C1 or D2) and Class S (change of use of an agricultural building to use as a state-funded school or registered nursery) all require that the building in question must have been solely used for the specified pre-existing use on a stated date or, in the case of a building which was in use before that date but was not in use on that date, when it was last in use.

Two points may arise from this wording. First, a question might arise as to whether these words might be construed as implying that the pre-existing use could have been entirely lost or abandoned before the stated date and yet still qualify the building for the relevant permitted change of use under Part 3. Secondly, a question could perhaps arise as to whether in the case of a building that was still in use for the specified pre-existing use on the stated date, this use must then continue until the proposed change of use under Part 3 takes place.

It is the author's view that, in both cases, the use (or at least the right, in planning terms, to use the building for that purpose) must still subsist until the change of use permitted by Part 3 takes place. If, by this time, there is no longer any existing right, in planning terms, to use the building for the specified qualifying use, then there is no longer a use upon which the right to make a permitted change of use under Part 3 can be based.

There certainly appears to be no basis on which it could be argued that, simply by reason of the fact that that the building in question had been used for the specified use when it was last in use, a previous use that has been lost or abandoned for any of the reasons mentioned in *paragraph A.2* above could still be relied upon as a qualifying use for the purposes of any of the classes of permitted development in Part 3 listed above. Previous use rights that have been lost or abandoned must be treated for all purposes as being at an end and incapable of revival, other than by means of a fresh planning permission (except in the very limited circumstances prescribed by section 57 of the 1990 Act, which in practice are unlikely to apply in the present context).

On the other hand, recent active use of the building for the qualifying use may not be necessary, provided that any discontinuance of that use has not amounted to abandonment of the use and provided that the relevant use rights, in planning terms, have not been lost in any of the other ways discussed in *paragraph A.2*, so that in law the pre-existing use is still in being.

A.4   Unlawful buildings and uses

By Article 3(5), the permission granted by Schedule 2 does not apply in the case of permitted development allowed in connection with an existing building, if the construction of that building was and remains unlawful. Similarly, it does not apply in the case of permitted development allowed in connection with an existing use if that use is unlawful. This is an important point that should not be overlooked.

Where permitted development is dependent on a building being in use within a specified use class on or before a particular date, the pre-condition for that permitted development will only be met if the relevant use was lawful or had become lawful by that date.

However, the rule in Article 3(5) does not prevent permitted development in cases where operational development or a change of use that was originally unlawful has subsequently become lawful, under the 4-year rule in relation to operational development or a change of use to use as a single private dwelling, or under the 10-year rule in relation to any other change of use.

Very briefly, the 4-year rule is satisfied if four years have passed since the substantial completion of building, engineering or other operations, or after four years' continuous use following a change of use to use as a single private dwelling. The 10-year rule is satisfied after ten years' continuous use following any other change of use, or after ten year's continuous breach of a condition, although a breach of planning control that consists solely of a breach of condition would not render the development as a whole unlawful unless it resulted in a development so different, in the form and manner in which it has been carried out, from what was authorised (assuming proper compliance with that condition or those conditions) that it is not within the scope of the planning permission. Needless to say, such cases are likely to be very rare in practice.

The finer points relating to these two rules lie beyond the scope of the present work, but it should be borne in mind that a breach of condition prohibiting permanent use as a separate dwelling which does in practice result in a change of use to use as a single dwelling is subject to the 4-year rule (not 10-year rule) (*Arun DC v FSS* [2007] 1 W.L.R. 523).

Where it is claimed that an existing development has become lawful, either under the 4-year rule or the 10-year rule, the owner or occupier of the property should be aware that this may be defeated if the development can be said to have been deliberately concealed. This can arise under the rule in *Welwyn Hatfield v SSCLG* [2011] UKSC 15 (applying the *Connor* principle) where the developer has deliberately misled the local planning authority as to the true position. It may alternatively lead (within certain time limits) to an application by the LPA to the magistrates' court for a Planning Enforcement Order under sections 171BA to 171BC of the 1990 Act.

A.5 *Removal of permitted development rights by condition*

Article 3(4) provides that nothing in the GPDO permits development contrary to any condition imposed by any planning permission. Permitted development rights may therefore be removed by a condition attached to a planning permission, and this is quite commonly done.

There is therefore no doubt that a condition, if appropriately worded, can restrict the use or uses to which the development authorised by a planning permission can be put. There is, however, an element of doubt and dispute as to whether a condition attached to a planning permission can preclude the operation of section 55(2)(f) and Article 3(1) of the Use Classes Order (so as to prevent the use of the site for other purposes falling within the same use class in the UCO), unless it specifically refers to the UCO, and also whether such a condition can prevent changes of use in accordance with Article 3(4) of the GPDO, unless the condition specifically refers to the GPDO as such. What can be said with certainty, however, is that if a condition is expressly worded so as to preclude the effect of either or both of these Orders, then it will be effective to limit the use of the property in that way.

The model conditions recommended in Appendix B to Circular 11/95 (which remain extant, although the rest of the circular was cancelled in March 2014) read:

"[48] The premises shall be used for.........and for no other purpose (including any purpose in Class........... of the Schedule to the Town and Country Planning (Use Classes) Order 1987, or in any provision equivalent to that Class in any statutory instrument revoking and re-enacting that Order with or without modification."

and

"[50] Notwithstanding the provisions of the Town and Country Planning (General Permitted Development) Order 1995 [2015] (or any order revoking and re-enacting that Order with or without modification) no..... .[specified development]........shall be [carried out]."

If so worded, there can be no doubt that such conditions do preclude the operation of these statutory provisions (subject to one possible exception discussed below). However, an element of doubt may occur where a condition purports to limit a use without referring in any way to either the UCO or the GPDO. There are two judgments that would strongly suggest that the effect of the UCO and/or of the GPDO can only be precluded by express reference to the relevant statutory instrument in the wording of the condition. As Sir Douglas Franks QC put it in *Carpet Decor (Guildford) Ltd v SSE* [1981] J.P.L. 806:

"As a general principle, where a local planning authority intends to exclude the operation of the Use Classes Order or the General Development Order, they should say so by the imposition of a condition in unequivocal terms, for in the absence of such a condition it must be assumed that those orders will have effect by operation of law."

The Court of Appeal reached a similar conclusion in *Dunoon Developments Ltd v SSE* [1992] J.P.L. 936. Article 3(4) of the GPDO (which rules out permitted development contrary to any condition imposed by any planning permission) had been called in aid by the LPA, but Farquharson LJ held that:

"The purpose of the General Development Order is to give a general planning consent unless such consent is specifically excluded by the words of the condition. The Schedule [now the Second Schedule to the GPDO 2015] identifies the activities included in this general consent..........Therefore it is apt to include the provisions of this particular planning permission unless the condition was wide enough to exclude it."

In agreeing with this judgment, the Vice-Chancellor, Sir David Nicholls, added:

"Of its nature, and by definition, a grant of planning permission for a stated purpose is a grant only for that use. But that cannot per se be sufficient to exclude the operation of a General Development Order. A grant of permission for a particular use cannot per se constitute a condition inconsistent with consequential development permitted by a General Development Order. If it did, the operation of General Development Orders would be curtailed in a way which could not have been intended. Thus to exclude the application of a General Development Order, there has to be something more."

There have, however, been other cases in which it was held that a condition which did not specifically refer either to the UCO or to the GPDO did nonetheless preclude their effect. The first of these was *City of London Corporation v SSE* (1971) 23 P. & C. R. 169 (which predated both *Carpet Decor* and *Dunoon Developments*). In that case, the wording of the condition was that *"the premises shall be used as an employment agency and for no other purpose."* This was held to operate effectively to exclude the operation of the Use Classes Order. Two later cases (*Rugby Football Union v SSETR* [2001] EWHC 927, and *R (Royal London Mutual Insurance Society Limited) v SSCLG* [2013] EWHC 3597 (Admin)) were similarly decided.

In the first of these two cases a condition relating to stands at Twickenham Rugby Football Ground required that the stands *"shall only be used ancillary to the main use of the premises as a sports stadium and for no other use."* The argument that the words did not exclude the Use Classes Order was rejected by the court on the ground that the words *'for no other use'* were clear. They had no sensibly discernible purpose than to prevent some other use which might otherwise be permissible without planning permission, for example under the Use Classes Order (by virtue of section 55(2)(f)). The judge was satisfied that those words met the test of being sufficiently clear for the exclusion of the Use Classes Order.

Royal London Insurance related to planning permission for the construction of a non-food retail park comprising five units. This permission contained a condition which provided that *"The retail consent shall be for non food sales only in bulky trades normally found on retail parks which are furniture, carpets, DIY, electrical goods, car accessories, garden items and such other trades as the council may permit in writing.*" The stated reason for the condition was to ensure that the nature of the scheme would not detract from the vitality and viability of the nearby town centre.

The Court upheld an inspector's decision that the use of the word *'only'* was effectively the same as the phrase *'and for no other purpose'*, especially when the condition was read in its entirety. When read alongside the reason for the imposition of the condition and in the context of the permission as a whole, the Inspector found that the condition prevented the exercise of rights under the Use Classes Order (to use the premises for other purposes falling within Use Class A1). The judge regarded the use of the word "*only*" as emphatic. It meant solely or exclusively. That was its plain and ordinary meaning. This would prevent any retail sales other than those stipulated of a non food nature.

The Court stressed that the reason for imposing a condition is important in understanding the objective of the condition. This condition was intended to provide an ongoing mechanism to maintain the retail health of the town centre. In the Court's judgment, this is what a reasonable reader of the condition would discern - namely, a non food retail consent only, with sales permitted of bulky goods within certain main sectors so as not to cause any material harm to the retail health of the town centre.

The use of a form of words excluding other uses within the same use class, however, (based on standard condition 48) may not necessarily be so restrictive as a literal interpretation of the words might suggest. In *Tendring DC v SSCLG* [2008] EWHC 2122, a condition required that "*The premises shall be used only for a nursing home and for no other purpose, including any other purpose in Class C2 of the Schedule of the Town & Country Planning Use Classes Order 1987.*"

The High Court upheld an inspector's decision quashing an enforcement notice which had alleged that there had been a breach of this condition when the premises came to be used (according to the LPA) as an institution for the provision of residential accommodation and care to persons in need of continuous supervision and for the provision of medical and/or psychiatric treatment of behavioural and learning difficulties. This, it was alleged, fell outside the definition of a "nursing home" and was more in the nature of a hospital, a use within Use Class C2 but one which was precluded by the condition.

The Inspector, and subsequently the High Court, decided that (having regard to the definition of the word "care" in Use Class C2) it is difficult to distinguish a 'nursing home' from 'use for the provision of residential accommodation and care to people in need of care', and they are effectively one and the same thing. A nursing home can encompass a wide range of activities involving personal care. The very limited definition of "nursing home" which had been advanced by the LPA was firmly rejected. The only appreciable effect of the condition was to prevent the use of the premises as a hospital, residential school, college or training centre, out of the other activities set out in Use Class C2.

In a planning appeal decided in March 2015, relating to prior approval in respect of the residential conversion of an office building under what was then Part 3, Class J (now Class O), the Inspector rejected the LPA's assertion that this was precluded by a condition in a previous planning permission requiring that the premises be used only for purposes falling within Class B1 of the Use Classes Order. The LPA had relied on article 3(4) of the GPDO but the Inspector held that the condition only referred to the building being used within Use Class B1(a) and no words conclusively or unequivocally prevented the operation of the GPDO. Article 3(4) did not therefore prevent the proposed change of use. This decision was specifically based on the judgments in *Carpet Decor* and *Dunoon Developments* cited above.

In contrast to this, an example of a permitted change of use being prevented by a condition in a planning permission is provided by a decision in a planning appeal in June 2015 in Hampshire against the refusal of prior approval for the proposed change of use of an office used by a firm of undertakers to a registered nursery under former Class K (now Class T) of Part 3. The condition in question required that the premises were to be for office use only and not for any other purpose (including any other activity associated with the undertaker's funeral business). The stated reason for the imposition of the condition was that any other use would be inappropriate and could place "unacceptable pressures" on the site and locality.

The argument on behalf of the applicant was that the purpose of the condition was simply to restrict the use of the premises to a limited ancillary use in connection with the undertaker's business, without its being used for the wider purposes of that business. It was also argued that the absence of any mention in the condition of development under the GPDO did not have the effect of removing the permitted development rights under Article 3(4).

However, the judgment in *Royal London Mutual Insurance* (cited above) was considered by the Inspector to apply in this situation. He drew attention to the use of the word 'only' in the condition. The stated reason for the imposition of the condition also explained the planning reason for its imposition. The effect of the condition was wider than that contended for by the applicant. Notwithstanding the lack of any explicit reference in the condition to the GPDO, this clearly worded condition was effective to remove permitted development rights in accordance with the Article 3(4).

This issue has also been tested in Dorset by way of an application for a Lawful Development Certificate, and a subsequent appeal against its refusal. The appeal was dismissed in September 2015 on the grounds that Article 3(4) prevented permitted development in that case, which involved the proposed residential conversion of offices under Class O (following a prior approval application having originally been made under Class J in the 1995 Order).

The appeal had been made primarily on the basis that the LPA had failed to determine the prior approval application within the 56-day period, but there was a condition in the planning permission for the erection of the offices which required that the use of the building was to be for purposes falling within Class B1 of the Use Classes Order, and for no other purpose whatsoever, without express planning consent from the local planning authority first being obtained.

The appellants argued that no reference was made to the GPDO by this condition, so that the condition did not have the effect of removing the permitted development rights under Part 3, Class O. The Inspector considered the judgments on this issue discussed above and pointed out that the condition made specific reference to the Use Classes Order in limiting the authorised use to Class B1 only, coupled with the admonition that the use of the building was to be for that purpose and for no other purpose whatsoever. This clearly precluded the operation of any Development Order that might otherwise apply.

A blanket exclusion of the whole of the GPDO would have been too wide, but the condition in the form in which it had been drafted did preclude the operation of Part 3, and of Class O in particular.

Notwithstanding these recent appeal decisions, the judgments in *Carpet Decor* and in *Dunoon Developments* should not be lightly set aside or overlooked. It is the author's view that the only justifiable exception to the rule laid down in those two judgments is the decision in *Royal London Insurance*, where there was a clear and overriding planning reason for the imposition of the restrictive condition which, when read together with the condition, indicated a clear intention to preclude the operation of (in that case) section 55(2)(f) In the absence of such clear evidence of the intention of the condition, the omission of any reference to the GPDO from such a condition should usually indicate that the condition does not bring Article 3(4) into operation.

A.6   *Planning obligations under section 106*

The use of a property may also be controlled or constrained by means of a deed entered into under section 106 of the 1990 Act (a 'planning agreement' or 'planning obligation'). This would not have the legal effect of actually removing permitted development rights under Article 3 of the GPDO, but if carrying out the permitted development would amount to a breach of a covenant in a deed entered into under section 106, such a breach of covenant could be restrained by injunction. Whether a covenant in a section 106 agreement is in practice enforceable depends on construing the wording and the legal effect of the deed, and is beyond the scope of the present work. Although rare now, there might in some cases be a subsisting agreement under section 52 of the 1971 Act which, if it is still enforceable, could have a similar effect.

A.7   *Restrictive covenants*

Even where there is no planning obligation in place under section 106 (or section 52 of the 1971 Act) which might restrict the use of a property, there may be restrictive covenants in the title deeds of the property which could constrain the development that can be carried out on the site (including changes of use). Such covenants are not always enforceable, but will require investigation. If there is no-one who could in practice enforce the covenant, an indemnity policy may suffice to protect the developer.

If the covenant is still enforceable, it might possibly be argued that it is obsolete due to changes in the character of the property or the neighbourhood, that its discharge or modification would not injure the persons benefiting from it, or that it prevents the use of the land for public or private purposes and does not secure any practical benefit of substantial value to those benefitting from it. In such a case an application can be made to the Lands Tribunal [the Upper Tribunal (Lands Chamber)] under section 84 of the Law of Property Act 1925 to modify or discharge the restrictive covenant.

However, as several developers have found to their cost, it cannot be assumed that the Lands Tribunal will necessarily agree to discharge the covenant. A graphic example was provided by *George Wimpey Bristol Ltd and Gloucestershire Housing Association Ltd* [2011] UKUT 91 (LC). Detailed planning permission had been granted for residential development on a large site which included land affected by the covenant. The offending houses that had already been built on that part of the site ultimately had to be demolished.

A further example is provided by the decision of the Court of Appeal in *Zenios v Hampstead Garden Suburb Trust Ltd* [2011] EWCA Civ 1645. In this case, planning permission had been granted for the erection of an extension of the house above an existing garage. The Court of Appeal dismissed an appeal against the Land Tribunal's refusal to discharge the covenant. A similar result was reached in the later case of *Shebelle Enterprises Ltd v Hampstead Garden Suburb Trust Ltd* [2013] EWHC 948 (Ch).

The cited examples both related to operational development, but restrictive covenants may quite frequently constrain the uses to which a property may be put, and a change of use that would be a breach of covenant could, if the covenant proves to be enforceable by a neighbouring owner, be restrained by injunction, notwithstanding the fact that the change of use is permitted development under the GPDO.

A.8   Article 4 Directions

A condition attached to a planning permission may be an effective means of precluding permitted development in respect of a particular property, but if a local planning authority wishes to preclude permitted development throughout its area or over a specified part of that area it may make a direction to that effect under Article 4 of the GPDO. The powers granted by Article 4 may be exercised either by a local planning authority or by the Secretary of State.

An Article 4 Direction does not prevent development of the specified type being carried out; it simply has the effect of preventing that development being carried out unless planning permission is obtained. Upon the making of the direction the permission granted by Article 3 no longer applies to the development of the Part or the Class or paragraph in question in the area specified in the direction (the whole or a specified part of the LPA's area) or to a particular development which is specified in the direction, and so a planning application will then be the only way of obtaining authorisation for that development.

The local planning authority for this purpose is the authority having power to grant planning permission for the particular type of development covered by the direction. So an Article 4 Direction in respect of development involving minerals or waste can be made only by a County (or unitary) planning authority. However, in conservation areas the power to make an Article 4 Direction can be exercised by the county planning authority, in addition to the LPA or the Secretary of State.

The precise procedural requirements for the making of an Article 4 Direction (which are set out in Schedule 3 to the GPDO) lie beyond the scope of the present work, but the LPA is required to give notice of the direction, which includes a description of the development and the area to which the direction relates, or the site to which it relates, and a statement of the effect of the direction, and to allow a period of at least 21 days (stating the date on which that period begins) within which any representations concerning the direction may be made to the LPA, as well as specifying the date on which it is proposed that the direction will come into force (which must be at least 28 days but no longer than two years after the date on which the consultation period commenced). An Article 4 Direction cannot have retrospective effect, and will not therefore affect permitted development that has already been carried out.

A material change of use is a single event (see *Cynon Valley BC v SSW* (1987) 53 P. & C. R. 68), and so once this has taken place, the resultant use will not be affected by the subsequent making of an Article 4 Direction which prevents a change of use to that use without planning permission. However, where permitted development is for a purely temporary use (e.g. under Part 4 or under Part 5, Class A of the Second Schedule to the GPDO), it was established by the decision of the Court of Appeal in *S Bucks DC v SSE* [1989] 1 P.L.R. 69, [1989] J.P.L. 351 that the development permitted by the Order is a series of separate developments, involving a fresh change of use each time. Thus the making of an Article 4 Direction has the effect of preventing further exercise of the right to make temporary changes of use, notwithstanding that the rights under the GPDO have previously been exercised for the same purpose on the same land.

An Article 4 Direction no longer has to be confirmed by the Secretary of State, even where objections are made to it, although the LPA is required to send a copy of the direction and notice, and other specified details, to the Secretary of State on the same day that notice of the direction is first published or displayed in accordance with Schedule 3 to the GPDO.

The direction will come into force on the date specified in the notice but must first be confirmed by the LPA, who are required to take into account any representations received during the consultation period. The direction must not be confirmed until at least 28 days following the latest date on which any notice relating to the direction was served or published, or such longer period as may be specified by the Secretary of State following the LPA's notification of the direction to the Secretary of State. The LPA must then (as soon as practicable after a direction has been confirmed) give notice of the confirmation of the Article 4 Direction and the date on which it will come into force, and send a copy of the direction, as confirmed, to the Secretary of State.

An LPA may cancel an Article 4 Direction at any time, by making a subsequent direction; and the Secretary of State also has power to make a direction cancelling or modifying any Article 4 direction made by an LPA at any time, either before or after its confirmation, and must notify the LPA of this. The Secretary of State has on occasion used this power to cancel Article 4 Directions made by LPAs which were thought to be too wide in their extent or effect. For example, an Article 4 Direction made by the London Borough of Islington preventing permitted development under what was then Part 3, Class J (now Class O) was cancelled by the Secretary of State because it was too wide in its effect. A second attempt by the LPA covering a reduced area of the Borough was also struck down by the Secretary of State, because it was still too wide in its effect. (In that case, a less extensive Direction was subsequently made by the LPA, to which the Secretary of State raised no objection.)

Local planning authorities whose areas include any 'Article 2(5) land' (which is currently exempt from permitted development under Part 3, Class O) can be expected to make Article 4 Directions preventing future changes of use under Class O in some or all of the currently exempted areas in sufficient time to enable 12 months' notice of those Directions to be given before the exemption under Article 2(5) is removed on 30 May 2019.

Schedule 3 to the GPDO provides for certain Article 4 directions to take immediate effect. This provision applies where an Article 4 Direction relating to development permitted by any of Parts 1 to 4, or Class B or C of Part 11, of Schedule 2 has been made by the LPA and the authority consider that the development to which the direction relates would be prejudicial to the proper planning of their area or constitute a threat to the amenities of their area.

(An Article 4 Direction can also be brought into immediate effect within the whole or part of a conservation area if the authority consider that it should have immediate effect, but this applies only where the development to which the direction relates fronts a highway, waterway or open space and comes within certain categories in the Second Schedule to the GPDO which are not relevant to the subject matter of this book. The Secretary of State may not make a direction under Schedule 3 cancelling an Article 4 Direction that comes within any of these specified categories.)

Compensation may be payable by the LPA where an Article 4 Direction has been made withdrawing permitted development rights. However the compensation provisions lie beyond the scope of this book.

There is one important saving, which is contained in Article 4(2). This provides that an Article 4 Direction does not affect the carrying out of development permitted by any Class in Schedule 2 which is expressed to be subject to prior approval where, in relation to that development, the prior approval date occurs before the date on which the direction comes into force and the development is completed within a period of 3 years starting with the prior approval date.

The 'prior approval date' is the date on which the LPA notifies the applicant that their prior approval is not required, or that prior approval is granted or, alternatively, the date on which the 56-day period expires without the prior approval application having been determined, or without the LPA having notified the applicant of their determination. (See *Chapter 15.*) As noted above, this provision imposes a 3-year time limit for completion of the development, even in those cases where no completion date is imposed by the relevant Class in Part 3.

Section 17(2)(b) of the Interpretation Act 1978 (read together with section 23) provides that anything done under previous subordinate legislation which has been repealed and re-enacted continues to have effect as if it were made or done under the new provision. Thus where an Article 4 Direction was made under an earlier version of the GPDO (e.g. the 1995 Order) and came into effect before 15 April 2015, so as to exclude a particular class or classes of development from being permitted development under any part of Schedule 2 to the 1995 GPDO, it will apply equally to the corresponding class of development in the Second Schedule to the 2015 Order in exactly the same way as it applied to the previous class of development under the earlier Order. Attention is also drawn in *paragraph 1.6* of *Chapter 1* to the provisions in sections 16 and 23 of the 1978 Act, which save the effect of other actions taken under the 1995 Order.

A.9   Revocation or amendment of a development order

Permitted development rights can be cancelled by the revocation or amendment of the GPDO (and by the revocation or amendment of other development orders), and there are several examples of permitted development rights which formerly existed but were later withdrawn by an amendment to the Order; but an amendment to the GPDO cannot have retrospective effect, and will not therefore affect permitted development that has already been carried out.

In the same way as in the case of Article 4 Directions (see *paragraph A.8* above), once a material change of use has taken place, the resultant use will not be affected by a subsequent amendment of the GPDO cancelling the right to make such a change of use without planning permission. However, where permitted development is for a purely temporary use (e.g. under Part 4, or under Part 5, Class A of the Second Schedule to the GPDO), the decision of the Court of Appeal in *S Bucks DC v SSE* [1989] 1 P.L.R. 69, [1989] J.P.L. 351 would apply. This established that the development permitted by the Order is a series of separate developments, involving a fresh change of use each time. Thus an amendment of the GPDO cancelling the right to make temporary changes of use without planning permission would have the effect of preventing further exercise of the right to make those temporary changes of use, notwithstanding that the right to make such temporary changes of use under the GPDO as it previously applied had already been exercised for the same purpose on the same land.

Compensation may be payable in certain circumstances in respect of the cancellation of permitted development rights by an amendment to the GPDO or other development order. However the compensation provisions lie beyond the scope of this book.

A.10   Exclusion of permitted development by the GPDO itself

There are several examples of permitted development being excluded by the GPDO itself where other permitted development has taken place.

Permitted development under all classes of Part 1 of the Second Schedule (various development within the curtilage of a dwellinghouse, as well as alteration or enlargement of the house itself) is entirely excluded where there has been development under Part 3, Class M (residential conversion of shops, financial or professional services and similar premises), Class N (residential conversion of an amusement arcade or centre or of a casino), Class P (residential conversion of a storage building), or Class Q (residential conversion of an agricultural building).

Similarly, in Part 6, permitted development is excluded if it would consist of the erection or extension of any agricultural building (under Class A or Class B of that Part), where there has been development under Part 3, Class Q (residential conversion of an agricultural building) anywhere on the same agricultural holding within the previous 10 years. (See *paragraph 9.9* in *Chapter 9*.)

These are not the only examples of the exclusion of permitted development rights by other provisions within the GPDO itself. Other examples have been quoted in earlier chapters relating to the particular Classes of permitted development where they occur.

Compensation is not payable for the removal of permitted development rights in this way.

A.11 Development requiring an Environmental Impact Assessment

Although it is unlikely in most cases to affect changes of use permitted by Parts 3, 4 or 5 of the Second Schedule to the GPDO, Article 3(10) of the 2015 Order provides that (with the limited exceptions set out in Article 3(12), none of which applies to changes of use) development falling within either Schedule 1 or Schedule 2 of the Town and Country Planning (Environmental Impact Assessment) Regulations 2011 ("the EIA Regulations"), i.e. development that may require an EIA, *is not permitted by the GPDO* unless the local planning authority has adopted a screening opinion under Regulation 5 of the EIA Regulations that the development is not EIA development, or the Secretary of State has made a screening direction under Regulation 4(7) or 6(4) of those Regulations to the same effect, or alternatively that the Secretary of State has given a direction under Regulation 4(4) of the EIA Regulations that the development is exempted from the application of those Regulations.

By Article 3(11), where the LPA has adopted a screening opinion under Regulation 5 of the EIA Regulations that the development is EIA development and the Secretary of State has neither made a screening direction to the contrary in relation to that development, under Regulation 4(8) or 6(4) of those Regulations, nor directed under Regulation 4(4) that the development is exempted from the application of those Regulations; or if he has directed that development is EIA development, then again this is development which *is not permitted by the GPDO*.

A.12 Change of use after only a brief period of existing use

In the case of changes of use under Class J (change of use of a shop, financial or professional services or similar premises to a use within Use Class D2 - assembly and leisure), Class M (residential conversion of shops, financial or professional services and similar premises), Class N (residential conversion of an amusement arcade or centre or of a casino), Class O (residential conversion of an office building), Class P (residential conversion of a storage building), Class Q (residential conversion of an agricultural building), Class R (change of use of an agricultural building to a flexible use within Use Class A1, A2, A3, B1, B8, C1 or D2) or Class S (change of use of an agricultural building to use as a state-funded school or registered nursery), the building to be converted must have been in use for the qualifying use on or before a specified date, and in the case of Class P there must also have been not less than four years of qualifying use before the change of use can be made. But apart from those Classes listed above, there is no requirement in the GPDO that the building should have been used for its existing use on or by a given date or for any specified period.

However, whether the existing use derives either from a planning permission or from some previous permitted development under Part 3, any change of use (or further change of use) under Part 3 will be governed by the rule in *Kwik Save Discount Group Ltd v SSW* [1981] J.P.L. 198. It was held in that case that a change of use, although it was permitted by Part 3 of the Second Schedule to the GPDO, could not lawfully be made less than two months since the existing use had itself been implemented. The existing use had to be more than purely nominal. The existing use in the *Kwik Save* case was as a car showroom (a *sui generis* use). At that time, it was possible to change the use of a car showroom to use as a shop within Use Class A1 (although this is no longer permitted by Part 3, as noted in *Chapter 2*, at *paragraph 2.1*). Notwithstanding this provision in Part 3, the change of use of the premises to use as a shop was held not to be permitted by Part 3 after so brief a period of use that the purported use of the premises as a car showroom had been no more than nominal.

There was also a planning appeal decision that related to a (non-material) change of use of a building that had been erected within the curtilage of a dwellinghouse under Part 1, Class E of the Second Schedule to the GPDO for a purpose incidental to the enjoyment of the dwellinghouse as such, whereby it was subsequently used for purposes that were no longer purely 'incidental' but were part of the primary residential use. The Inspector opined in that case that the original incidental use would have to continue 'for a year and a day' before the outbuilding could lawfully be used for purposes forming part of the primary residential use of the house. There would appear to be no judicial authority to support the Inspector's insistence that the original use should continue for at least a year before a further change of use could be made; nevertheless, this appeal decision serves as a practical example confirming that a use must continue for a sufficient time as to be seen to be more than purely nominal, before a further change of use can lawfully be made, either within the same Use Class under section 55(2)(f) or to use within a different Use Class under Part 3 of the GPDO.

Appendix B

The planning unit and the concept of 'curtilage'

Before any meaningful consideration can be given to a change of use of a building and/or land, it is essential to answer this preliminary question - change of use of *what*? The identification of the precise area of land or the part of the building in question, the use of which is to be changed, is fundamental to establishing the physical extent of the permitted development in such cases.

In attempting to grapple with this issue, the courts developed the concept of the 'planning unit'. No mention of a 'planning unit' will be found in the legislation - it is entirely judge-made law, but is nonetheless an essential conceptual tool in planning law.

A second important legal concept which is encountered in relation to the use of a building, and which is essential in understanding the planning status of the land immediately surrounding that building is its 'curtilage'. This is a term that is to be found in a number of places in Schedule 2 to the GPDO, but for which (with one limited exception, mentioned at the end of *paragraph B.2.1* below) there is no statutory definition.

'Planning unit' and 'curtilage' are two separate and entirely distinct concepts, and the one must not be confused with the other. It is particularly important in the planning context not to use the word 'curtilage' loosely to refer to the entirety of the surrounding land forming part of a property. As explained in *part B.2* of this Appendix, the actual curtilage of a house or other building may cover only part of the land owned or occupied with that building. In the same way, it should not be assumed that all the land within a single property is necessarily within one and the same planning unit.

B.1 The Planning Unit

The planning unit needs to be identified in order to understand precisely what area of land or what part of a building benefits from a particular class of permitted development. Similarly, when considering the lawful use of a property (whether or not this derives from a planning permission), it is essential to identify the precise extent of the land or buildings (or the part of a building) in question.

B.1.1 The planning unit created by a planning permission

In many cases, the relevant planning unit will have been defined by the red line on the site plan which was one of the approved drawings on the original grant of planning permission for the current development or use on the site.

This site forms the planning unit that benefits from that planning permission and (unless a smaller planning unit is to be created out of it by the proposed permitted development) it will be this planning unit to which the relevant permitted development rights apply (except where the permitted development right applies only to a "building and its curtilage" - see *part B.2* of this Appendix below).

It is worth noting that there may also have been a blue line on the original approved drawings, showing other land owned by the applicant at that time, but which does not form part of the site which benefits from the original planning permission and which does not form part of the resulting planning unit under that planning permission.

The case of *Barnett v SSCLG* [2009] EWCA Civ 476 demonstrates, however, that there are circumstances in which the red line, even on an approved drawing, cannot always be taken to define correctly the planning unit in respect of which planning permission was granted, although the situation that occurred in *Barnett* is likely to remain a rare exception to the general rule that the red line, once planning permission is granted, defines the planning unit.

In that case, a house had been erected with planning permission, and a reasonable area of land had been included within the red line, showing the planning unit to which it was intended that this planning permission should apply. Three years later, an application was made for an extension of the house. The footprint of the extension fell wholly within the planning unit defined by the approved application plan in the original planning permission, but the site plan that accompanied the application for the extension showed a greatly increased area of land within the red line on that plan. It was argued on behalf of the owner that the planning permission for the extension had therefore had the effect of extending the area of the planning unit to incorporate all the extra land shown on the approved site plan in this later planning permission.

Both the High Court and the Court of Appeal rejected this argument. The planning unit had been defined by the original planning permission for the erection of the house in 1995. When planning permission was granted for the extension in 1998, the house itself was already in existence, and it was not a necessary implication of permitting the extension or alteration of that house that the planning unit would be extended beyond that which had been permitted in 1995.

There was nothing on the site plan accompanying the application for the extension which suggested that the red line should be interpreted as defining the extent of such an extension. To put it another way, the permission for the extension was not granting permission for any new use beyond the established residential site. The court therefore concluded that the 1998 permission for the extension did not grant planning permission for an extension to the residential use so as to enlarge the planning unit beyond that shown in the approved site plan in the 1995 permission for the erection of the house.

B.1.2 The rule in **Burdle**

Although a planning permission will initially define the extent of a planning unit, as explained above, subsequent changes can take place (with or without planning permission) which alter the extent of the planning unit, either by taking in extra land or by subdividing the original planning unit into separate planning units. It was in order to address this problem that the concept of the planning unit was developed by the courts.

The leading case in which the planning unit was defined was *Burdle v SSE* [1972] 3 All E.R. 240, at page 244. This judgment suggests that there may be three possible situations which can be identified when considering the planning unit:

– First, there may be a single main purpose, to which any secondary activities are ancillary or incidental. In that case, the whole unit of occupation is the planning unit.

– Secondly, there may be a variety of activities, which do not have a primary/ancillary relationship to each other, e.g. a composite use with fluctuating component activities, not in separate and physically distinct areas. In that case, again, the entire unit of occupation is the planning unit, and one is looking at a mixed use of the whole planning unit.

– Finally, there may be separate and distinct areas occupied for substantially different and unrelated purposes. In that case, these areas are separate planning units and each is to be considered by itself.

The general rule which can be derived from these examples is that *the unit of occupation is the appropriate planning unit to consider, until or unless a smaller unit is identified which is in separate use, both physically and functionally.*

B.1.3 The 'agricultural unit'

There are references both in Part 3 and Part 6 of the Second Schedule to the General Permitted Development Order to an "agricultural unit". In Part 6, "agricultural unit" is defined by paragraph D.1 of that Part as agricultural land which is occupied as a unit for the purposes of agriculture, and this includes any dwelling or other building on that land occupied for the purpose of farming the land by the person who occupies the unit, or any dwelling on that land occupied by a farmworker.

The reference to "agricultural land" means land which, before development permitted by Part 6 is carried out, is land in use for agriculture and which is so used for the purposes of a trade or business, but excludes any dwellinghouse or garden. There is no contradiction here, because the permitted development in that Part of the Second Schedule to the GPDO relates to the carrying out of development on "agricultural land" (i.e. excluding a dwelling or its garden) in an "agricultural unit" (which, taken as a whole, may include one or more agricultural dwellings).

In Part 3, an "established agricultural unit" is defined by paragraph X of that Part as agricultural land occupied as a unit for the purposes of agri-culture - for the purposes of Class R, on or before 3 July 2012 or (if its use commenced after that date) for ten years before the date the development begins, or for the purposes of Classes Q or S, on or before 20 March 2013 or (if its use commenced after that date) for ten years before the date the development begins.

In quite a few cases an agricultural unit may not necessarily be co-extensive with a single planning unit. This is particularly likely to be the case where a large agricultural enterprise is spread over a number of separate parcels of land, possibly over several whole farms. These may potentially form one agricultural unit, but will constitute several separate planning units, especially where parts of the land comprising the agricultural unit are not contiguous. (See, for example, the decision of the Court of Appeal in *Fuller v SSE* (1988) 56 P. & C. R. 84; [1988] 1 P.L.R. 1.)

Notwithstanding this point, where references are made in Part 3 to an "established agricultural unit", this term clearly applies to the entirety of the agricultural enterprise, even if it extends over more than one farm. The only exception to this might occur where separate agricultural holdings certificates have been issued by DEFRA (or by their predecessor, MAFF).

The term "established agricultural unit" in Part 3 is used only in the context of the qualifying criteria for the development that is permitted by this Part and also in the context of the restrictions on further development on that agricultural unit that are imposed where permitted development is carried out under Part 3. The change of use itself which is permitted by Part 3 is confined to the new planning unit created by this permitted development, which comprises the building that is to be converted and any land within its curtilage (the curtilage in this case being very restrictively defined - see *paragraph B.2.1* below).

The creation of the new residential planning unit does not in itself prejudice or affect the continuing existence of the established agricultural unit, provided that the agricultural use continues on the rest of the holding; nor does an agricultural unit cease to be an agricultural unit merely by reason of the fact that some other separate planning unit has been carved out of it and put to a non-agricultural use (e.g. an office within Class B1(a)), provided that the remainder of the agricultural unit continues to be in agricultural use, and continues to comply with the statutory definition of an "established agri-cultural unit". The existence of a different use within the boundaries of the agricultural holding does not create a mixed use, so long as the area occupied by the non-agricultural use is both physically and functionally separate, and/or forms a separate unit of occupation (and therefore constitutes a separate planning unit). (See *paragraph B.1.2* above).

B.2 The 'curtilage' of a building and its significance in planning terms

The term 'curtilage' is to be found in several places in both primary and subordinate planning legislation, and is used in various contexts in Part 3 of the Second Schedule to the GPDO, as well as in other Parts of that Schedule. This one word has been the source of endless difficulty and confusion and continues to cause doubt and uncertainty.

As mentioned at the beginning of this Appendix, it is particularly important in the planning context not to use the word 'curtilage' loosely to refer to the entirety of the surrounding land forming part of a property. For the reasons explained below, the actual curtilage of a house or other building may cover only part of the land owned with that building. It follows that the curtilage of a building is *not* necessarily co-extensive with the planning unit.

If one is dealing with a building on a comparatively small plot, then the curtilage may in fact cover the whole property, and it may be this which has led to the widespread habit of using the word 'curtilage' in this rather loose and, in fact, inaccurate way. However, where a building stands in larger grounds, the curtilage almost certainly will not include the whole of the land surrounding the building. It is in these cases where the difficulty of defining what is or is not within the curtilage of the building arises.

B.2.1 The definition of 'curtilage'

Although (with one limited exception, mentioned below) there is no statutory definition of the word 'curtilage', the courts have been called upon to construe the meaning of the word on several occasions.

The leading authority on this issue is *Sinclair-Lockhart's Trustees v Central Land Board* (1950) 1 P. & C. R. 195, where it was held that:

"The ground which is used for the comfortable enjoyment of a house or other building may be regarded in law as being within the curtilage of that house or building and thereby as an integral part of the same although it has not been marked off or enclosed in any way. It is enough that it serves the purpose of the house or building in some necessary or useful way."

Whether a particular area of land near a building is used for its comfortable enjoyment, or serves the purpose of that building in some necessary or useful way, is bound to be a question of fact and degree in each case, but one point which can clearly be derived both from decided cases in the courts and from inspectors' appeal decisions is that the curtilage can properly be said to extend to those parts of the land around a building which include forecourts, parking areas, servicing bays or other servicing areas (and, in the case of a house, the grounds around a house which include formal gardens - mown lawns and herbaceous borders, and also kitchen gardens or a vegetable patch, provided that there is no significant physical separation of any such area from the rest of the curtilage, i.e. by any intervening uncultivated ground).

However, if something like a tennis court or a swimming pool is separated from the house by an area of rough grass or is situated in a field or paddock which is clearly not part of the formal gardens closer to the house, then it is very unlikely to be seen as falling within the curtilage of the house, and the same would apply to any part of the servicing areas associated with any other building which are similarly separated from it. (For examples of this, see *Collins v SSE* [1989] P.L.R. 30 and *McAlpine v SSE* [1994] E.G.C.S. 189. In *Collins* an area of rough grass was held not to be part of the curtilage because it did not serve the dwellinghouse in some necessary or useful manner, echoing the words used in *Sinclair-Lockhart's Trustees*.)

In contrast to the definition adopted in *Sinclair-Lockhart's Trustees*, the definition of 'curtilage' in the Oxford English Dictionary is:

"a small court, yard, garth or piece of ground attached to a dwellinghouse, and forming one enclosure with it, or so regarded by the law; the area attached to and containing a dwellinghouse and its outbuildings"

In *Dyer v Dorset County Council* [1989] 1 Q.B. 346, the Court of Appeal adopted the dictionary definition mentioned above, but this decision can no longer be treated as authoritative. In particular, the use of the word "small" in the dictionary definition is misleading, and was held to be irrelevant by the Court of Appeal in *Skerritts of Nottingham Ltd v SSETR (No. 1)* [2001] QB 59; (2000) 80 P. & C. R. 516, who decided that *Dyer* had gone too far in adopting the dictionary definition word for word. The definition of 'curtilage' is therefore a matter of fact and degree in each individual case, and this was the principal point established by *Skerritts of Nottingham*. One has to look at all the circumstances of the particular case in question.

The one limited exception to the lack of any statutory definition of the word 'curtilage' is to be found in Part 3 of the Second Schedule to the General Permitted Development Order 2015, in relation to permitted development comprising the conversion of agricultural buildings to certain other uses. Paragraph X sets out an extremely restricted definition of "curtilage" for the purposes of Classes Q, R or S, and the same restrictive definition is found in paragraph P.3 in relation to Class P.

For the purposes of these four classes of permitted development only, "curtilage" is defined as the piece of land, whether enclosed or unenclosed, immediately beside or around the agricultural building, closely associated with and serving the purposes of the agricultural building, or an area of land immediately beside or around the agricultural building no larger than the land area occupied by the agricultural building, *whichever is the lesser*. [In the case of Class P, read "storage building" in place of "agricultural building".]

However, this definition of "curtilage" has no application outside the narrow confines of that particular provision, and the statutory definition of 'curtilage' for the purposes of those four Classes of development under the GPDO cannot be taken in any way to influence the definition of 'curtilage' for any other purpose.

B.2.2 *The curtilage of a listed building*

The precise identification of a building's curtilage may be of particular importance in relation to a listed building, due to various prohibitions and restrictions imposed by the planning legislation on development within the curtilage of a listed building. This is most graphically illustrated by reference to a number of disputes with local planning authorities which have arisen in determining the curtilage of a farmhouse (or former farmhouse) that is a listed building. Are nearby farm buildings, such as barns, within the curtilage of the farmhouse?

This can be of some importance if it is proposed to convert a neighbouring barn to form one or more new dwellings. If the barn was within the curtilage of the farmhouse when it was listed, then the barn, as a curtilage building, is also listed. Subsequent separation of the barn from the curtilage of the listed farmhouse cannot alter the barn's listed status. The question that arises, however, is whether the barn really was within the curtilage of the farmhouse at the time of listing.

Notwithstanding that the farmhouse may form part of the same agricultural unit as the rest of the farm (see *paragraph B.1.3* above), in most cases the barn will not be within the same planning unit as the farmhouse, because a farmhouse is not an agricultural building; it is by nature and purpose a single private dwellinghouse, and so the dwelling and the land occupied with it as part and parcel of the same planning unit (usually just the garden and maybe also some form of forecourt) necessarily falls within Use Class C3. This is not an agricultural use.

In quite a few cases, the farmhouse (together with the land occupied with it - i.e. its garden) is separate from the neighbouring farm both physically and functionally, and it is this which is the relevant unit of occupation (see *paragraph B.1.2.* above). As a separate private dwelling, the occupation and use of the farmhouse for exclusively residential purposes cannot be said to be ancillary or incidental to the use of any of the neighbouring land.

Equally, the neighbouring farm is not ancillary or incidental to the residential use and occupation of the farmhouse. (See *Westminster City Council v*

British Waterways Board [1985] A.C. 676; [1984] 3 All E.R. 737.) This alone would preclude a building in one planning unit being within the curtilage of a building in a different, though adjoining, planning unit.

Even if the farmhouse could be said to be part of one and the same planning unit as the farm with which it is associated, it is clear from the judgment in *R (Egerton) v Taunton Deane BC* [2008] EWHC 2752 (Admin) that the farm buildings are very unlikely to be within the curtilage of the farmhouse in any event (bearing in mind the criteria explained in *paragraph B.2.1* above).

In *Egerton*, from a date prior to the listing of the farmhouse in 1984, the farmhouse was enclosed by a wall. The other buildings (including various barns, etc.) were located on the other side of that wall. Beyond these there were a number of larger agricultural buildings which stretched away further to the west. It had been contended that the curtilage of the farmhouse was not defined by the wall on its western and southern sides, but extended so as to incorporate the nearby barns. However, there was no readily discernible feature which might serve to define the curtilage to either the west or the south of the farmhouse other than the wall, and it had been accepted in argument that the curtilage could not extend so as to include the whole of the farm.

The court did not accept the submission that any of the barns or other agricultural buildings were within the curtilage of the farmhouse. In 1984 there was a clear distinction between the farmhouse and its curtilage and the farmyard with its barns and other agricultural buildings. The judge accepted that there will not necessarily be such a physical distinction in each and every case but, on the evidence, there was such a distinction in this case.

This view was reinforced by evidence as to the use and function of the barns at the time of listing in 1984. The nearby barns were always used in conjunction with the farming activities carried on at the farm. Thus, it could be seen that these barns were not being used for purposes that were ancillary to the use of the farmhouse as a dwellinghouse; they were being used for the purposes of the general farming enterprise which was being carried on at the farm. They, and the agricultural buildings to the west, were being used for agricultural purposes. They were not being used, for example, to garage the farmer's car, to store his domestic items, as a children's playroom, staff quarters etc. Thus neither of the barns fulfilled the criteria set out in *Sinclair Lockhart's Trustees* (see *paragraph B.2.1* above).

The alternative submission was that the farmhouse was not simply a dwellinghouse; it was the hub from which the agricultural business at the farm was being conducted. The judge readily accepted that the farm was being run from the farmhouse in 1984, but the whole of the farm, and all the agricultural buildings upon it, could not sensibly be regarded as being within the curtilage of the farmhouse on that account. The primary use of the farmhouse was as a house. The farm, as a whole, was not listed; only the farmhouse itself was listed. Its curtilage, as a house, was clearly defined by the wall which separated the residential use within the wall from the agricultural use that was being carried on in the agricultural buildings, and in the fields beyond.

For these reasons, although the whole of the farm, including the farmhouse and all the agricultural buildings, was in common ownership when the farmhouse was listed in 1984, the listed farmhouse and its residential curtilage was both physically separated from, and functionally distinct from, the agricultural land and buildings on the other side of the wall. The fact that they were all constituent parts of the same farming enterprise at this farm did not mean that either of the nearby barns or any of the other agricultural buildings beyond the wall were within the curtilage of the farmhouse.

In giving judgment in *Egerton*, the court also considered the earlier decision in *A-G (ex rel Sutcliffe) v Calderdale B.C.* [1982] 46 P. & C. R. 399, where it had been held that there were three factors to be considered when identifying the curtilage of a (listed) building. These were: (1) the physical 'layout' of the listed building and the structure, (2) their ownership, past and present, and (3) their use or function, past and present.

Stephenson LJ had said in that case:

"Where they are in common ownership and one is used in connection with the other, there is little difficulty in putting a structure near a building or even some distance from it into its curtilage. So when the terrace was built, and the mill was worked by those who occupied the cottages, and the millowner owned the cottages, it would have been hard, if not impossible, to decide that the cottages were outside the curtilage of the mill."

In that case the cottages were physically linked to the mill.

In giving judgment in the *Taunton Deane* case, Sullivan J considered all three of the factors promulgated in *Calderdale*. However, he clearly did not accept that historical association alone would be sufficient to allow the land or buildings in question to be regarded as being within the curtilage of the farmhouse itself. The functional relationship (if any) of the land and buildings in question with the farmhouse at the material date (1984) was clearly the ultimate determining factor, even when the other two factors were also taken into account.

This point has been discussed here in some detail because it is often assumed, wrongly, that a barn situated close to a listed farmhouse is thereby also listed by virtue of its being within the curtilage of the farmhouse. There may be a few cases where this is so (if the barn really was in domestic use at the time when the farmhouse was originally listed) but, for the reasons explained above, and as very clearly demonstrated in *Egerton*, there will be many cases in which the barn in question has never been within the curtilage of the farmhouse and so is not itself listed.

Although this point has been illustrated here by reference to the curtilage of a listed farmhouse (or former farmhouse), it is of general application, and is therefore material to the identification of the curtilage of all listed buildings where this is relevant to the applicability or otherwise of the prohibition or restriction of development within the curtilage of a listed building.

B.2.3 Other buildings attached to a listed building

The situation in the preceding paragraph deals with a detached building which is allegedly within the curtilage of a listed building. A similar query may be raised in a situation where the other building is actually attached to the listed building. In this case, it is clear from section 1(5) of the Listed Buildings Act that any structure fixed to a listed building forms part of the listed building (although it seems to have been generally accepted before the judgment in *Richardson*, cited below, that this only applied to a building that was fixed to the listed building at the time of its original listing).

Furthermore, the House of Lords in *Debenhams plc v Westminster LBC* [1987] A.C. 396 put a gloss on section 1(5), by insisting that a structure fixed to a listed building would itself be listed only if it was subordinate or ancillary to the building that was actually listed. An obvious example is a terrace of houses; the listing of just one of the houses in the terrace clearly does not apply to the houses on either side if these are in separate ownership or occupation, even though they are structures that are "fixed to a listed building".

However in *Richardson Development Ltd v Birmingham City Council* [1999] J.P.L. 1001 it was held that Section 1(5)(a) of the 1990 Act does not apply only to extensions to listed buildings which exist at the date of listing. The words in subparagraph (a) "any object or structure fixed to the building" are unqualified as to date. The result is that the words in section 1(5)(a) must be given the same meaning whether the extension existed before or was added after the listing of the original building.

Counsel for Richardson accepted that section 1(5)(a) of the 1990 Act applies to extensions to listed buildings which have already been constructed at the date of listing of the original building, but submitted that it does not apply to extensions made after the original building has been listed. He argued that the reasoning of Lord Keith in the *Debenhams* case should be treated as limited to cases in which the extensions predate the listing, and that in cases where the extensions postdate the listing, the dictum of Lord Mackay should be applied.

Dyson J did not accept this submission. The words in subparagraph (a) "any object or structure fixed to the building" are unqualified as to date. In this respect there is a striking contrast with subparagraph (b), which requires a qualifying object or structure within the curtilage to have formed part of the land since before July 1, 1948. If Parliament had intended an object or structure fixed to the land to be treated as part of the building only if it was fixed at the date of listing, it could, and surely would, have so provided.

Dyson J added that there is no suggestion in *Debenhams* or any of the cases in which section 1(5)(a) has been considered that the interpretation contended for by Richardson is correct. His lordship's attention had been drawn to *Shimizu (UK) Ltd v Westminster City Council* [1997] 1 W.L.R. 168 and *City of Edinburgh Council v Secretary of State for Scotland* [1977] 1 W.L.R. 1447.

The result was that the words in section 1(5)(a) must be given the same meaning whether the extension existed before or was added after the listing of the original building and that meaning is the one which had been determined by the House of Lords in *Debenhams*. In Dyson J's view, Parliament intended, when enacting section 1(5)(a), to specify as the only criterion for determining whether an extension to a listed building should be treated as part of a listed building, that it should be fixed to the building, and, as the House of Lords has held, that it should be ancillary to it.

Section 1(5) is clearly intended to provide a complete code of what Parliament intended to be comprised in a listed building. This intention must be respected, particularly as listed buildings are in any event exclusively creatures of statute. It is plain that the words "and includes any object or structure fixed to that building" are intended to reflect and bear the same meaning as the same words in section 1(5)(a) of the Act.

The practical application of these rules was illustrated by a planning appeal in West London in July 2015 against a refusal of prior approval for the proposed residential conversion of an office building under Class O. The LPA had contended that the building in question was itself listed by reason of its being physically linked to an adjoining listed building. They relied on the judgment in *Debenhams* (cited above) as authority for this. However, the Inspector concluded that in view of the much larger size of the office block compared with the smaller listed building its relationship to the listed building was not ancillary, and so it was not itself a listed building.

On the other hand, the Inspector held that the office building was in fact within the curtilage of the listed building. Both buildings, as well as being inter-connected, were used together by a single business with a garden occupied in common, and this appears to have been the case at the time of the original listing of the listed building in the 1980s. The office building was therefore disqualified from conversion under Class O.

B.2.4 Extension of the curtilage

The curtilage of a building is not fixed for all time; its physical extent is readily capable of changing at any time, subject to its meeting the criteria discussed in *paragraph B.2.1* above.

It has become clear from the decision of the High Court in *Sumption v Greenwich LBC* [2007] EWHC 2776 (Admin) that land can very easily be incorporated in the curtilage. There is no qualifying period for the incorporation in the curtilage of land which already lawfully forms part of the same planning use as the house. The incorporation of land within the domestic curtilage is not subject either to the 4-year rule or to the 10-year rule, because it is not a 'use' of land for planning purposes.

In giving judgment in *Sumption*, Collins J observed that it is necessary to determine the status of the land from the factual situation existing at the present time (in that case, the date on which an application was made for a Lawful Development Certificate). In *Sumption*, the land had been acquired in 2004; it had been fenced and it was useable and was intended to be used as an extension of the garden of the residential property in question. Collins J concluded that once the wall was erected and the garden use confirmed so that the land did indeed form part of the garden of that property it would be well nigh impossible to contend that it was not within the curtilage.

The position explained above is, however, subject to the proviso that land can only be treated as part of the curtilage of a building if its *use* (as part of the planning unit comprising the building and the land occupied with it) is lawful. In the case of *Sumption*, the extra land taken into the garden was already lawfully in residential use. Let us suppose, however, that neighbouring land previously in agricultural use has been taken into the planning unit and has been incorporated in the property as part of the domestic garden. If this change of use was not authorised by planning permission, it will not become lawful until 10 years' continuous use as part of the residential property. Until such time as its use becomes lawful under the 10-year rule, no part of this land can be regarded as coming within the curtilage of the house, even if it would otherwise meet the test set out in *Sinclair-Lockhart's Trustees*.

This last point may be relevant in the context of Article 3(5) of the GPDO, as discussed in *paragraph A.4* of *Appendix A*.

B.2.5 References to 'curtilage' in Parts 3, 4 and 5 of Schedule 2 to the GPDO

The importance of identifying whether a particular part of a property is within the 'curtilage' of a building becomes clear when considering the effect of the various provisions in the GPDO which refer to the curtilage of a building. The relevant provisions are briefly summarised below.

In a number of cases, Part 3 of the Second Schedule to the GPDO grants permission in respect of "a building and any land *within its curtilage*". It is therefore important to identify the extent of the curtilage for this purpose. Attention has already been drawn (in *paragraph B.2.1* above) to the very restrictive definition of "curtilage" that applies in respect of development under Classes P, Q, R and S, but the general definition discussed in *paragraph B.2.1* applies to identification of the curtilage of the building in other cases.

In a number of Classes of permitted development under Part 3 of the Second Schedule to the GPDO such development is specifically precluded in respect of a listed building or land *within the curtilage* of a listed building.

In this context, Section 1(5) of the Listed Buildings Act is also relevant. This provides that, where a building has been listed under that Act, any object or structure *within the curtilage* of the building which, although not fixed to the building, forms part of the land and has done so since before July 1, 1948, is to be treated for the purposes of the Act as part of the building. In this case, the curtilage is to be defined as at the date of the original listing of the building.

Thus the protection afforded by the listing extends to any pre-1948 object or structure that is within the curtilage of that building, even though the curtilage may later have been extended or reduced in size (for example by part of the land having subsequently been sold off). This is a point that should be clearly borne in mind where there has been any change in the size of the curtilage of a listed building at any time since its original listing. (For further discussion of this point, see *paragraphs B.2.2* and *B.2.3*, and also *B.2.4*, above.)

Part 4, Class B of the Second Schedule to the GPDO permits the temporary use of land for certain purposes for not more than 28 (or in some cases 14) days in any one year. However, this development is not permitted if the land in question is *within the curtilage* of a building.

In relation to Part 5 of the Second Schedule to the GPDO, section 2 of the Caravan Sites and Control of Development Act 1960 provides that no site licence is required for the use of land as a caravan site in any of the circumstances specified in the First Schedule to that Act. Paragraph 1 of the First Schedule applies to use *within the curtilage* of a dwellinghouse. A site licence is not required for the use of land as a caravan site if the use is incidental to the enjoyment as such of a dwellinghouse *within the curtilage* of which the land is situated. However, the permitted development right granted by Part 5 of the Second Schedule to the GPDO which applies to uses within paragraphs 2 to 10 of that schedule does *not* extend to a use within paragraph 1 (i.e. *within the curtilage* of a dwellinghouse).

Appendix C

The Use Classes Order

C.1   Specific exclusions from the Use Classes Order

The Town and Country Planning (Use Classes) Order 1987 (which has been much amended since 1987, most recently on 15 April 2015) greatly simplifies the identification and classification of various uses of land and buildings. However, the Order is not comprehensive. Thus, if a use does not come within any of the classes specified in the Order, it is a *sui generis* use (a use of its own kind).

In addition to this, there are some uses that are specifically excluded from the Order, by Article 3(6). All of these uses are also therefore *sui generis* uses. They comprise the following uses:

(a)   *as a theatre;*

(b)   *as an amusement arcade or centre, or a fun fair;*

(c)   *as a launderette;*

(d)   *for the sale of fuel for motor vehicles;*

(e)   *for the sale or display for sale of motor vehicles;*

(f)   *for a taxi business or business for the hire of motor vehicles;*

(g)   *as a scrap yard, or a yard for the storage or distribution of minerals or the breaking of motor vehicles;*

(h)   *for any work registrable under the Alkali, etc. Works Regulation Act 1906;*

(i)   *as a hostel;*

(j)   *as a waste disposal installation for the incineration, chemical treatment, or land fill of certain waste;*

(k)   *as a retail warehouse club being a retail club where goods are sold or displayed only to persons who are members of that club;*

(l)   *as a night club;*

(m)   *as a casino;*

(n)   *as a betting office;*

(o)   *as a pay day loan shop.*

"Pay day loan shop" means premises from which high-cost short-term credit is provided principally to visiting members of the public and includes premises from which such credit is provided in addition to other financial or professional services, and which (but for provision made in Article 3(6)), would fall within Class A2 (financial and professional services).

C.2   Mixed uses

A particular point to be borne in mind is that the use of the planning unit for a mixed use falling within more than one of the classes in the Use Classes Order is a *sui generis* use, notwithstanding that each of the elements of that use is in itself a use that would come within the UCO. It is quite common for such a mixed use to be described for convenience as (for example) "a B1/B8 use", but this is in fact a *sui generis* use. (See, for example, *Belmont Riding Centre v FSS* [2003] EWHC 1895 (Admin).) [The sole exception to this rule is a B1/B2 use, as provided by article 3(4) of the Use Classes Order – see *paragraph 4.1* in *Chapter 4.*]

This has important consequences, because it means that certain changes of use that are permitted development under the General Permitted Development Order where a use falls wholly within a particular use class are not permitted development if the existing use of the property does not fall wholly within the scope of that single use class. As noted above, this applies to any combination of uses that do not fall within a single use class, even if each of the elements of that mixed use is in itself a use that would come within the UCO.

On the other hand, a use which is included in and ordinarily incidental to any use in a specified use class is not excluded from the use class in which the primary use falls, merely because the same use is specified elsewhere in the UCO as a separate use (see Article 3(3)). Thus an incidental or ancillary use when considered in conjunction with the primary use will not amount to a mixed use, always provided that the incidental or ancillary use has not grown to such an extent as actually to become a mixed use together with what was originally the primary use (see, for example, *Wallington v SSW* [1990] J.P.L. 112).

C.3   Physical and legal extent of uses within the UCO

By Article 2 of the UCO, where the term "site" is used in this Order, it means the whole area of land within a single unit of occupation (effectively the planning unit - see *part B.1* of *Appendix B*).

By Article 3(1) of the UCO, subject to the provisions of that Order, where a building or other land is used for a purpose of any class specified in the Schedule to the UCO, the use of that building or that other land for any other purpose of the same class is not to be taken to involve development of the land. This repeats the effect of section 55(2)(f) of the 1990 Act.

Article 3(2) makes it clear that the use of a building within a specified use class is taken to include land occupied with the building and used for the same purposes; in other words it includes all the land within the same planning unit. This was confirmed by the Court of Appeal in *Brookes & Burton Ltd v SSE* [1978] 1 All E.R. 733. Furthermore, a use which is included in and ordinarily incidental to any use in a specified use class is not excluded from the use to which it is incidental merely because it is specified elsewhere in the UCO as a separate use (see Article 3(3)).

Paragraph 12 of Circular 03/2005 stated that in identifying the use of a property (and therefore whether it falls into a particular use class and, if so, which) it is the primary purpose of the use which must be considered, but it is not simply a question of whether the primary use comprises more than 50% of the business. A primary/ancillary relationship between uses is not dependent on the proportion or ratio of one use to the other, either in terms of turnover, or in terms of the floorspace devoted to the respective elements of these uses, but is dependent on their functional relationship. (See *Main v SSE* (1998) P. & C. R. 300; [1999] J.P.L. 195.)

C.4   The Use Classes

The use classes are organised in four groups (A to D), but this is of no legal significance. Each use class is self-contained, and so a change of use from, say, A1 to A3 constitutes development in exactly the same way as a change of use from A1 to B1 or from A1 to D2, and thus it requires planning permission (although that planning permission may in practice be granted by the GPDO).

There are currently 15 separate use classes, which are discussed briefly in the following paragraphs of this Appendix. They comprise:

A1   Shops

A2   Financial and professional services

A3   Food and drink

A4   Drinking establishments

A5   Hot food take-aways

B1   Business

B2   General industrial

B8   Storage or distribution

C1   Hotels, guest houses, etc.

C2   Residential institutions

C2A   Secure residential institutions

C3   Dwellinghouses

C4   Houses in multiple occupation

D1   Non-residential institutions

D2   Assembly and leisure

For most purposes, any sub-classes identified in respect of a particular Use Class are unimportant, because both section 55(2)(f) of the 1990 Act and Article 3(1) of the UCO provide that where a building or other land is used for a purpose of any class specified in the Schedule to the UCO, the use of that building or that other land for any other purpose of the same class is not to be taken to involve development of the land, but Class O in Part 3 of the Second Schedule to the GPDO requires that, in order to qualify for residential conversion under that Class, a building must have been used specifically as an office within Use Class B1(a). It will not qualify under Class O if it was used for any other purpose within Use Class B1, or any combination of uses within that Use Class, even if one of those uses was within Class B1(a). However, this may possibly change when the residential conversion of buildings in light industrial use is introduced in May 2016.

Each of the current Use Classes listed in the Schedule to the UCO is set out below. The detailed consideration of the many ramifications of these various types of use will be the subject of a further book in due course.

C.4.1 Use Class A1 - Shops

Class A1 comprises use for all or any of the following purposes :

(a)   *for the retail sale of goods other than hot food,*

(b)   *as a post office,*

(c)   *for the sale of tickets or as a travel agency,*

(d)   *for the sale of sandwiches or other cold food for consumption off the premises*

(e)   *for hairdressing*

(f)   *for the direction of funerals*

(g)   *for the display of goods for sale*

(h)   *for the hiring out of domestic or personal goods or articles*

(i)   *for the washing or cleaning of clothes or fabrics on the premises*

(j)   *for the reception of goods to be washed, cleaned or repaired*

(k)   *as an internet café, where the primary purpose of the premises is to provide facilities for enabling members of the public to access the internet.*

In all cases, use within Class A1 is subject to the sale, display or services being to visiting members of the public.

C.4.2 Use Class A2 - Financial and professional services

The type of offices to which Class A2 relates are the type of town centre offices that offer what are sometimes referred to as 'retail services'. This use class comprises use for the provision of:

(a) financial services; or

(b) professional services (other than health or medical services); or

(c) any other services which it is appropriate to provide in a shopping area.

In each of these cases, use within Class A2 is subject to the services being provided principally to visiting members of the public.

In the 2015 amendment to the UCO, betting offices and pay day loan shops have been removed from Use Class A2, and have been added instead to the list of *sui generis* uses in Article 3(6).

C.4.3 Use Class A3 - Food and drink

The re-organisation of the catering use classes in 2005 resulted in the scope of Use Class A3 being cut down to the following:

"Use for the sale of food and drink for consumption on the premises"

C.4.4 Use Class A4 - Drinking establishments

This is one of the two new use classes introduced by the re-organisation of the catering use classes in 2005. It is confined to:

"Use as a public house, wine-bar or other drinking establishment"

C.4.5 Use Class A5 - Hot food take-aways

This is the second of the two new use classes introduced by the re-organisation of the catering use classes in 2005. It comprises:

"Use for the sale of hot food for consumption off the premises"

This, as the heading indicates, means a 'hot food take-away', but it also includes a use where hot food is delivered to the customers, rather than being collected.

C.4.6 Use Class B1 - Business

This use class comprises use for all or any of the following purposes:

(a) use as an office (other than within Class A2);

(b) use for research and development of products or processes; and/or

(c) use for any industrial process,

being a use which can be carried out in any residential area without detriment to the amenity of that area by reason of noise, vibration, smell, fumes, smoke, soot, ash, dust or grit.

An important use within this use class is as an office (Class B1(a)). Note that an office use within Class A2 is excluded from the definition of an office within Class B1(a).

An "industrial process" is defined by Article 2 of the UCO as a process for or incidental to any of the following purposes:

(a)   *the making of any article or part of any article (including a ship or vessel, or a film, video or sound recording);*

(b)   *the altering, repairing, maintaining, ornamenting, finishing, cleaning, washing, packing, canning, adapting for sale, breaking up or demolition of any article; or*

(c)   *the getting, dressing or treatment of minerals; in the course of any trade or business other than agriculture, and other than a use carried out in or adjacent to a mine or quarry.*

Some of the processes listed above will come within Use Class B1, if they can be carried out in any residential area without detriment to the amenity of that area by reason of noise, vibration, smell, fumes, smoke, soot, ash, dust or grit, but many of them will fall within Use Class B2 (below).

C.4.7   Use Class B2 - General industrial

This use class comprises:

Use for the carrying on of an industrial process other than one falling within Class B1 above.

The definition of an "industrial process" has been quoted in *paragraph C.4.6* above and, as noted there, many of the listed industrial processes will fall within Use Class B2.

When considering Use Class B2, it should be borne in mind that Article 3(6) of the UCO expressly excludes from the use classes in the Order the following uses, which are therefore *sui generis*:

(g)   *as a scrap yard, or a yard for the storage or distribution of minerals or the breaking of motor vehicles,*

(h)   *for any work registrable under the Alkali, etc. Works Regulation Act 1906,*

and also

(j)   *as a waste disposal installation for the incineration, chemical treatment, or land fill of certain waste.*

Special Industrial Groups A to E (which formerly comprised Use Classes B3 to B7 and covered certain particularly noisome or noxious industrial processes) have been abolished, and these uses are now subsumed within Use Class B2. As noted above, however, this use class still excludes any work registrable under the Alkali, etc. Works Regulation Act 1906 and any waste disposal installation for the incineration, chemical treatment, or land fill of certain waste, so that any of such uses will be *sui generis*.

Article 3(5) of the UCO originally excluded from the Order any use involving notifiable quantities of any hazardous substance, but this paragraph was removed by an amendment order in 1992 (S.I. 1992 No.657). The presence of a hazardous substance on site is now controlled by the Planning (Hazardous Substances) Act 1990, which came into force on the same date as this amendment to the UCO . This is a topic that lies beyond the scope of this book.

C.4.8 Use Class B8 - Storage or distribution

This use class comprises:

Use for storage or as a distribution centre.

For this purpose the storage use must be the primary use of the site. This Use Class is discussed in more detail in *paragraph 8.3* of *Chapter 8*. If storage of various items is merely ancillary to other uses, this would take it outside Use Class B8.

It should also be noted that a "retail warehouse" used to be an A1 shop (see former Circular 13/87, para 23) but, as a result of an amendment of the UCO in 2005, this is now a *sui generis* use.

C.4.9 Use Class C1 - Hotels

This use class comprises:

Use as a hotel or as a boarding or guest house where, in each case, no significant element of care is provided.

"Care" means personal care for people in need of such care by reason of old age, disablement, past or present dependence on alcohol or drugs or past or present mental disorder, and in Use Class C2 also includes the personal care of children and medical care and treatment. The reference to the absence of any significant element of care is therefore intended to distinguish this use class from Use Class C2.

A hostel, which at one time was with this use class, is now among the *sui generis* uses listed in Article 3(6).

C.4.10 *Use Class C2 - Residential institutions*

This use class comprises:

Use for the provision of residential accommodation and care to people in need of care (other than a use within Class C3 (dwellinghouses)

Use as hospital or nursing home

Use as a residential school, college or training centre

The definition of "care" in this context has already been mentioned in *paragraph C.4.9* above in relation to Use Class C1.

The wording of Use Class C2 makes it clear that this use class applies only to care homes that do not fall within Use Class C3 (dwellinghouses). That use class includes Class C3(b), which covers *use as a dwellinghouse (whether or not as a sole or main residence) by not more than six residents living together as a single household (including a household where care is provided for residents)*. It seems clear from the wording of the Order that there is intended to be no overlap between these two use classes, and that a care home with no more than six residents falls into Class C3(b) (unless it involves personal care of children or medical care and treatment), so that only those care homes accommodating more than six adult residents, or which involve personal care of children or medical care and treatment, fall within Use Class C2.

If no significant element of care is provided, then the use may (by definition) fall within Use Class C1, unless it is in fact a hostel, and therefore a *sui generis* use or comprises one or more single dwellings within Use Class C3.

C.4.11 *Use Class C2A - Secure residential institutions*

A new use class was introduced in 2006 (and amended in 2010), which comprises:

Use for the provision of secure residential accommodation, including use as a prison, young offenders institution, detention centre, secure training centre, custody centre, short-term holding centre, secure hospital, secure local authority accommodation or use as military barracks.

C.4.12 *Use Class C3 - Dwellinghouses*

Use Class C3 comprises:

Use as a dwellinghouse (whether or not as a sole or main residence) by

(a) *a single person or by people to be regarded as forming a single household;*

(b) *not more than six residents living together as a single household where care is provided for residents; or*

(c) *not more than six residents living together as a single household where no care is provided to residents (other than a use within Class C4).*

For the purposes of Class C3(a) [*but not C3(b) or C3(c)*], the 2010 amendment to the UCO provides that "single household" is to be construed in accordance with section 258 of the Housing Act 2004 (which sets out when persons are to be regarded as *not* forming a single household for the purposes of section 254 of that Act). The ramifications of this definition are complex, and are beyond the scope of this book.

C.4.13 Use Class C4 - *Houses in multiple occupation*

Use Class C4 was created on 6 April 2010. It comprises:

Use of a dwellinghouse by not more than six residents as a "house in multiple occupation".

For the purposes of Class C4 a *"house in multiple occupation"* does not include a converted block of flats to which section 257 of the Housing Act 2004 applies but otherwise has the same meaning as in section 254 of the Housing Act 2004.

Section 254 of the 2004 Housing Act contains a comprehensive definition of a "house in multiple occupation", supplemented by the *Licensing and Management of Houses in Multiple Occupation and Other Houses (Miscellaneous Provisions) (England) Regulations 2006* (S.I. 2006 No. 373).

Section 254 sets out three tests and two other alternative criteria for identifying and defining an HMO, but the last of these (that it is a converted block of flats to which section 257 applies) does *not* apply for the purposes of the Use Classes Order. With this one exception, a house is an HMO within Use Class C4 if any one of the tests is met. These are 'the standard test', the 'self-contained flat' test and the 'converted building test'. The property will also be an HMO if an "HMO declaration" is in force in respect of it under section 255. These provisions are extremely complex and are beyond the scope of the present book.

C.4.14 Use Class D1 - *Non-residential institutions*

This use class comprises:

Any use <u>not</u> including a residential use -

(a) *for the provision of any medical or health services, except the use of premises attached to the residence of the consultant or practitioner,*

(b) *as a crèche, day nursery or day centre,*

(c) *for the provision of education,*

(d) *for the display of works of art (otherwise than for sale or hire)*

(e)   *as a museum,*

(f)   *as a public library or public reading room*

(g)   *as a public hall or exhibition hall,*

(h)   *for, or in connection with, public worship or religious instruction,*

(i)   *as a law court*

This is a very wide-ranging use class, which embraces various institutions or buildings visited by the public on a non-residential basis, but (unlike, for example, Use Class D2) it is not open-ended and is confined to uses falling within those categories listed above.

C.4.15 Use Class D2 - Assembly and leisure

This use class comprises use as:

(a)   *a cinema;*

(b)   *a concert hall;*

(c)   *a bingo hall;*

(d)   *a dance hall; or*

(e)   *a swimming bath, skating rink, gymnasium or area for other indoor or outdoor sports or recreations, not involving motorised vehicles or firearms.*

Use Class D2(e) is very wide (but not unlimited) in the uses that it embraces.

It should be borne in mind that the following leisure or leisure-related uses are listed in Article 3(6) as *sui generis* uses:

(a)   *as a theatre;*

(b)   *as an amusement arcade or centre, or a fun fair;*

and also

(l)   *as a night club; and*

(m)   *as a casino*

so that these uses do not fall within Use Class D2, or within any other use class in the UCO.

Index

M

Q

S

U